THE NEW SOCIETY FOR UNIVERSAL HARMONY

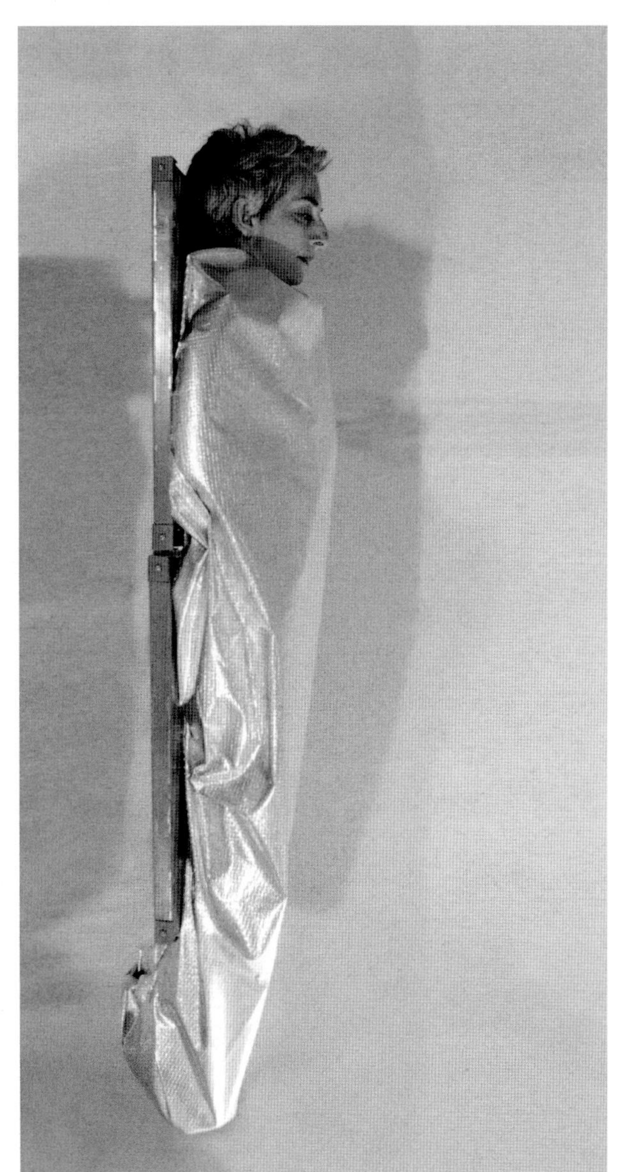

THE NEW SOCIETY

FOR UNIVERSAL HARMONY

LENORE MALEN

GRANARY BOOKS, INC.   NEW YORK CITY

2005

Design by Julie Harrison and Russell Hassell
Printed and bound in Canada

Library of Congress Control Number: 2005920940
ISBN 1-887123-67-9

Granary Books, Inc.
307 Seventh Avenue, Suite 1401
New York, NY, 10001 USA
www.granarybooks.com

The New Society for Universal Harmony
www.thenewsociety.org

Distributed to the trade by
D.A.P./Distributed Art Publishers
155 Avenue of the Americas, Second Floor
New York, NY 10013
Orders: (800) 338-BOOK
Tel: (212) 627-1999 Fax: (212) 627-9484
www. artbook.com

Also available from
Small Press Distribution
1341 Seventh Street
Berkeley, CA 94710
Orders: (800) 869-7553
Tel: (510) 524-1668 Fax: (510) 5224-0582
www.spdbooks.org

The strange magnetic force
That holds lovers to their course
Still shows the truth; if you will but aspire
You will attain to all you desire.

— Farid-Ud-Din Attar, *The Conference of the Birds*

For Josh,
and for Ilana and Dave

CONTENTS

1

THE NEW SOCIETY FOR UNIVERSAL HARMONY

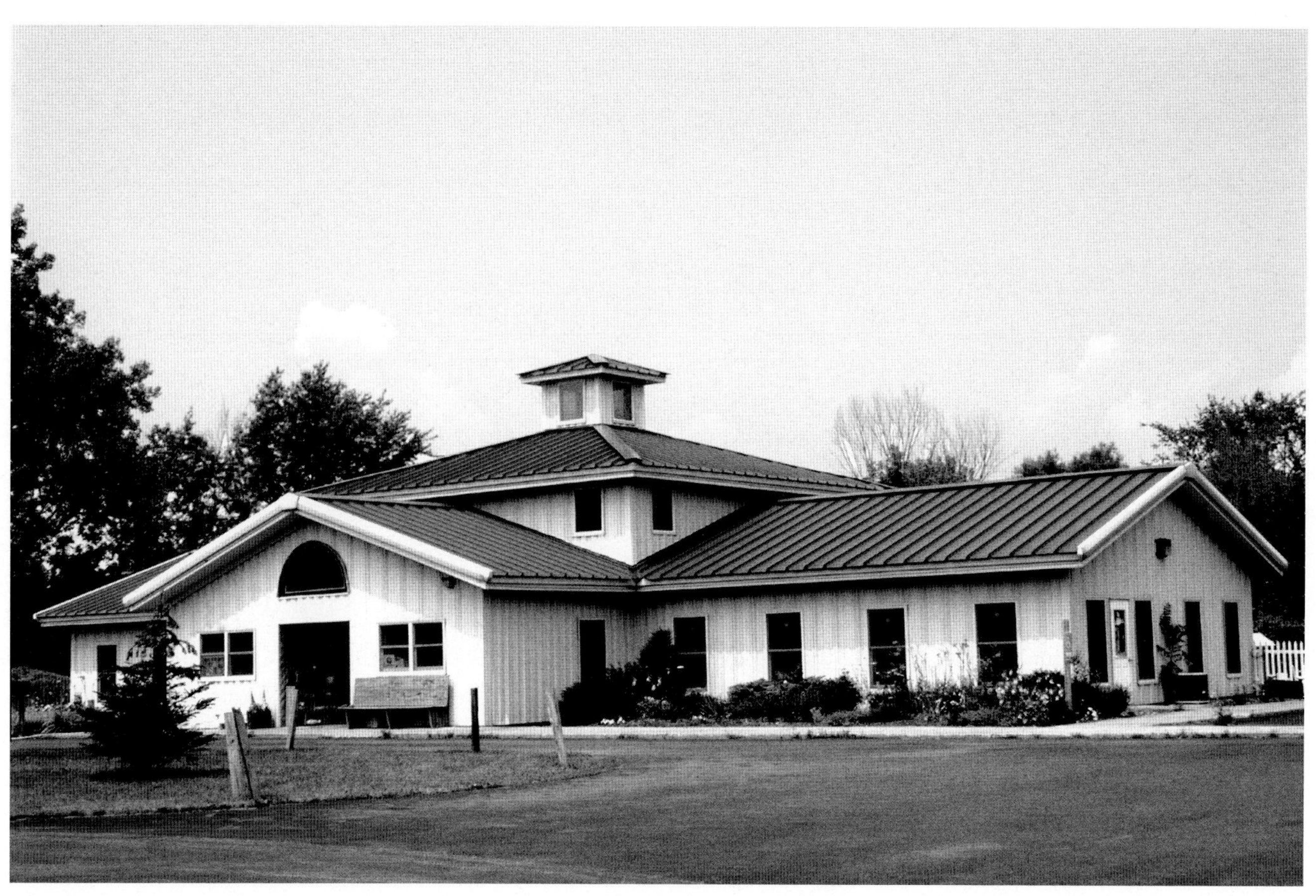

Athol Springs, New York

HOW I LEARNED ABOUT THE NEW SOCIETY

Certum est, quia impossibile est.
(It is certain because it is impossible.)
—Tertullian, *De carne Christi* [1]

IT WAS SEPTEMBER 1999. When the moon was in its first quarter, I could not easily take the elevator to my tenth-floor apartment.[2] Its rapid acceleration and deceleration caused me to nearly faint. To control my anxiety I had to touch the red emergency button while the elevator was in motion. When people asked me why, I said I was resting my finger. At night I had a recurring dream that the elevator was going through the roof.

Another thing. I seemed to be fixated on the compass points: The windows in my apartment faced east and west, and it annoyed me that they didn't face north and south. The grid of the streets, a geometric purity I used to love, threw me into despair. Now I saw only endless impassable facades with canyons between them. I would walk for hours looking for the parking lots that make diagonal shortcuts from street to street or the ground-level stores that run through buildings, with an entrance on one block and an exit on another.

On a Sunday in October I was at the Brooklyn Museum. I noticed a flock of starlings perched on the branches of a tree near the entrance. Suddenly they flew out, making a black shape in the sky. There were hundreds of them. They swirled up and disappeared. The next week I began to research the migration of the birds and their connection to magnetism. Magnetite crystals are found near their olfactory nerves.

What did that mean?

At the same time as I began noticing these changes — these symptoms — in myself, I started losing my friends. I kept calling them, asking, "Is it gravity or is it magnetism?" "There's nothing wrong with you," they said. But I continued calling anyway and, one by one, over a period of months, they stopped calling me back.

Depressed and confused, I thought that it might help to get away for a while. After the holidays I summoned what little remaining energy I had to visit my cousins in Buffalo, New York. On Saturday, February 5th, we sat in their kitchen lingering over the local newspaper, *Ananova.* The cover story, by C. Palm, referred to Doctor F.A. Mesmer, the founder of The New Society for Universal Harmony, located on County Route 122 in Athol Springs, which my cousins told me was only eight miles away. According to Palm, the Society was situated on a 1,250-acre estate, with a magnificent view of Lake Erie.

The article went on to say:

"We live in a network of institutional settings, each one with its own rules, goals, and rewards, the ensemble of which mediates our existential reality. The cumulative effect has long been identified under the rubric of alienation for which the corporate institutional power brokers have supplied their own palliative, epitomized in the term 'spectacle,' whose main manifestation has been television.

"For many, however, the existential pain is too strong and they seek other more authentic solutions. A small coterie of these seekers has come together around the charismatic figure of Doctor F.A. Mesmer, who has established a therapeutic community expanding and updating the principles of her illustrious eighteenth-century eponym, Franz Anton Mesmer, the physician/founder of the original *Société de l'harmonie universelle*. The contemporary group seeks solutions for spiritual dislocation through symbolically mediated magnetic treatments devised by F.A. Mesmer. They call themselves the Harmonites."

The next day we took the short drive to The New Society.

FEBRUARY 6, 2000

County Route 122 turned out to be a beautiful road and the Society stood there gracefully alone, with nothing on either side of it for miles. We parked in the small front lot and, seeing no one, entered the main building whose door was unlocked. The waiting room was plain except for a nice Oriental carpet on the floor.

Our eyes fell on a bulletin board wedged in the corner that listed upcoming weekend lectures:

February 26th: From Aristotle to Mesmer
March 4th: New Analysis of the Michelson-Morley Experiment
March 11th: Fourier's Passional Attraction
March 18th: The Cure at the Sanctuary at Pergamum (Aelius Aristides)
March 25th: Early Martian Magnetism Tape-Recorded in Rock[3]

Off the entrance room were corridors lined with chalkboards on which were written numerous equations, citations, and quotations.

$$D(K)=\sum_{j=0}^{K}(-1)^{K-j+1}\binom{N-j}{K-j}\,Q(N-j),$$

$$Q(N-j) = -\sum_{\{i_1..i_j\}}\sum_{S} P(s_1\ldots s_N)\log_2\left(\sum P(s_1..s_N)\right)$$

$$\dot{p}_j = -\frac{\partial H}{\partial q_j} \qquad \dot{q}_j = \frac{\partial H}{\partial p_j}$$

$$E(K) = C\,\epsilon^{2/3}K^{-5/3}f(K\eta)$$
$$\eta = (\nu^3/\epsilon)^{1/4}$$

$$i\hbar\frac{\partial\psi}{\partial t} = H\psi$$

$$S(t) = -\iint f(\vec{r},\vec{v},t)\ln f(\vec{r},\vec{v},t)\,d\vec{r}\,d\vec{v}$$
$$\frac{dS(t)}{dt} \geq 0$$

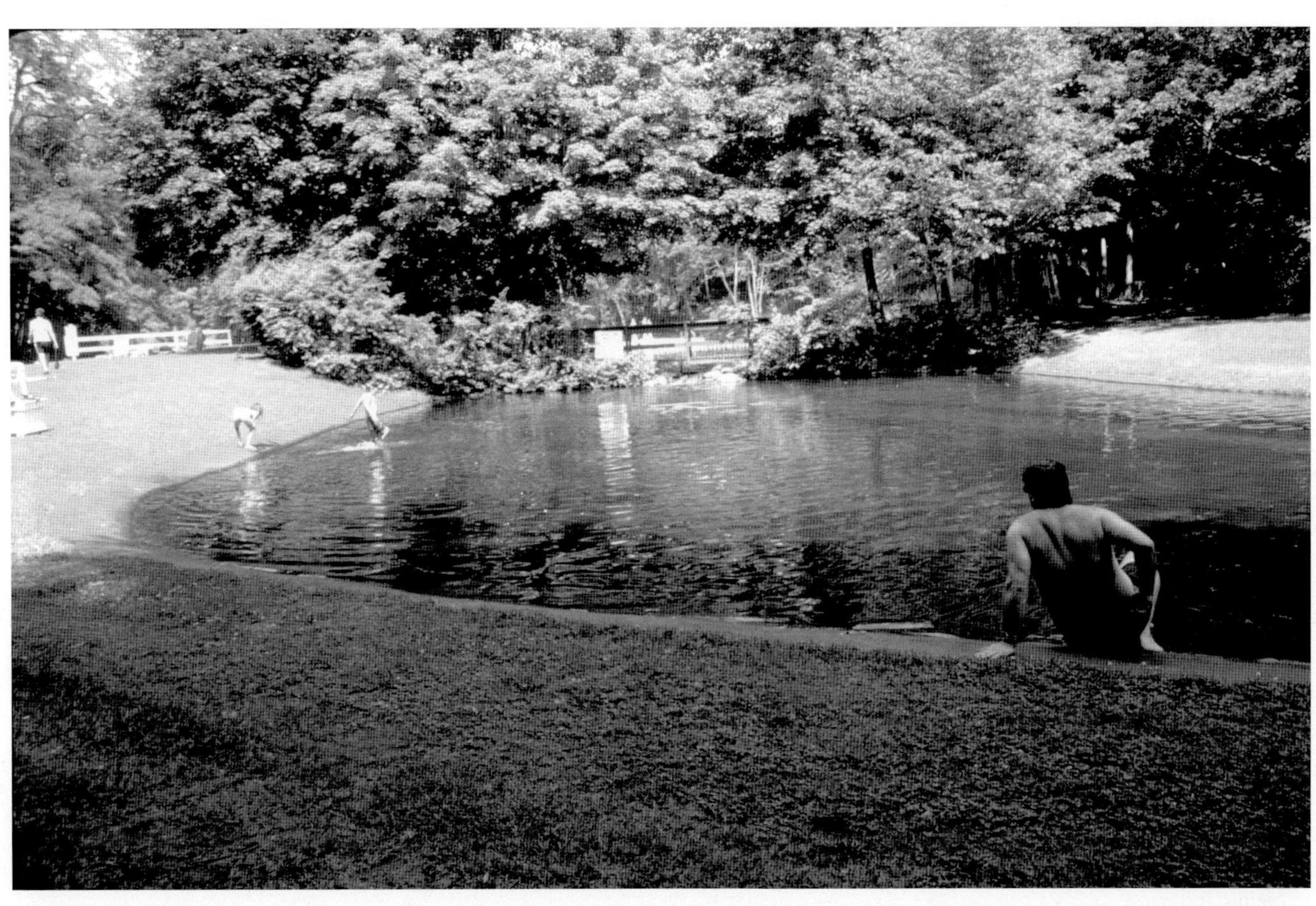

The chalkboards fascinated us. The equations had symbols we had never seen. There were quotes by Goethe and Rousseau. There was a line by Poe: "But there are gradations of matter of which man knows nothing; the grosser impelling the finer." We looked at the chalkboards, one after another, for a long time before retracing our steps down the hallways.

Standing outside in the near dark of late afternoon, I said to my cousins, "Something important is going on here." I knew I would come back.

MAY 10, 2000

The next time I visited The New Society I went alone. It was a brisk spring afternoon, the sky a light gray. I parked in the same small lot we had used before, and again seeing no one, walked freely on the grounds. Not far from the main building I discovered a vegetable garden; farther along, the path led to an old barn, freshly painted; then to a pasture with cows and their calves; and finally to a valley and sheep meadow, bordered on its near side by a stone wall. In the valley I could see dozens of sheep, all grazing, their heads turned, bells clinking as I walked by. I followed a logging trail and up it went, very steeply. I climbed for a long time in solitude beneath the high branches of old oaks, beeches, and maples.

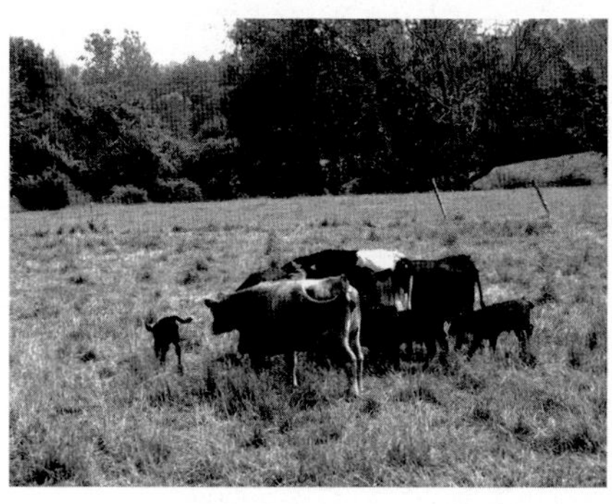

At dusk, at the edge of a field, I saw a group of men and women carrying iron pipes, jugs of water, and other mysterious objects toward a wooden tub.

"Could these be the Harmonites?" I wondered. I remembered Palm's article. Keeping a respectful distance, I stared for a while and then said loudly, "Excuse me." They didn't seem surprised. A young woman separated herself from the crowd and came toward me. She extended her hand and greeted me expectantly.

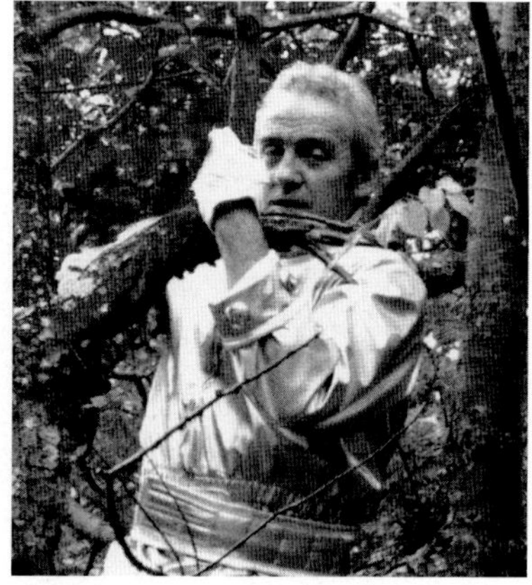

"Hello, I'm Maureen. I'm a cellular biologist." She had a long blond braid and pale blue eyes. She said quietly, "I worked at the spa Hygeology for twelve years, and when it closed Mesmer recruited me to treat the Harmonites." Her warm manner drew me to her.

Whispering into my ear she repeated what I had read in *Ananova*: "F.A. Mesmer is attempting to update and expand the principles of her illustrious forbearer, Franz Anton Mesmer, according to modern discoveries in physics and biology."

She spoke about animal magnetism.[4] Pointing to the wooden tub, Maureen said in a dreamy voice, "You see there, on our left, is the baquet, the bath. People are bathing in the magnetized water."

Walking slowly side by side we came to an apple orchard where I saw men and women tied to the apple trees with ropes. Maureen gestured broadly toward them. "Mesmer magnetizes trees[5] and then ties people to them in daisy-chain fashion. She is particularly keen on fruit-bearing trees."

"Is that so?" I replied.

"Listen," said Maureen. "Cure by the magnetized tree has a long therapeutic history. You can find references to it in many works by Franz Anton Mesmer and in the memoirs of his follower, the Marquis de Puységur." She paused. "Puységur cured the peasant Victor Race under the magnetized elm of Buzancy."[6]

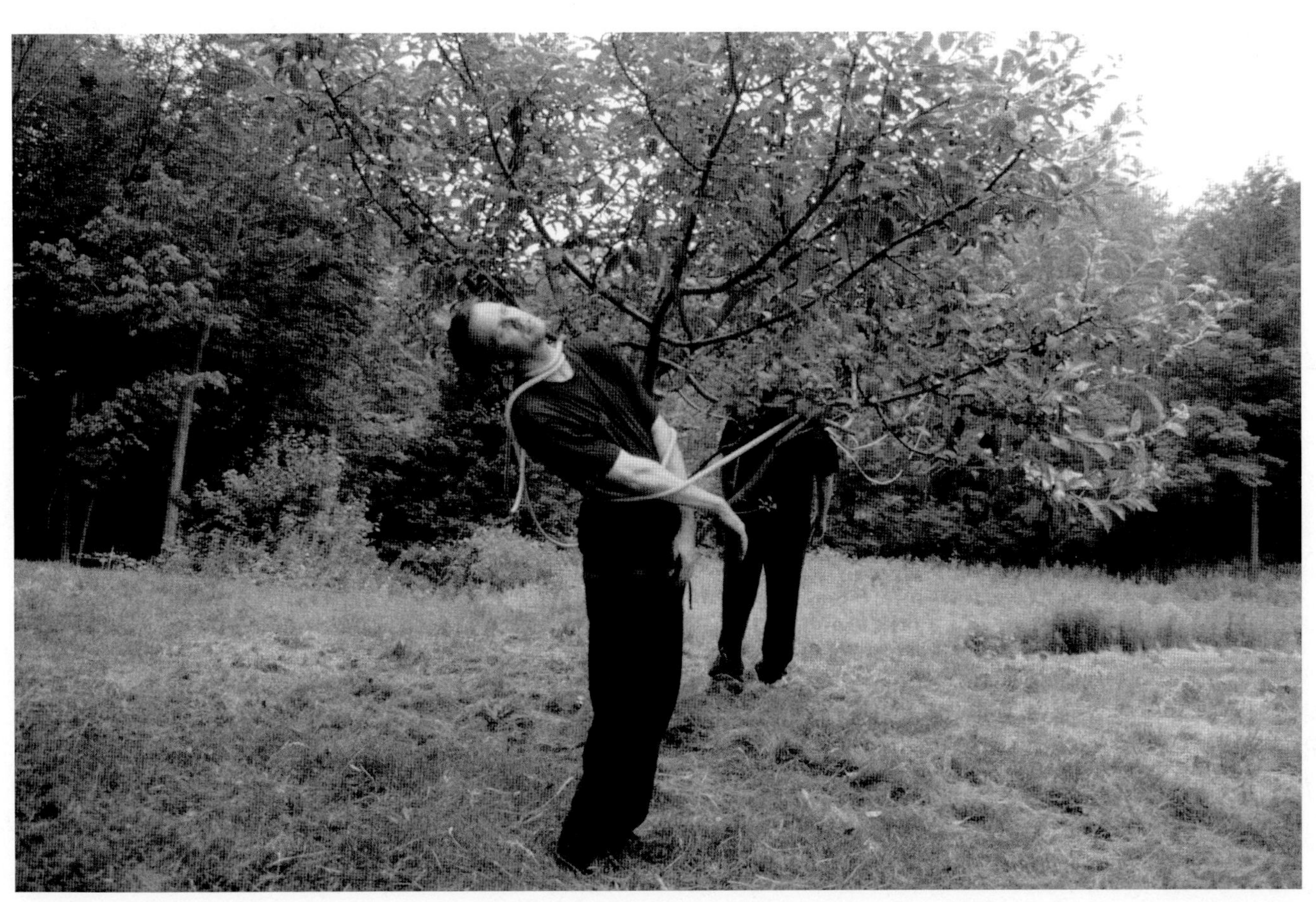

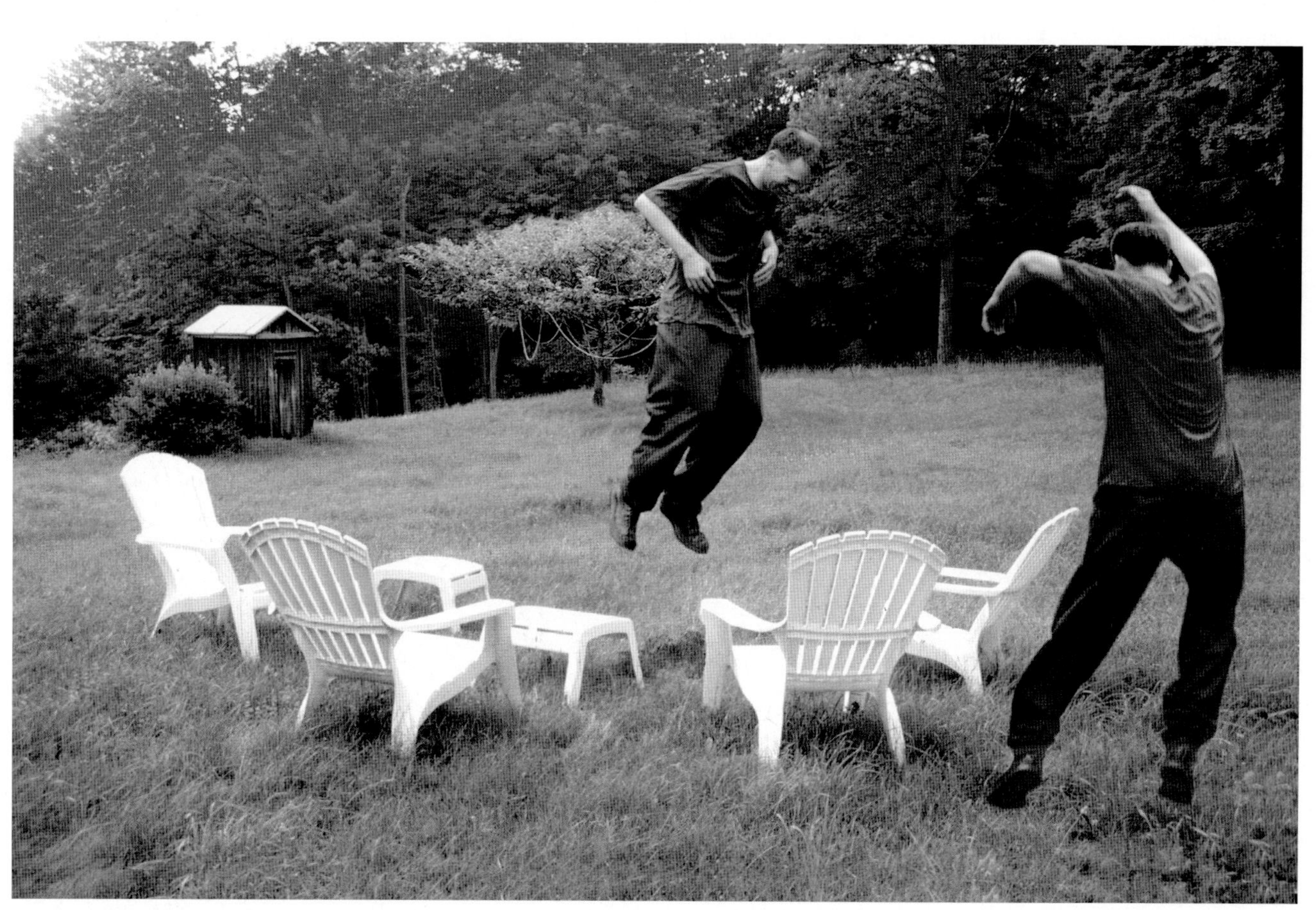

We continued walking and she did most of the talking. Maureen's thoughts were abstract. Inclining her head towards me, she said, "One of the most interesting technical problems may be called psychology. It is the central problem of the mind or the nervous system. Also, there is the physical problem common to many fields that is very old and that has not been solved. It is the analysis of circulating or turbulent fluids. Mesmer is addressing these issues. She believes that the route to the psyche is through the basic sciences."

She continued, "People want to be happy."

I nodded. "It makes perfect sense."

When we parted, she beamed. "Perhaps our paths will cross again."

I answered, "You never know."

JULY 15, 2000

On my next trip I immediately took the path to the logging trail without lingering near the main building. It was a long distance to the field. On the way there it suddenly became hot and windy. I looked up at the sun. It was fierce and bright. A man approached me. He was thin and very tall.

"I'm Ben," he boomed. The trees were rustling and bending furiously in the wind.

"I'm Lenore." I looked up at him. Our eyes met, and I didn't turn away. We stood in the intense heat and wind for some time.

"I'm an investigator," he said. "I research terahertz radiation, particularly the investigation of the terahertz spectral region — that's the wavelength that lies between 30 μm and 1 mm. I'm interested in terahertz radiation's ability to penetrate deep into many organic materials without causing the damage associated with ionizing radiation, such as x-rays."

Then he said with a grave look, "That wind, that heat. You are now witnessing an electromagnetic storm.

"The earth's regular magnetic patterns can be suddenly disrupted by storms that originate in the sun, causing magnificent light displays in the sky or, alternately, power outages and radiation exposure, and occasionally nervous excitation and arousal in human beings. Their bodies become receivers."

The following day I read a report about the storm in *The New York Times*. I was amazed.

AUGUST 12, 2000

I visited Athol Springs again in August and planned on staying a week or longer. I rented a room at the Lavender Lakeview Motel, which isn't really a motel, but more of a bed-and-breakfast. It's run by an energetic woman with very short hair who, with much waving of hands, told me about the interesting sights in the area: the numerous hikes to mountaintops and waterfalls, the old canals and caves, the museum that devotes an entire wing to the display of large taxidermied animals. She stuck her finger into the air. "They have wolves and mastodons and saber-toothed tigers!"

The motel was an Adirondack-style cottage, painted lavender-gray with a screened-in porch facing the lake. Two dormered

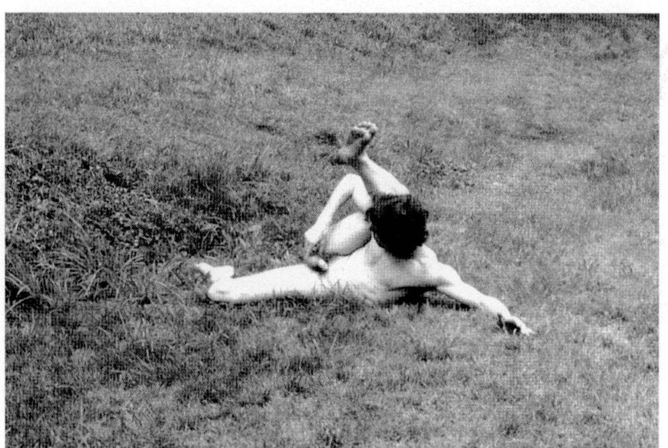

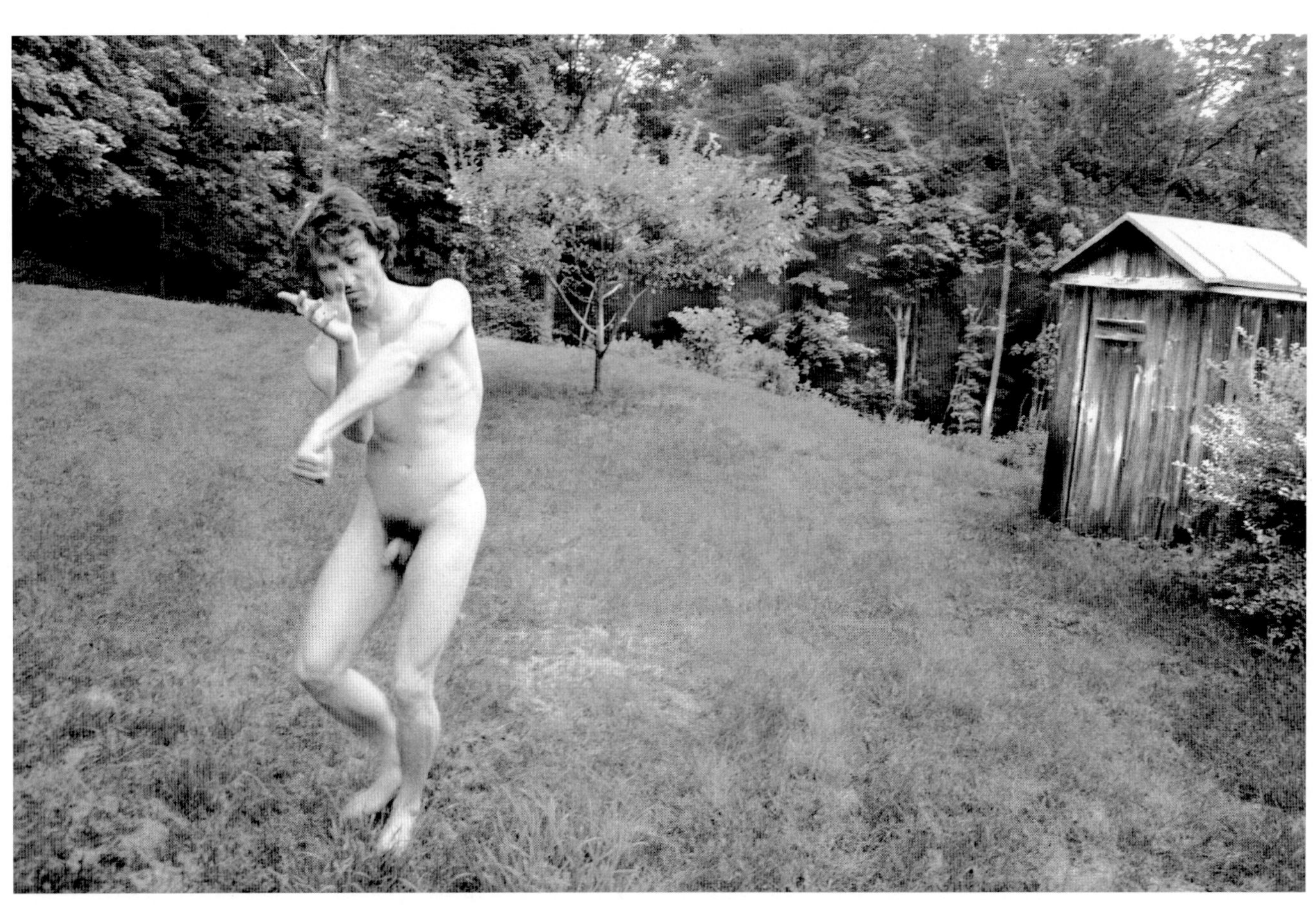

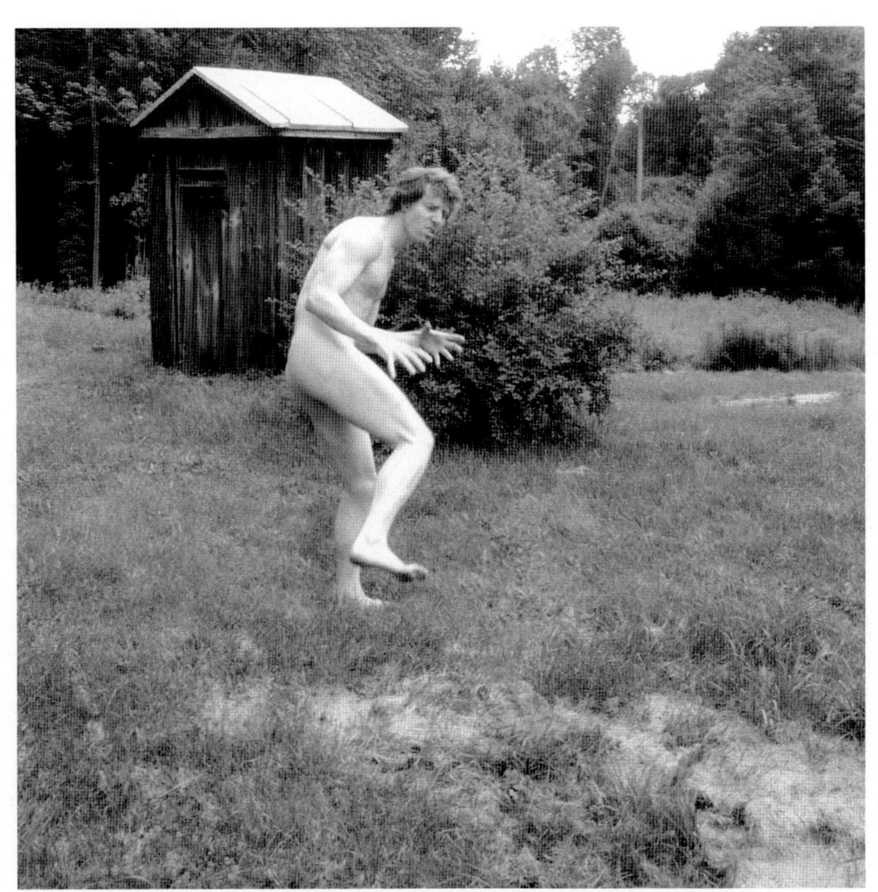

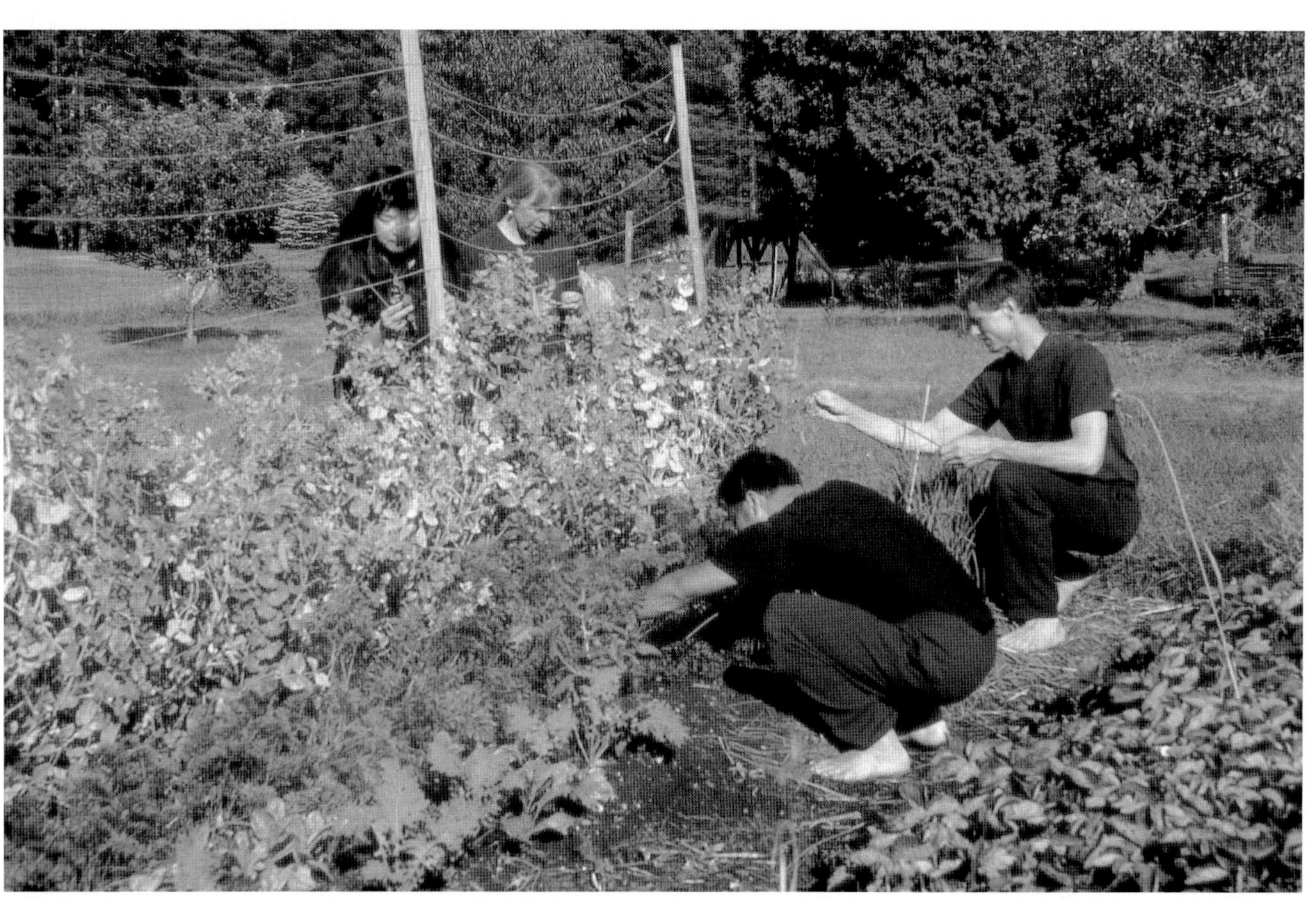

windows perched on its broad sloping roof. Barely fifty yards from the house was a babbling brook that ran into the lake. Upstairs my bedroom walls were lined with pine paneling polished to a golden brown. From my window I had a view of the lake. I tended to linger there at the window a little too long, staring at the lake's glassy surface. I kept rearranging the furniture. The armchair faced west, which was fine in the morning, but in the evening I turned it to face south. I asked the owner to remove an extra chest of drawers, which she did with a smile.

"You may use our kitchen," she told me enthusiastically. In the refrigerator I found an unopened bottle of lime juice and a bottle of tonic. I threw them away and carefully arranged my own food on the shelves.

I called The New Society to announce my visit and found, to my surprise, that they remembered who I was. Ben came to the phone.

"Please," he said, "take the tour."

The following morning Ramona, a helpful guide, showed me the assembly room, the conference room, and the bedrooms where the Harmonites rested after treatment. The atrium and the basement laboratories were off-limits. Ramona talked eloquently about all of the Societies of Harmony. "They were radicals," she said. "Right before the French Revolution, Mesmerism was a radical political theory; its initiation rites combined occult science and masonic-like rituals. In its heyday *La société* had many branches all over Europe. Mesmerism was widely known and respected throughout the nineteenth century in Europe and in America."

She spoke emphatically. "Remember this: The Harmonites are important people and they talk about significant things. They ask each other again and again, 'What is the nature of existence?' and 'Why have we fallen out of harmony?' I've heard them read aloud from Nicolas Bergasse." She paused briefly, putting her hand on my shoulder. "In the 1780s, he wrote, 'We have lost almost all connection with nature' and 'We owe almost all the physical ailments that consume us to our institutions.' Also, he said so prophetically, 'We are on the brink of a Great Revolution.' You know," she said, "Bergasse was a co-founder of the old *La société*."[7]

She raised her eyes. "There's something else you should know: Here we celebrate the Equinox. It's F.A. Mesmer's idea. Every fall on September 22 we meet at a quarry in northern Canada, paying homage to 'Year I' of the French Republic, which began on that very day in 1792. We take the oath: 'The year will begin — miracle of history — with the autumn equinox, a day on which equality belongs to nature.'"[8]

Ramona began telling me more about F.A. Mesmer. Breathlessly, she said: "We revere Mesmer for her brilliance, sensitivity, patience, and compassion, for the depth of her knowledge, but most of all because she believes that every question has an answer and every ailment has a cure."[9]

Lowering her voice, Ramona then politely inquired, "Would you like to take a treatment?"

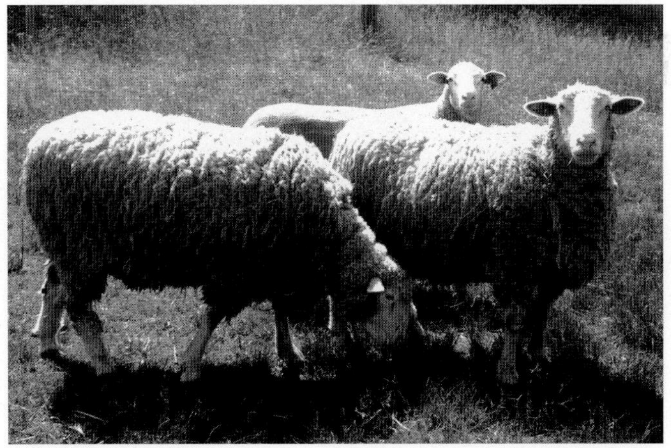

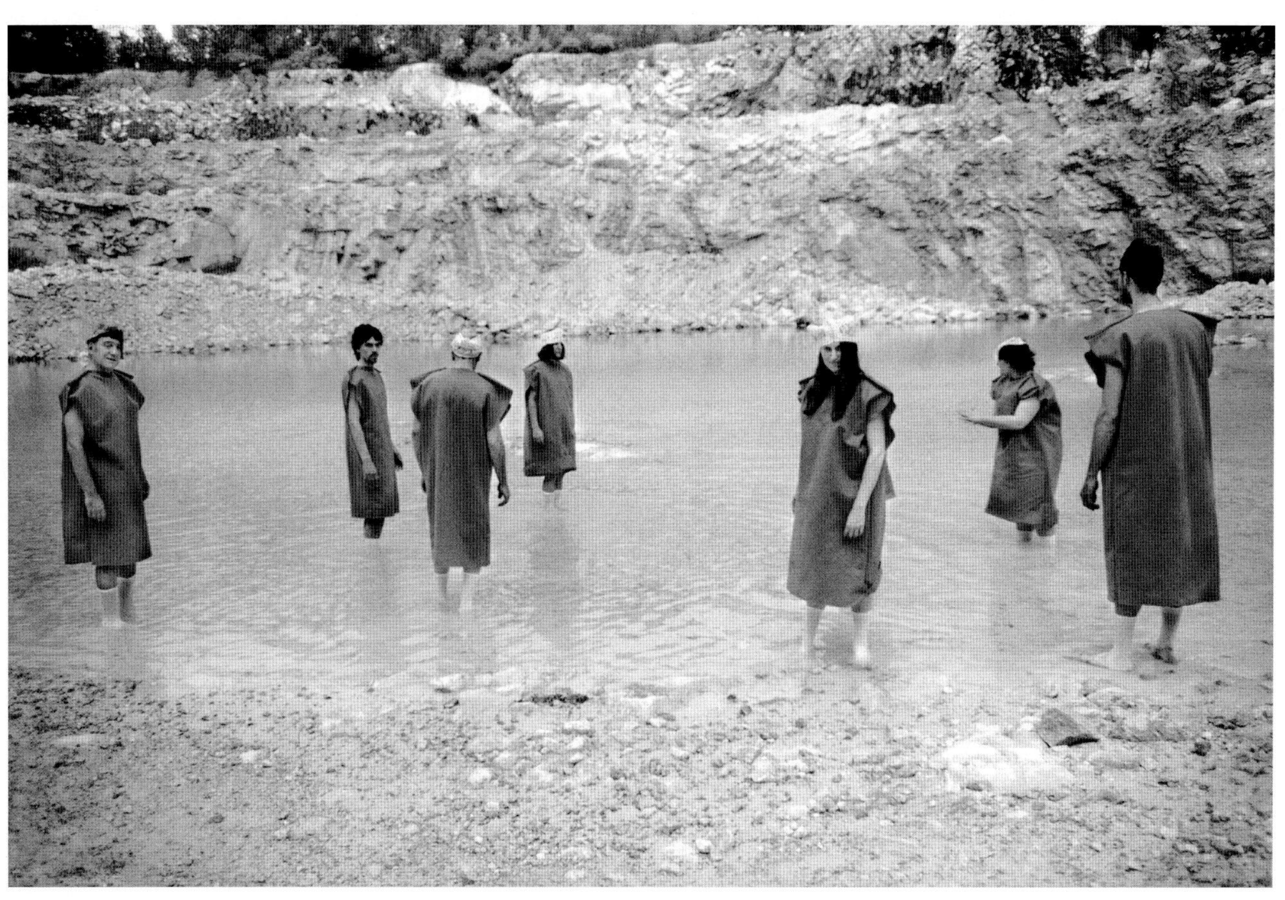

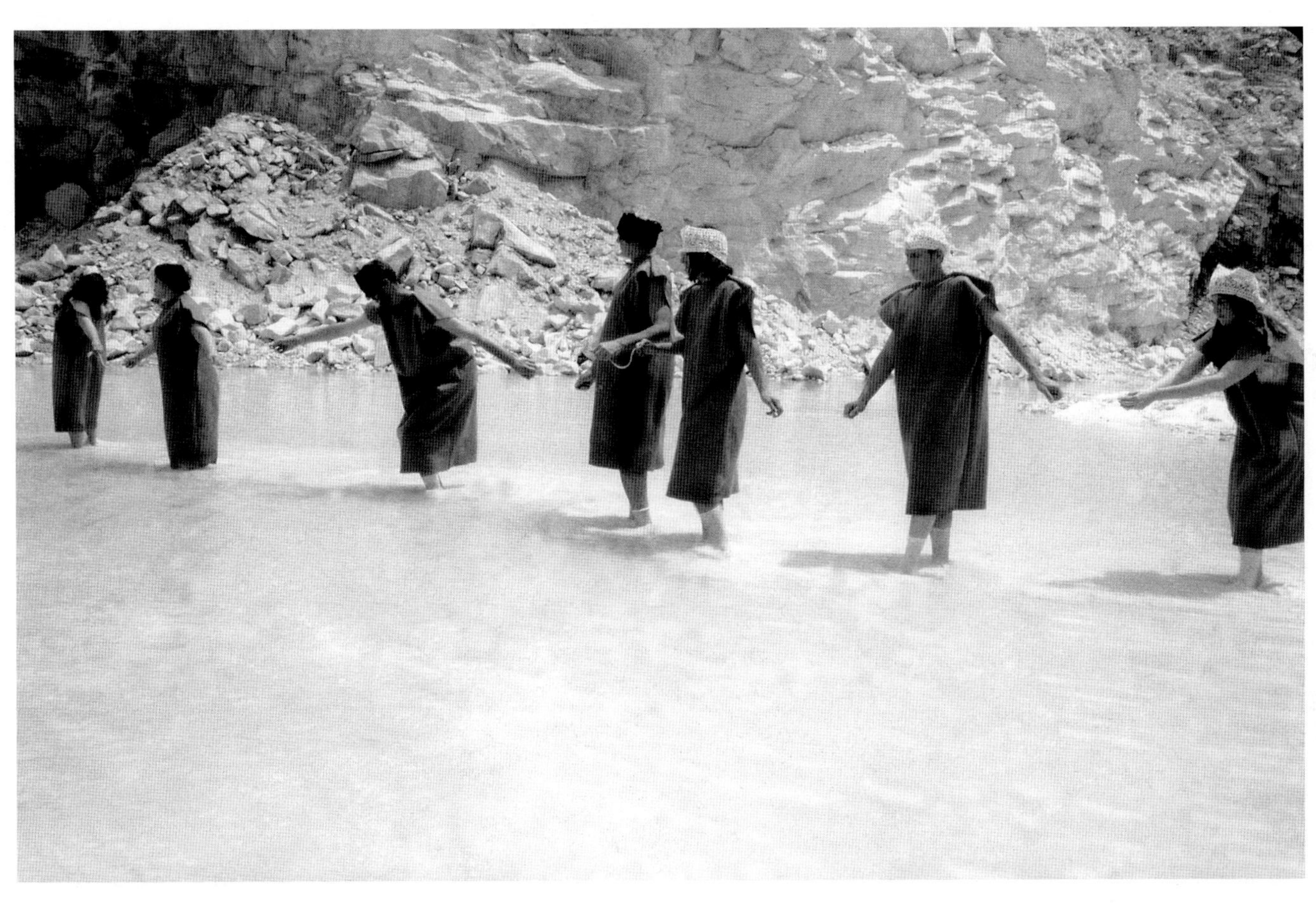

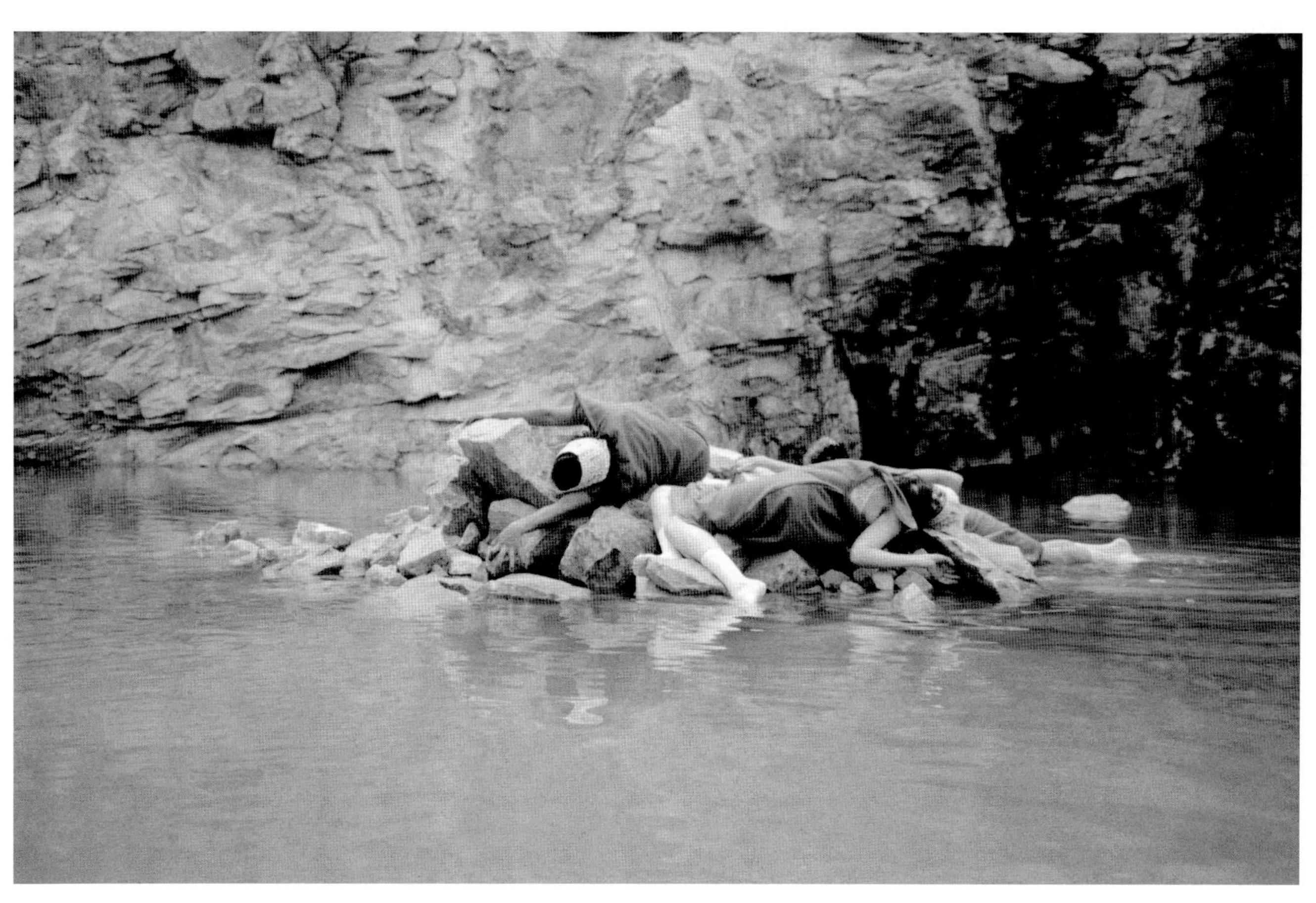

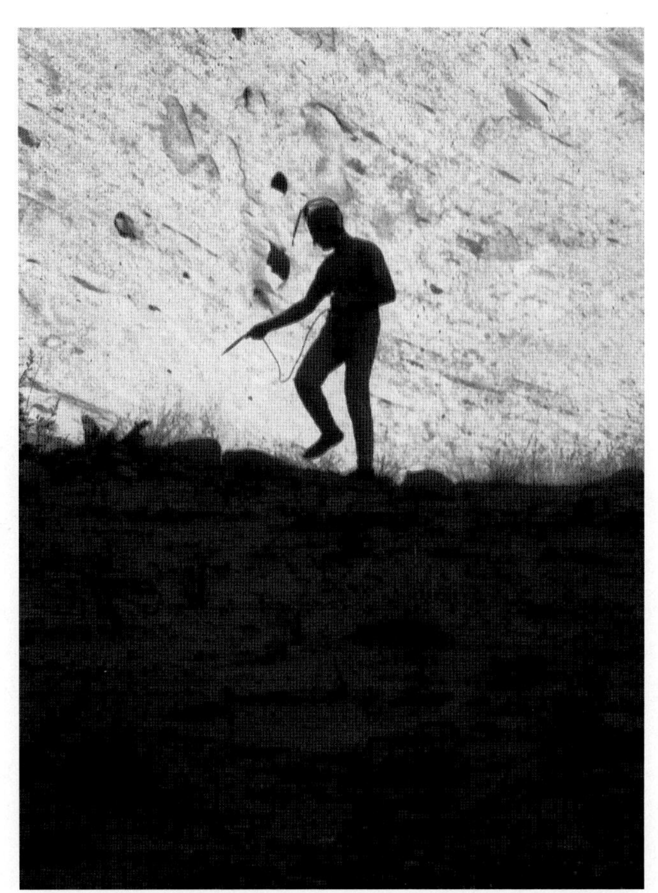

A bit startled, I tried changing the subject. "But where is F.A. Mesmer now?"

"In Sacramento, lecturing."

"I may write a story about the Society," I told her. She said, "If you come again, you can see the archives." "If I come back, may I also see the laboratories?" "Yes."

She left me alone for a few minutes, and I put my ear to the basement door over a sign that read: NO METALS OF ANY KIND. I opened another door onto a large corner room. The windows faced north and east, and when I looked out I could see the sun shining brightly. Inside, pictures of the heavenly bodies lined the walls, and notes tacked with long pins were placed above and below them. The notes held equations that looked like the ones that covered the chalkboards in the corridors. Magnets filled the shelves. Electricity was in the air. There were several armchairs and a couch, also a long table on which were globes of many sizes. At the far end of the table two marble busts were placed so that they appeared in conversation with one another. It was Mesmer's office.

I felt a sudden peacefulness and thought, "I can't bear to leave Athol Springs."

But as soon as I had this realization I chastised myself, "I must go home, resume my life, my work."

I went back and forth.

On the one hand, "I must go home."

On the other hand, "I mustn't go."

I felt that Mesmer was onto something big. I wanted to see the laboratories. I would take pictures. I wondered what I had to lose anyway? Better to stay here. Do what I had never done before.

I went home.

In New York City, at a rooftop party on Labor Day, I met an editor from a major publishing house. I raved about The New

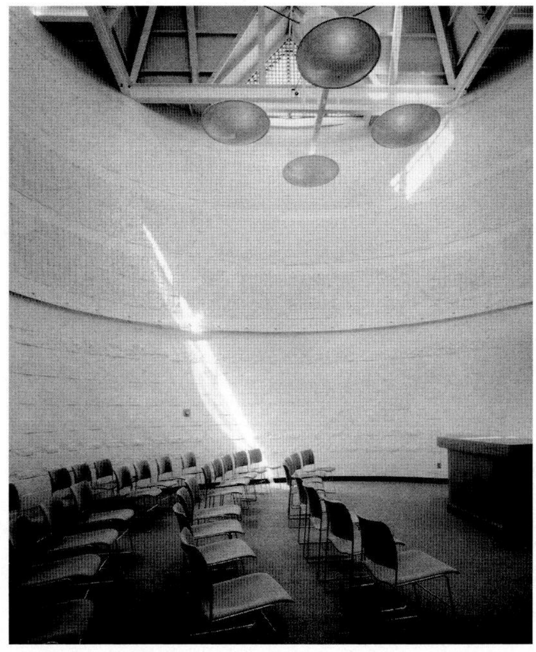

Society and told her about the mysterious Doctor Mesmer.

"There's nothing else like this. I'd like to photograph what I see and write a book about it, too."

"Maybe I can do something for you," she said.

I handed her my card. A few days passed and I received an e-mail from her asking to get together.

We had a long meeting and at the end she said, "There's a story here. Take the pictures. Write the book. Don't rush it. Get involved. Spend a year or longer if you need."

Several weeks later I received a contract with a sizable advance. I would write and I'd shoot the photos, too. I sublet my apartment and came back to Athol Springs. I took a month-to-month lease at the Lavender Lakeview Motel and moved there.

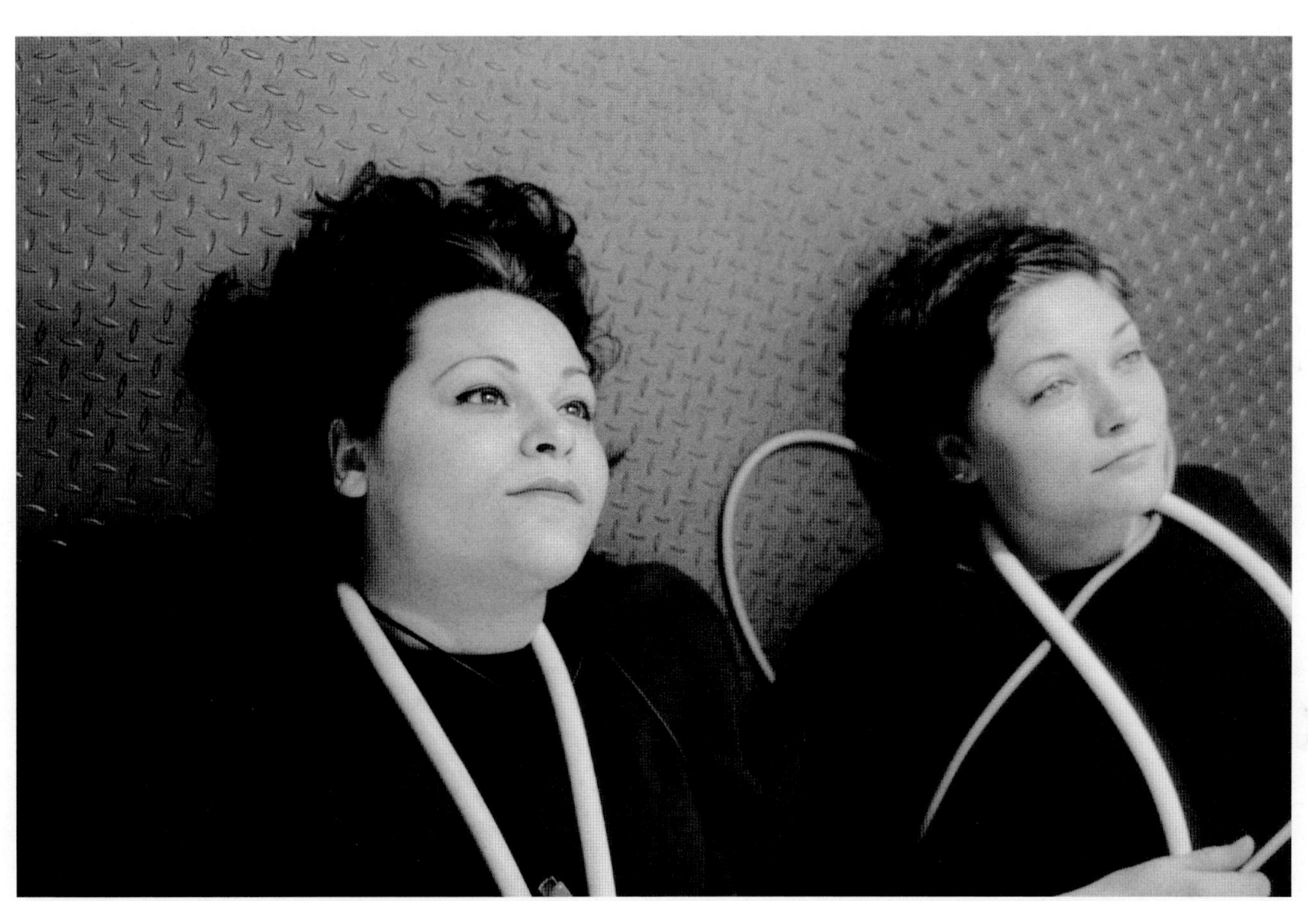

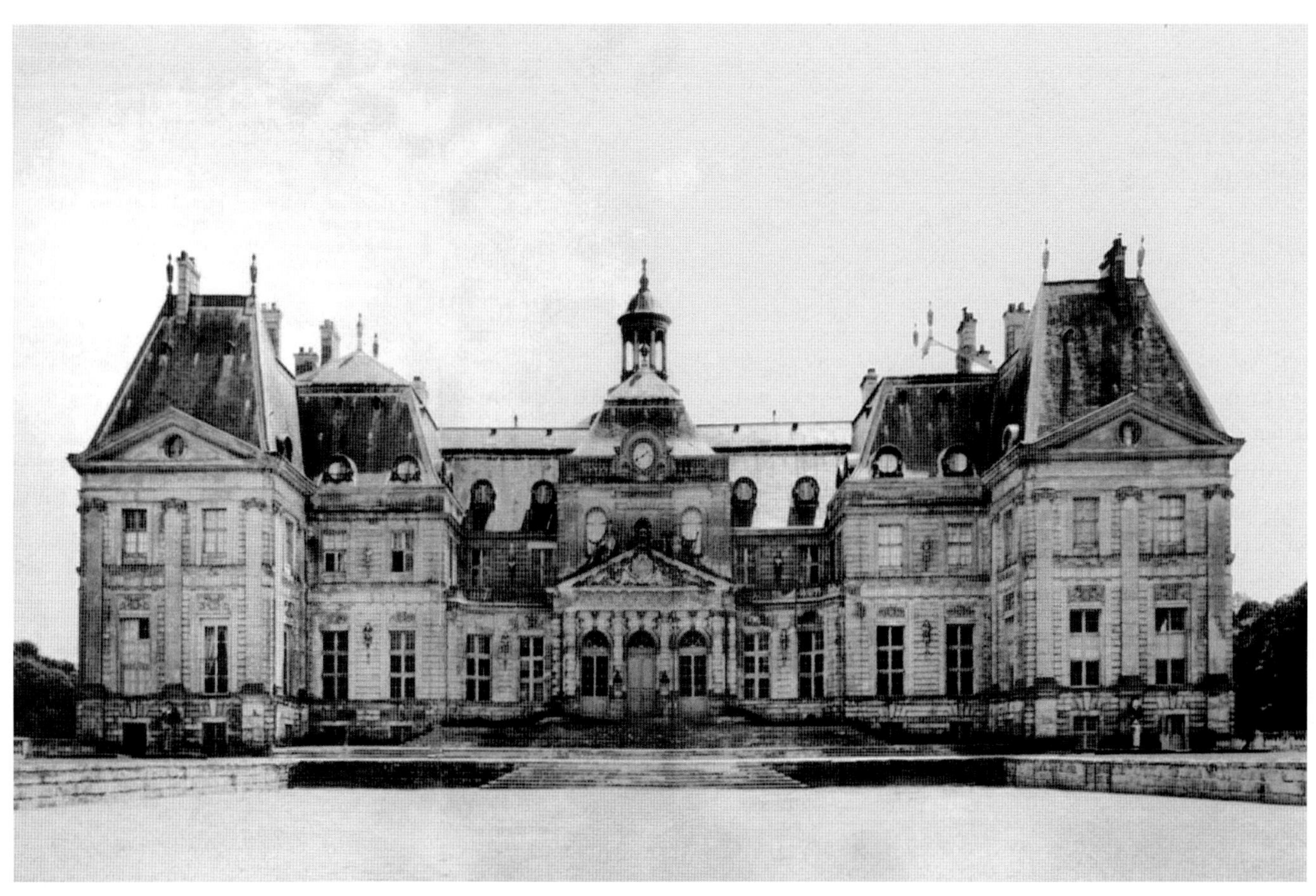

La société de l'harmonie universelle, Nantes

atholôtos untroubled, of water. Hes.
atholos not turbid, clear, Luc.

SEPTEMBER 11, 2000

I arrived at The New Society on Monday at 9:30 A.M. Maureen and Ben greeted me at the door.

"We're so pleased to see you," they both said cheerfully. They knew about my book proposal. "Mesmer welcomes you too, but she's away in Leeds."

After making their rounds and introducing me to the staff, they ushered me into a small office and said I could use it as my own. A computer and monitor occupied most of the desk, so I would have to work on what little space remained, laying things on the floor when necessary.

I was given the key to the Archives Room, where many shelves were stacked with files, books, photographs, and clippings, scores of boxes all organized chronologically.

The books were arranged according to topics too numerous to name. There were old, valuable works in many volumes and many languages, complete editions. I discovered all the works of Ernst Bloch, Charles Fourier, Robert Owen, Karl Mannheim, letters from John Humphrey Noyes, the papers of James Clerk Maxwell and Michael Faraday. Whole shelves were devoted to Mesmerism.

For the next four months I read every day, at first researching Mesmer and his legacy. I selected materials from the Archives Room and carried them back to my little office. I organized my reading carefully so that I read about Franz Anton and then Marquis de Puységur, James Braid, Hippolyte Bernheim, Jean Martin Charcot, and finally Freud.

From time to time I wrote in my diary. The entries were brief.

SEPTEMBER 20, 2000

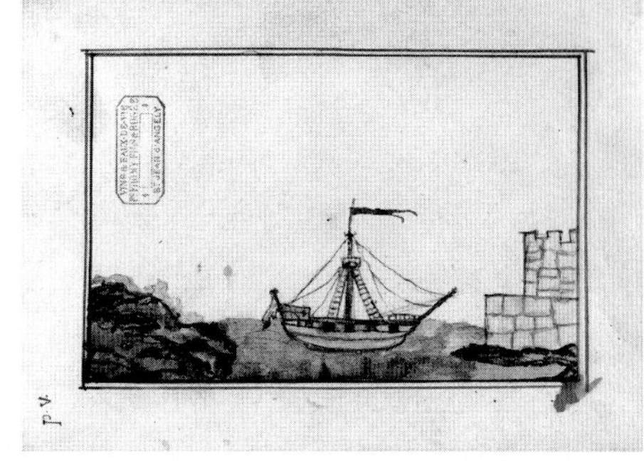

On Friday the moon was in its first quarter. It was affecting my ability to drive. No question about it. I could only drive on the left side of the road. That night I woke in the darkness and had no idea of where I was. The following day I went canoeing, tipped the canoe in the middle of the lake, and had to push it to the dock with my arms.

But when I settled in at The New Society, I felt good.

Mesmer — I read his *Dissertatio physico-medica de planetarum influxu*, 1766; the *Mémoire de F.A. Mesmer, docteur en médicine sur ses découvertes,* 1799; the *Précis historique des faits relatifs au magnétisme animal jusqu'en Avril,* 1781; and *"Catéchisme du magnétisme animal,"* in *L'Antimagnétisme, ou origine, progrès, décadence, renouvellement et réfutation du magnétisme animal,* 1784.

Drawing from Newtonianism and astrology, Mesmer argued in his dissertation that it was the gravitational attraction of the planets that played a role in human health by affecting an invisible fluid found in the body and throughout nature.

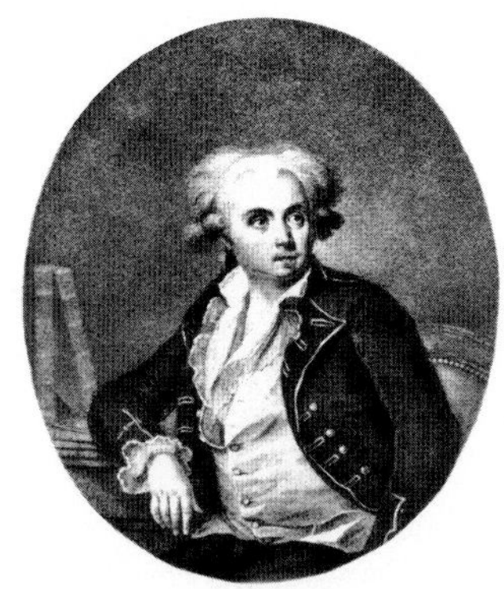

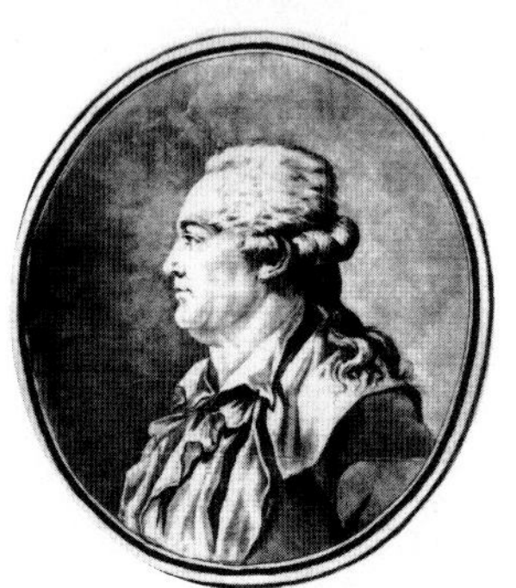

THÉORIE
du
MONDE
&
DES ÊTRES ORGANISÉS
Suivant les Principes
De M...
Gravée par D'A:-Ol:
A PARIS
1784

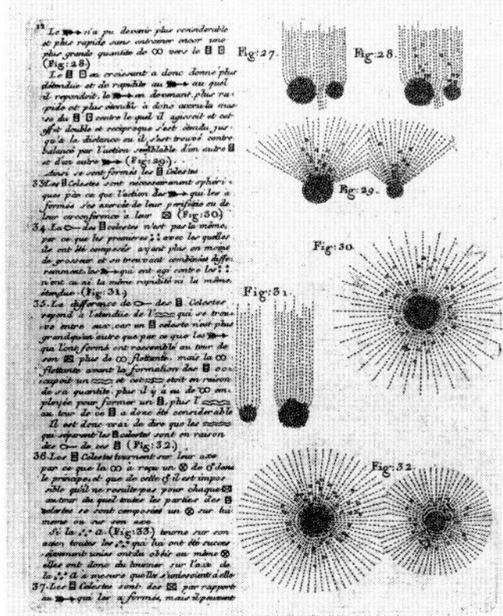

PAGE 29 Watercolor from *Principes du magnétisme,* ca 1786. Courtesy The Bakken Library, Minneapolis.
LEFT Nicholas Bergasse from Louis Bergasse, *Un défenseur des principes traditionnels sous la Révolution, Nicolas Bergasse* (Paris, 1910).
CENTER Franz Anton Mesmer, courtesy Bibliotèque National, Paris.
BOTTOM *Théorie du monde,* edited by Bergasse from Mesmer's lectures, from an edition of 100 engraved copies. Courtesy The Bakken Library, Minneapolis.
OPPOSITE Frontispiece from *Mémoires pour servir à l'histoire et l'establishment du magnétisme animal.* By A.M.J. De Chastenet, M. de Puységur. Third edition, Paris. J.G. Dentu, 1820. Courtesy The Bakken Library, Minneapolis.

Disease, he believed, was the result of obstacles in the fluid's ebb and flow and these obstacles could be broken by trancelike crises or convulsions. Mesmer initially used magnets as a curative agent, but eventually dispensed with them, considering himself to be an animal magnet.

I held in my hand engravings of Mesmer and his followers, Bergasse and Kornmann. Also emblems and diagrams of Bergasse's "physio-moral" laws of nature. I found pages torn from folios, also pictures of palaces and engravings that showed Mesmeric treatments from the 1780s through the 1850s, sheaves of paper with occult texts, slim books in French and German with marginalia written by F.A. Mesmer and others before her, dating back to 1784. Many pieces referred to the Societies of Harmony, to politics, and to the occult. It was all true. An underground current of radicalism ran through the Mesmeric movement.

I discovered a text undated, but probably written in the 1780s or 1790s — a discourse on Egyptian religion from *La société de l'harmonie* of Bordeaux.

Mesmer distanced himself from the occult. I began to sense that his ideas were modified early on and Mesmerism, as it evolved in the nineteenth century, had less and less to do with his original theses.

OCTOBER 15, 2000

Today I attended an outdoor lecture on rebuilding the body. How do we stay strong and healthy? How do we feed ourselves well and cheaply? I had hoped to meet Mesmer. "You will some day," said Ramona. "But this week Mesmer is in Argentina conducting seminars."

OCTOBER 22, 2000

Ramona took another job and was replaced by Sherry, a woman with curly red hair, very outgoing.

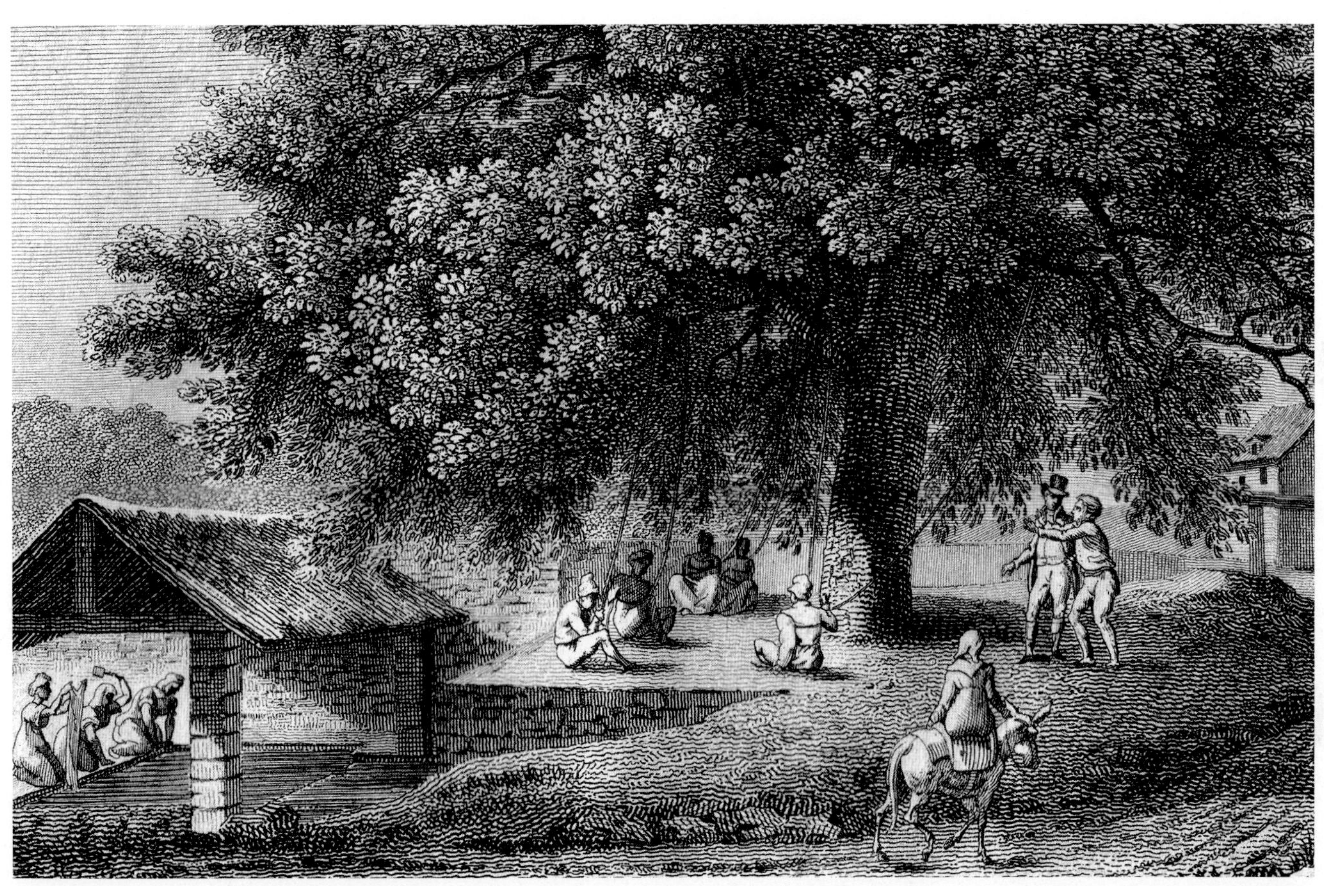

BOTTOM Animal Magnetism: The Operator Putting His Patient Into a Crisis. Engraving from *A Key to Physic, and the Occult Sciences,* by Ebenezer Silby, London. Printed for the author, 1796. Courtesy The Bakken Library, Minneapolis.
TOP Two sisters in Mesmeric communication. From Alison Winter, *Mesmerized: Powers of Mind in Victorian Britain.* Chicago, University of Chicago Press, 1998, p.142.
PAGE 33 Lethargy. From *Iconographie photographique de la Salpêtrière,* 1876–80.

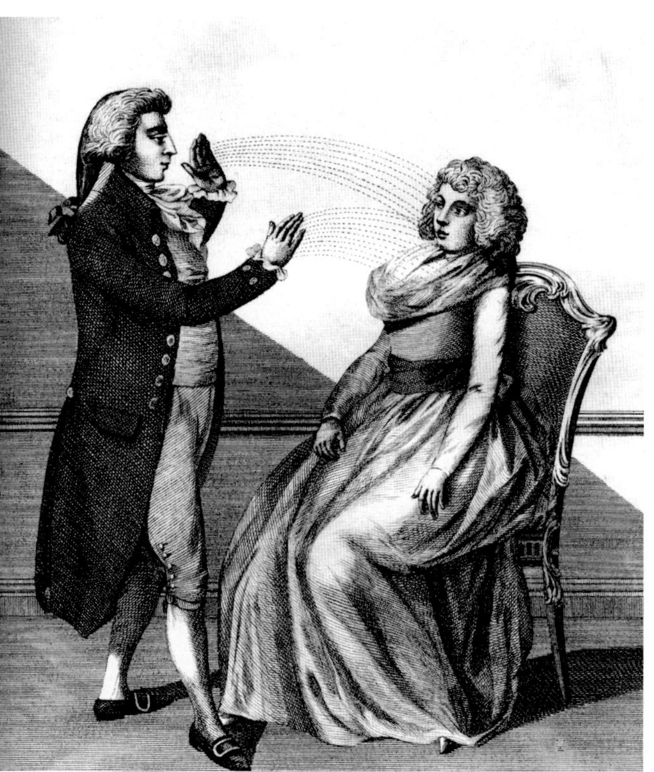

I've made friends with my landlady, who comes from St. Petersburg, Florida. She was divorced twice and her kids live in the West. We drove to the mall to buy some winter clothes.

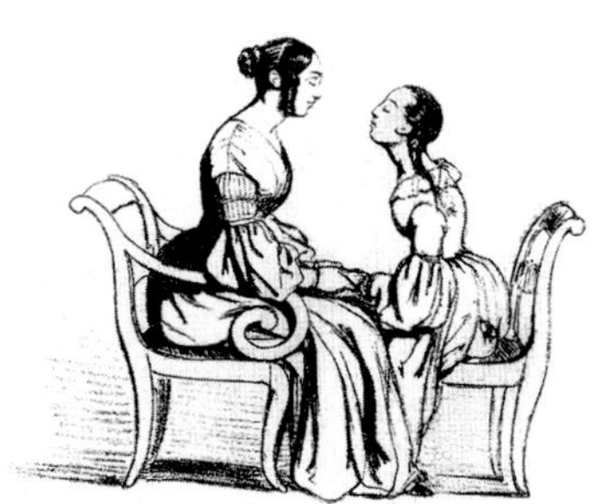

Maureen had suggested I read the memoirs of Puységur, Mesmer's follower. Here is what he said about the magnetized tree: "After attaching a rope to a tree I tried its effectiveness on some sick people. The first patient came and as soon as he had put the rope around himself, he looked at the tree and said with an air of surprise, which cannot be duplicated: 'What do I see there?' Next his head dropped and he was in a perfect state of somnambulism."

In 1784, while treating Victor Race, a peasant on his estate, Puységur discovered an unusual state of consciousness, in which the patient is "awake" while sleeping. He called this state "magnetic somnambulism." Mesmer's approach was physiological, but what Puységur described was a psychological relationship between magnetizer and patient.

NOVEMBER 17, 2000

Mesmer is in Stockholm delivering a paper. Last Thursday there was a crisis at The New Society. The lights began to flicker. Through the walls I heard the hushed voices of Maureen and Ben. "The basement generators are malfunctioning. Nothing to worry about," they told me. I saw a Harmonite in the front office sitting bolt upright with a lost look on his face.

Yesterday I attended a wonderful party in the conference room. With much laughter, hugging and kissing couples were wandering off. It was lunchtime and we were served tomatoes, red peppers, and carrots flavored with sambar curry powder. At

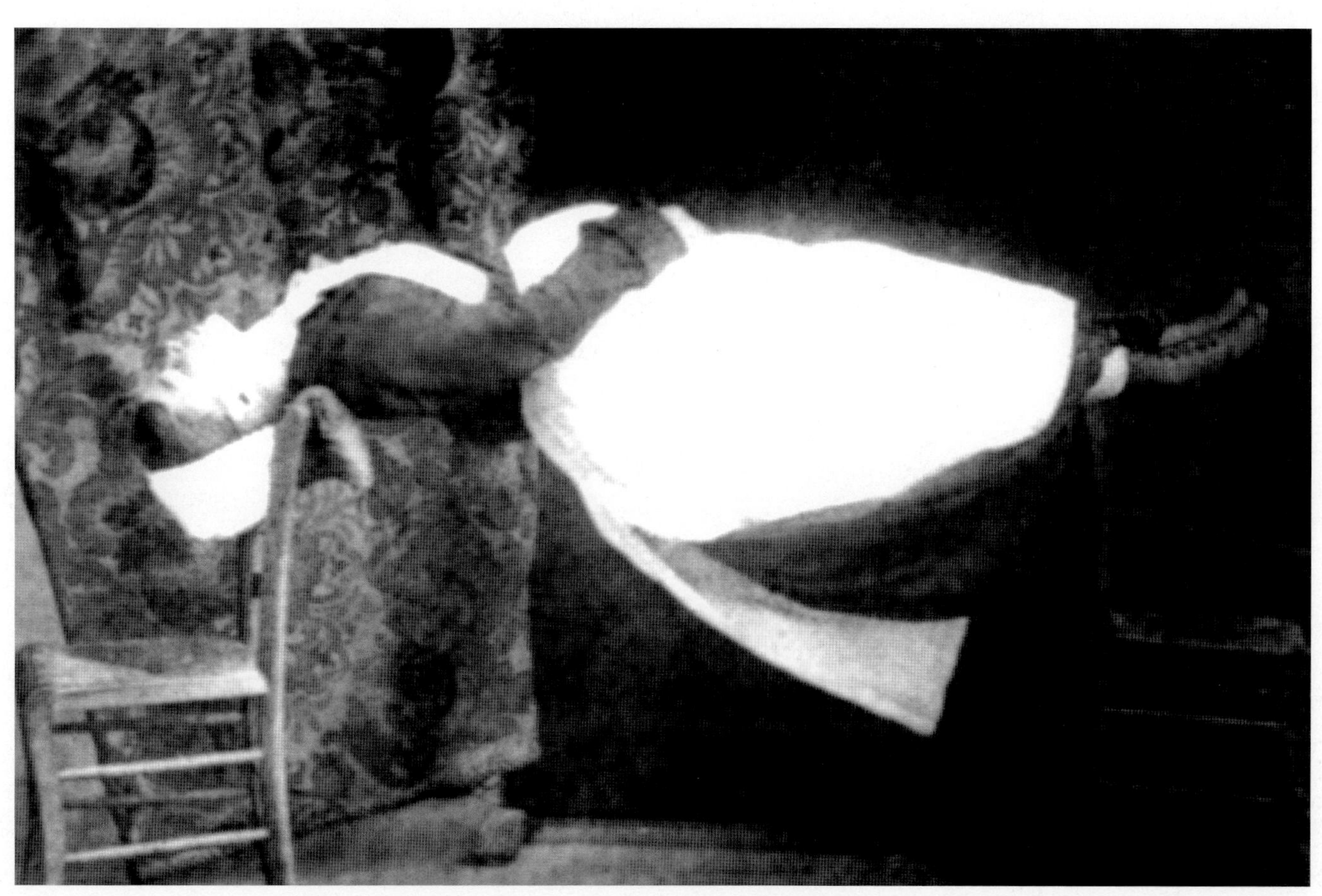

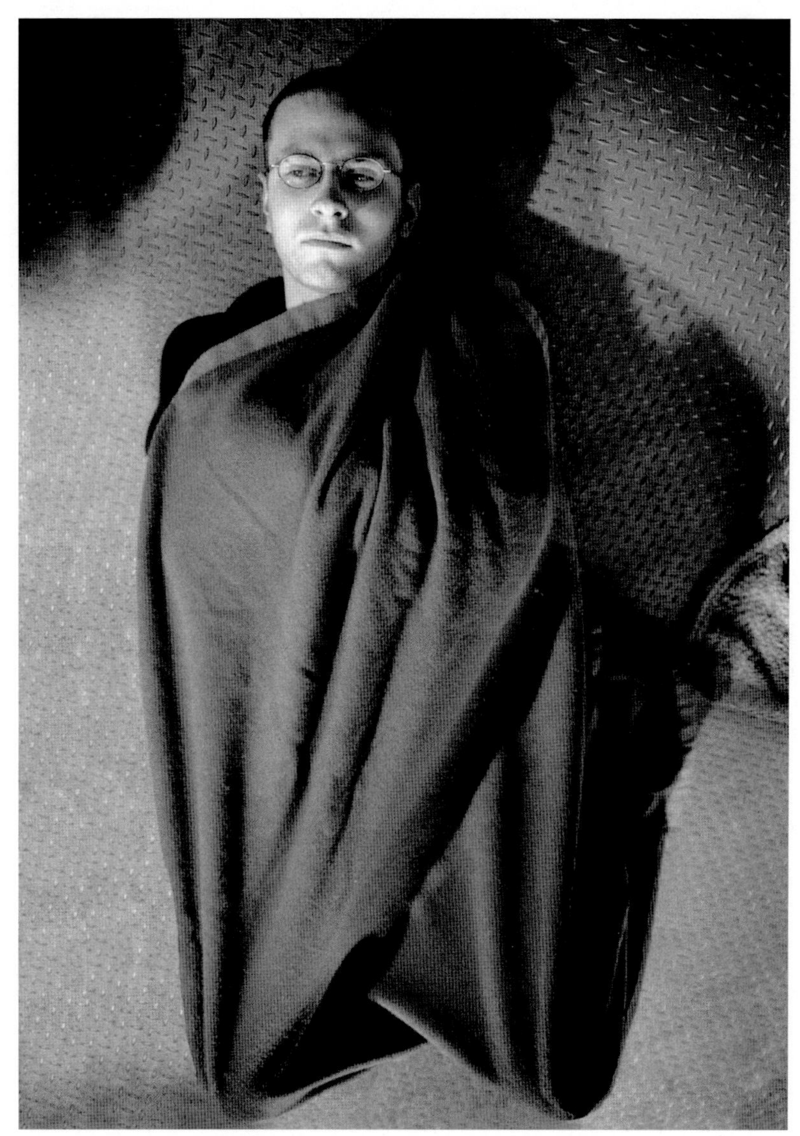

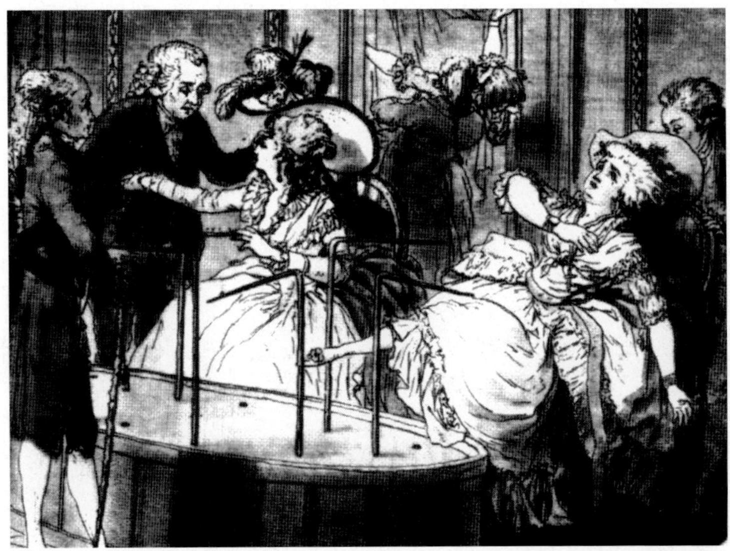

LEFT Detail of *The Magnetism*. Drawn by Sergent, engraved by Toyuca, ca 1785. Courtesy The Bakken Library, Minneapolis. Mesmer's *baquet* was a tublike apparatus filled with iron filings and powdered glass. Iron rods come from the tub, transmitting a magnetic fluid. As patients surround the tub, they hold hands. The magnetic fluid creates a magnetic bond between them. The woman on the right has experienced convulsions and is being carried away to a crisis room.

the party I met a handsome man named Kent. He sat down beside me and we talked for a while. He tried to kiss me, but I turned my head: "Not now."

I continued reading and discovered the work of James Braid. A nineteenth-century Scottish physician, Braid attended magnetic stage demonstrations while living in Manchester in the 1840s. Disavowing the popular notion of the magical passage of a fluid or other influence from the operator to the patient, Braid adopted a physiological view. He said that magnetic sleep is a state induced by fatigue resulting from the concentration necessary for staring fixedly at a bright, inanimate object. He coined the term "hypnosis," distancing himself from Mesmer.[1]

I came upon volumes on Mesmerism and animal magnetism in America resting in a corner of a high shelf. Widely practiced — many branches — thousands of practitioners. I pulled down from the shelf an edition of Charles Poyen's *Progress of Animal Magnetism in New England* (1837). Afterwards I read James Caldwell's *Facts in Mesmerism* (1842). I read John Dod's *The Philosophy of Electrical Psychology* (1850). In 1850 Dod lectured to the U.S. Senate on electromagnetism. Then there was Caldwell, a practitioner of phrenomagnetism. I read his book, *Facts in Mesmerism* (1842); also Stanley Grimes's *Etherology: Or the Philosophy of Mesmerism and Phrenology* (1845); and Andrew Jackson Davis's *The Divine Revelations* (undated).

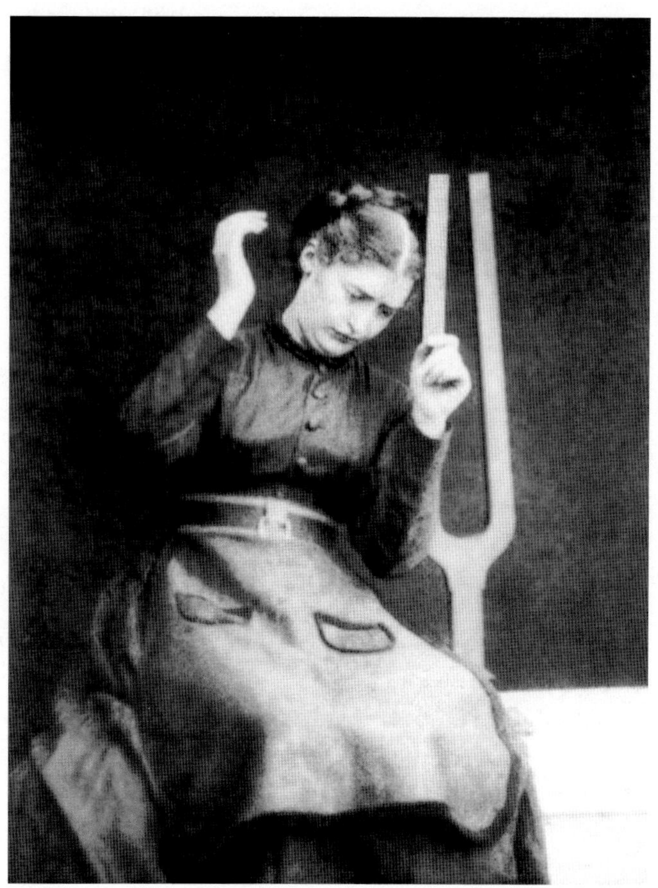

DECEMBER 2, 2000

Nothing happened with Kent. I met a woman named May who was brought to The New Society by her husband. I saw her in the dining room at lunch poised at the edge of her seat. She was softly reciting chapter four, verse thirty-two, of the *Acts of the Apostles:*

> And the multitude of them that believed were of one heart and of one soul: neither said any of them that ought of the things which he possessed was his own; but they had all things common.

I put my arms on her shoulders. "Greetings," I said. She turned towards me; her face brightened.

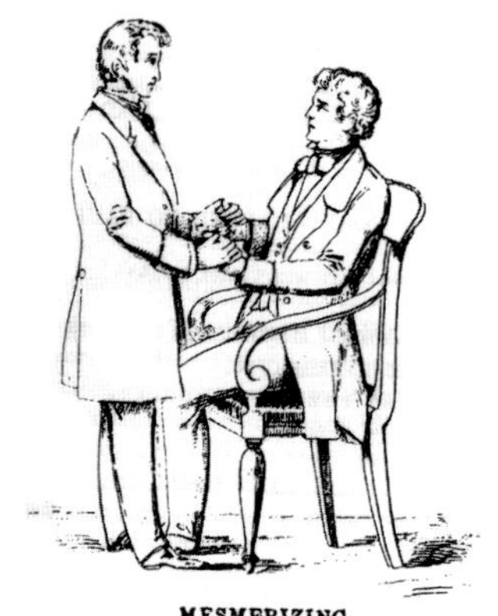

MESMERIZING.

In the Archives Room I found a folder titled "Ambrose August Liébeault" and one titled "Hippolyte Bernheim." Both men were magnetists and believed that their magnetic cures had a physiological basis. But around 1884 they repudiated animal magnetism for the more psychological concept of "suggestion." That became the cardinal principle of their School of Nancy. Put another way, the doctor "suggests" something and you believe it.

DECEMBER 9, 2000

A number of guests went to Buffalo last night to see a screening of the film *Fahrenheit 451*. I declined and spent the night reading Bernheim in my motel room.

Bernheim's ideas on suggestion were provocative. I've been thinking about them, but I remain wary. We live in a physical universe. We are animals, physical beings. Can you suggest to a dog: "YOU THINK THIS" or "YOU THINK THAT"?

Today I found a nineteenth-century volume called *La Salpêtrière*. An immense book filled with engravings, it describes the history of the so-named Parisian hospital where G.-B. Duchenne de Boulogne, the first neurologist, and Jean Martin Charcot, his pupil, did their work.

In the 1840s at *La Salpêtrière*, Duchenne demonstrated the relationship between facial expression and emotion by activating the muscles of the face with electricity and then photographing the patient. From the 1870s through the 1890s, while investigating the phenomenon of hypnosis at *La Salpêtrière*, Charcot and his students experimented with real mineral magnets, calling their treatment "metallotherapy."[2] Like Mesmer, Charcot believed that hypnosis and magnetic sleep (or somnambulism) were somatic rather than psychological in origin. The connection between the two men was duly noted by Charcot's students Charles Féré and Alfred Binet in their book *Le magnétisme animal* (1887). Hippolyte Bernheim, co-founder of the Nancy school of hypnotism, strongly distinguished his views from those of Charcot, and thus a protracted feud ensued between the two institutions: the School of Nancy and the Salpêtrière School.

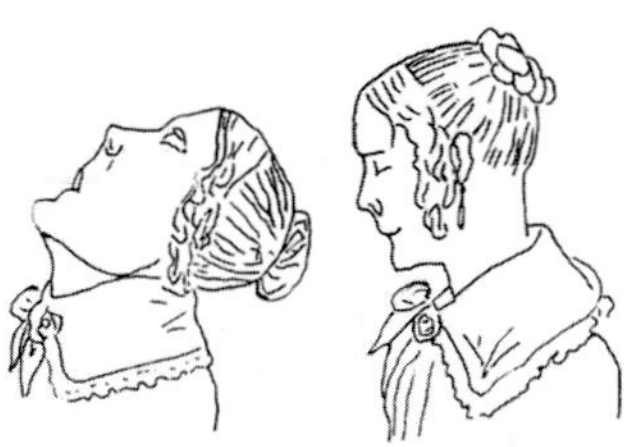

I wondered about Freud. In the fall of 1885, Charcot was Freud's teacher at *La Salpêtrière*. The young Freud wrote: "Charcot, who is one of the greatest physicians, a genius and a sober man, simply uproots my views and intentions."[3] Freud continued to lean toward Charcot's views until a visit to Nancy in 1889. In the 1890s he grew closer to Bernheim, rejecting the theories put forth at *La Salpêtrière*. We know from his writings that Freud was aware of Mesmer and magnetism.[4]

PAGE 36 Catalepsy. Provoked by the Sound of a Tuning Fork. *Iconographie photographique de la Salpêtrière,* 1876–1888.
PAGE 38 Plate 10 from *Mécanisme de la physionomie humaine,* G.-B. Duchenne de Boulogne, Paris, 1862.
PAGE 39 Plates 38 and 39 from *Mécanisme de la physionomie humaine.*

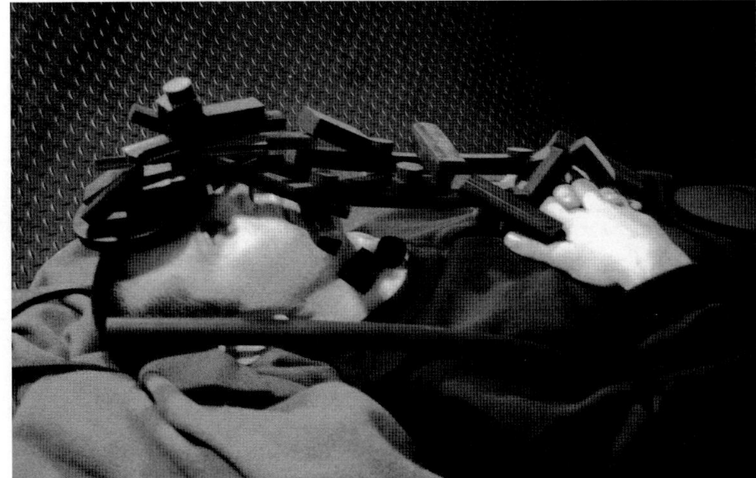

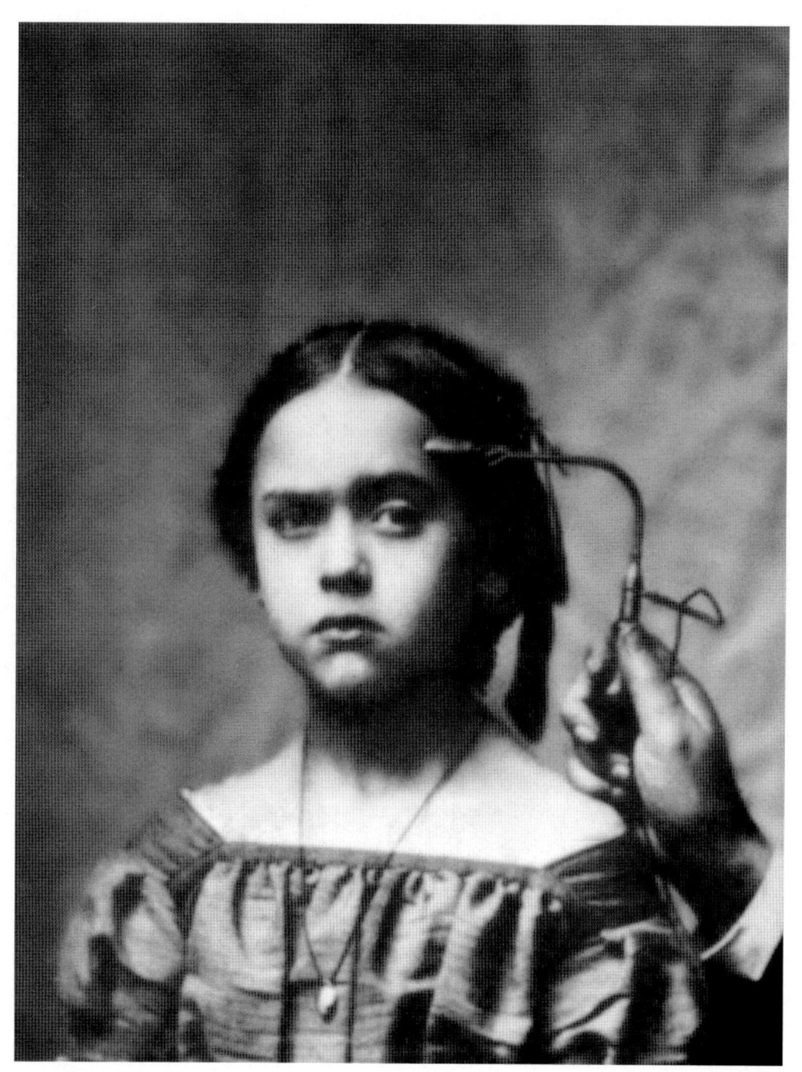

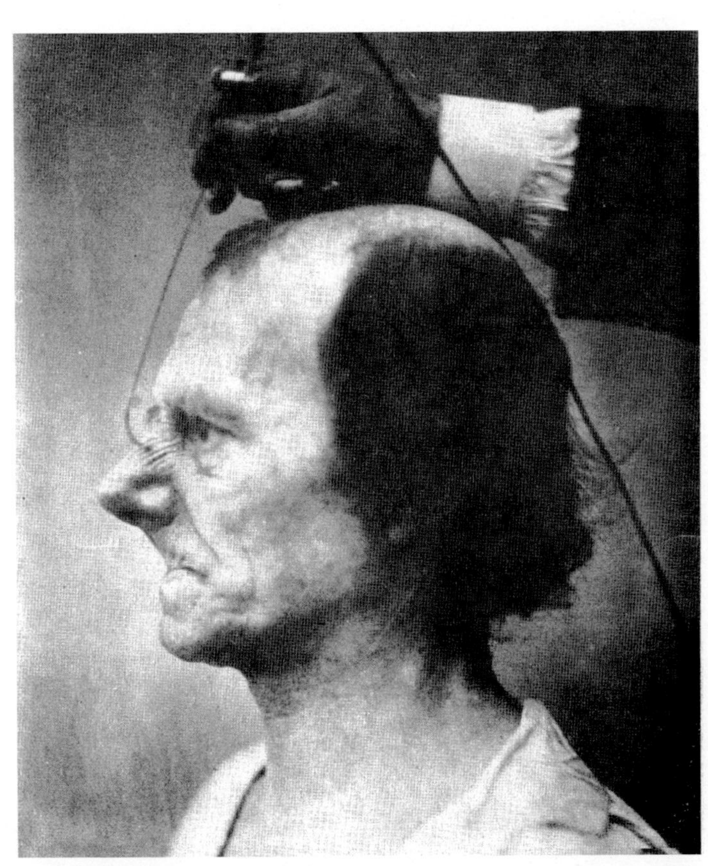

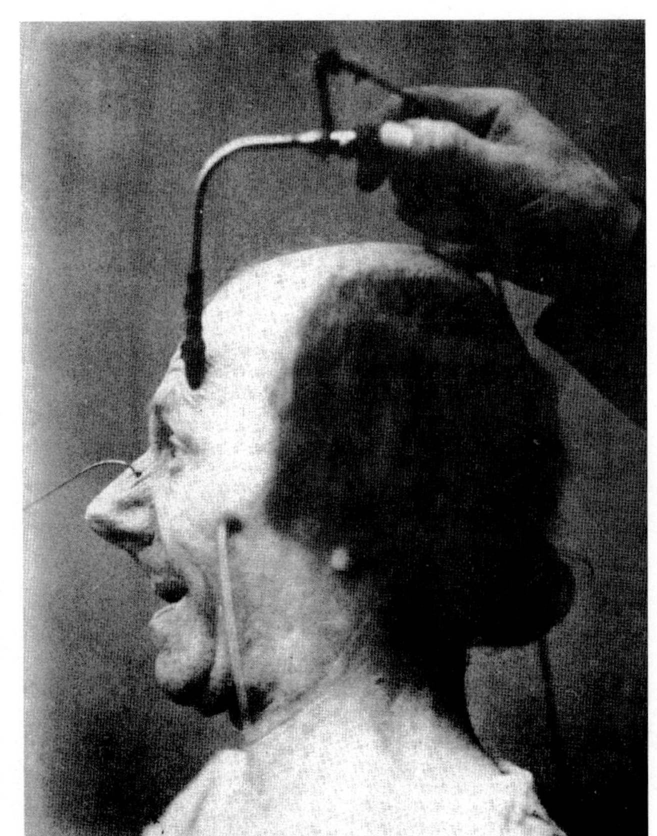

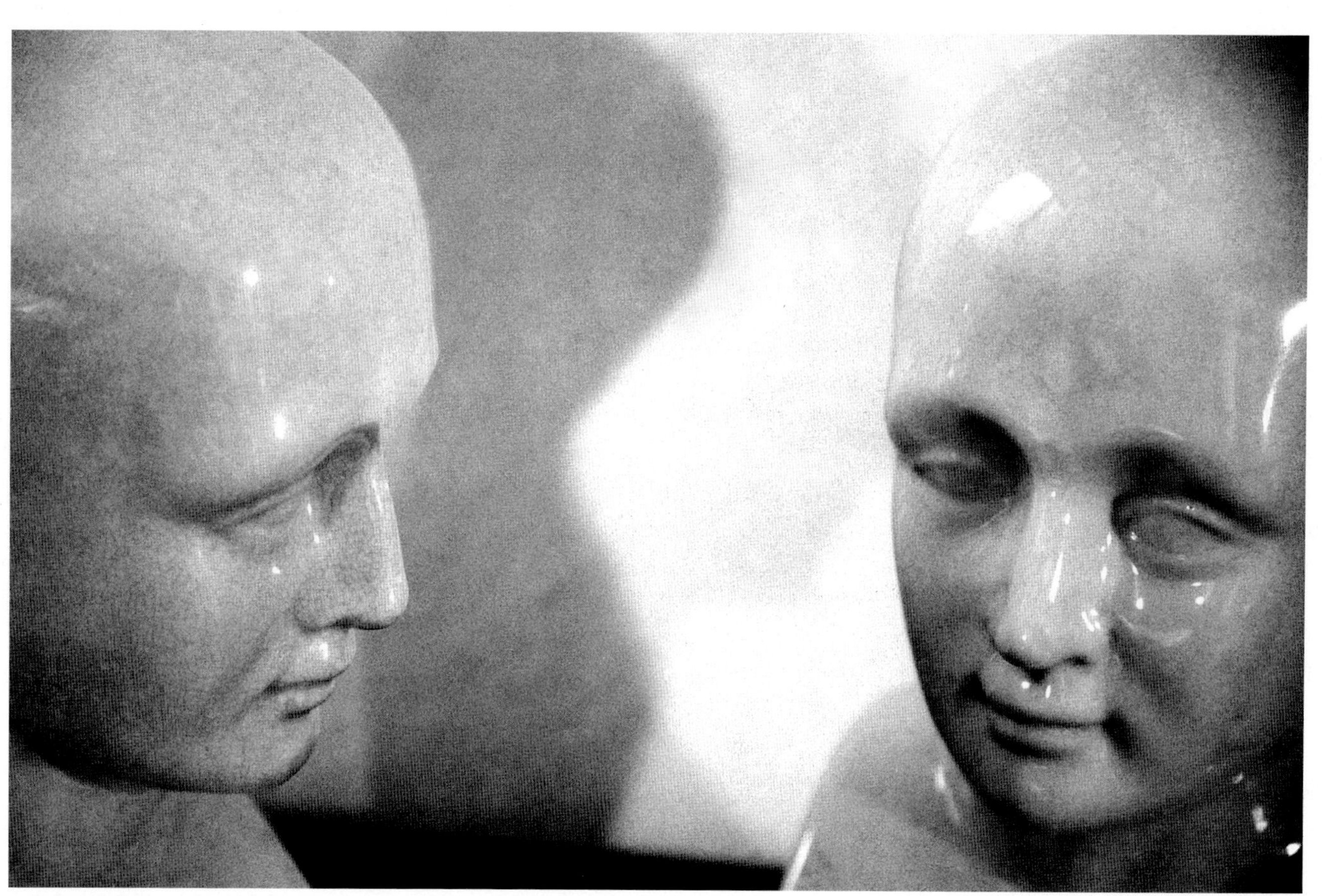

JULY 20, 2001

I had longed to meet Mesmer. How many times had I walked down her corridor thinking I would catch a glimpse, only to be disappointed? But then, one summer day, there she was. When I approached, to my surprise, she didn't turn away. I mentioned conducting an interview and she said yes.

At the appointed hour I knocked on her office door. She responded in a resonant tone, "Come in."

Standing some feet away from her desk, I stammered, "May I ask you . . . ?"

Putting down a pen, she looked up and said, "Unseen forces dismay us."

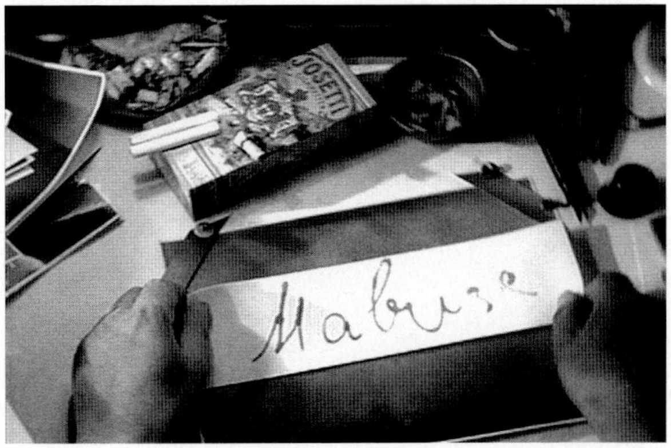

I expanded on what I had told her in the corridor. "I am writing a story about the Society and photographing it. I'd like to interview you. Also, I'm having problems with my orientation. I think it may be the moon."

She said, "It's good that you came to see me. A pigeon to eat is worth more than a peacock in the sky."

The window was open, and at that moment I could hear from outside the whistle of a woodthrush.

I asked her, perhaps thinking of my own unhappiness, "How do we achieve magnetic rapport?"

She answered, "Just as the hoopoe bird seeks *fana,* every person seeks harmony." She paused for a moment and then said, "Love is essential for the healing of souls."

What did that mean? I never mentioned love. I was about to ask her why she established The New Society when she interrupted and said, "The world is full of unharmonious fields and forces. Science can help initiate a utopian order." The interview was over. She opened the door and motioned me out.

AUGUST 5, 2001

I made an appointment to see Mesmer again last night at 8:00. A few minutes after the hour she emerged from her office wearing a plain white lab coat over a rose-colored dress.

She asked, "Shall we take a walk?" We strolled on the grounds while a faint moon rose in the sky. She patiently explained her theories from an astrological and geological perspective. She talked about Newton and Gilbert. From time to time she looked up at the sky and murmured, "From the firmament of heaven to the ephemeral insect, one law."

I wanted to know more about The New Society and why she founded it a year and a half ago. I summoned my courage and said, "Why did you reestablish *La société de l'harmonie universelle?*"

She steered the conversation in another direction. "The theories that I will explain to you originated with Franz Anton Mesmer. They are as true today as when he wrote them.

"But let me first tell you about Resolute Bay." She threw me a conspiratorial glance. As she talked her wide brown eyes grew wider and her reddish hair seemed to bristle with an electromagnetic charge.

"In 1998, as director of the MHD Institute,[1] I was working towards a practical application for my universal theory of magnetic reconnection, a cure which updated and expanded Mesmer's hypotheses. His own work left him nearly penniless and shunned by the scientific community of which he was once a respected member.[2] To make matters even worse, his followers misinterpreted his ideas so that what we know of Franz Anton Mesmer comes mainly from them, not him."

Mesmer and I walked into a field. Standing side by side, we watched satellites streak across the sky. She seemed lost in thought.

I implored, "Tell me more."

This time she willingly complied. "In 1999 I was grappling with some especially difficult formulas that combined the Navier-Stokes equations of fluid mechanics with Maxwell's equations on electromagnetism. My ideas were still unproven. I was in my office one afternoon, and I remembered an image from a science book I once owned that showed dotted magnetic field lines sprouting from the earth's poles. At that moment I made a decision. To confirm my hypotheses I would subject my own body to the earth's magnetic forces. But not just anywhere." "Where then?"

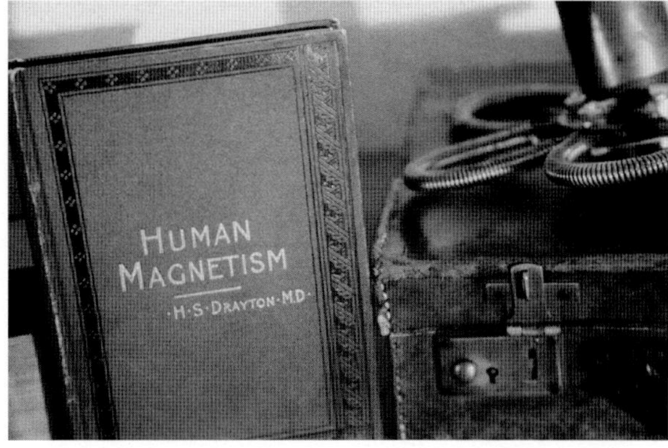

"I was going to the two places on earth where there is no magnetic deviation: Cape Agulhas — The Cape of Needles — at the southernmost tip of Africa, and a site that has no name, a short plane ride from Resolute Bay in the Arctic Ocean."

She looked straight at me.

"The earth's magnetic field results from a spinning molten metallic core. The concentration of metal in the northern part of the globe means that compass needles will point generally, but not exactly, north. The difference is called magnetic deviation."

I said, "Interesting, I never knew there was a difference. But where is the true magnetic pole?"

"The true magnetic pole in the Northern Hemisphere presently lies in the Northwest Territories in Canada, about 112.6 degrees south of the geographic North Pole and about 104.3 degrees west longitude; the nearest town is Resolute Bay.

"In May I flew to Resolute Bay in a Twin Otter from Edmonton and stayed for a week, making day trips to the Pole. The tee shirt sold at the local motel said 'Resolute is not the end of the world, but you can see it from here.'

"My pilot told me, 'We always do this kind of work in May. We need frozen conditions so that we can land an airplane anywhere on ice or snow, but not so cold that it's impossible to work outdoors. You're not the only one; tourists do visit. Last time I flew some folks here they said they wanted to have a baby. They set up a tent because they thought the region nurtured fertility.'

"But my experience was different. At the Pole I was completely overcome. I could barely breathe. My heart pounded violently. I sensed magnetic shifts in my electrons' spin. They were all pointing toward the pole, billions of them. That's how magnetism affects our bodies, it's through the electrons."

Mesmer raised her eyebrows. “Afterwards I had a dream. A staircase went into an arc in the distance and then it broke off. I could see my sister wrapped in a cloth. She was upside down. Her head was pointing north. Then I saw an enormous cloud hovering overhead.

“When I returned home, I opened my copy of Aristotle’s *On Sleep and Dreams*.

“‘The dreams may be signs,’ Aristotle wrote, ‘for they may presage illnesses or other imminent bodily conditions. Early intimations of these would be more noticeable in sleep.

‘It is true, then, that some dreams are causes, while others are signs, for example, of what is happening in the body. Even medical experts say that one should pay extremely close attention to dreams. For movements occurring during daytime, unless they are very big and powerful, pass unnoticed alongside those of the waking state, which are bigger. But during sleep the opposite happens. For then even slight movements seem to be big.’

“Aristotle goes on to say, ‘People think it is lightning and thundering when faint echoes are sounding in the ears, or that they are enjoying honey and sweet flavors when a tiny drop of phlegm is running down the throat, or that they are walking through fire and feeling extremely hot when a slight warmth is affecting certain parts of the body. But as they wake up it is obvious to them that those things have the above character. Seeing that the beginnings of all things are small, so too, clearly are those signs of illnesses and other affections imminent in our bodies. Plainly then, these must be more evident during periods of sleep than in the waking state.’”[3]

We walked in silence for a long time. Mesmer suddenly said, “Aristotle convinced me that the dream was a sign.”

Another long silence.

She gestured with her hands. “The staircase was a field line. My sister was a magnet. The cloud was a vapor of electrons. A voice inside me said, ‘Go back to Athol Springs and establish your own institute, an institute for universal harmony based on Franz Anton Mesmer’s magnetic theories and your own.’” I said, “So that’s when you decided. . .”

She interrupted me: “I understood the role of the electrons, but there were still some astrological puzzles that had to be sorted out.”

Mesmer had the look of a highly intelligent person talking to an eager child. I gave a smile, but did not reply.

“My next trip was to the Cape,” she said. “I wanted to fly there directly from Edmonton, but complications in my personal life distracted me. By the time I arrived at Cape Agulhas it was already July. The Cape is the southernmost point of Africa, the only place on earth where all compasses point true north. Portuguese navigators discovered this fact in the 1480s. The Cape is extremely wild and windy and needle-sharp cliffs overlook the sea. For two nights I stayed in nearby Arniston, a small fishing village. The white cottage of the Arniston Lodge is not very inviting, but I visited the massive nineteenth-century lighthouse.”

By then it was dark; one by one the stars had come out.

Mesmer hooked her arm in mine and led us quickly toward the main building. "I'm late," she said. "Another time. We'll talk again."

AUGUST 19, 2001

Two weeks passed. Mesmer agreed to see me for a third time on August 15 at 9:00 P.M.

We sat together on a bench in the warm night air. She remembered exactly where we had left off. "Last time we talked about Cape Agulhas." I nodded, "Yes."

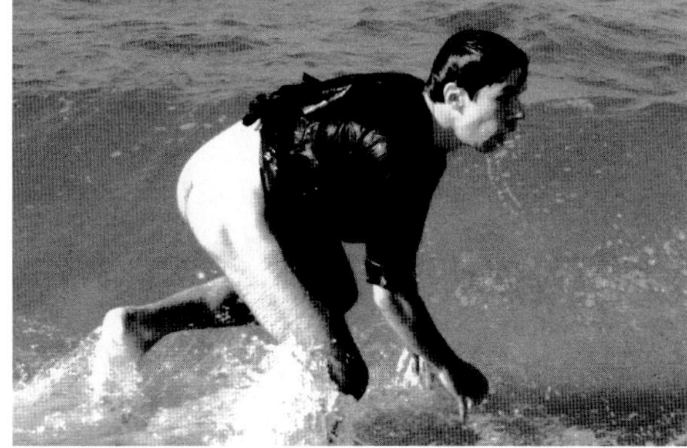

"At the Cape, in that old lighthouse, I saw the geomagnetic storm of Saturday, July 10, 1999. It was very windy that day, like a gale. The sea turned turgid and gray. The white sky almost blinded me. I stayed in the lighthouse until the storm died down. Afterwards I was determined to replicate that experience in the controlled environment of Athol Springs.

"Perhaps now you understand how the observations I made during my trips directly propelled me to establish The New Society.

"As I told you, I was after a practical application for my Universal Theory — basic science applied to human psychology. Magnetic forces surround us. They emanate from the sun and the moon and from the earth's core."

I said, "What an incredible coincidence. My third visit to Athol Springs took place a little over a year later, during the electromagnetic storm on July 16, 2000. But I still don't understand the theory."

Mesmer continued, "The geomagnetic storm relates to my Universal Reconnection Theory. Reconnection begins in the high chaparral of space where magnetic fields drive huge storms, heating the atmosphere of the sun. Here turbulent electrically charged gases of space, called plasmas, stick to magnetic fields. For decades we have been trying to understand how this happens.

"We now think that the field lines brush together, cut each other, and then whip around suddenly in a new configuration, creating a solar flare or eruption of gases into space. This accounts for the magnetic storm I saw in July 1999 and you saw in July 2000. It also explains solar flares."

"I still don't understand," I said meekly. "If the huge storms heat the atmosphere, then what about the plasma?" I thought to myself: Mesmer holds the key to my happiness. I need to know. Maybe it's the sun that is affecting me and not the moon.

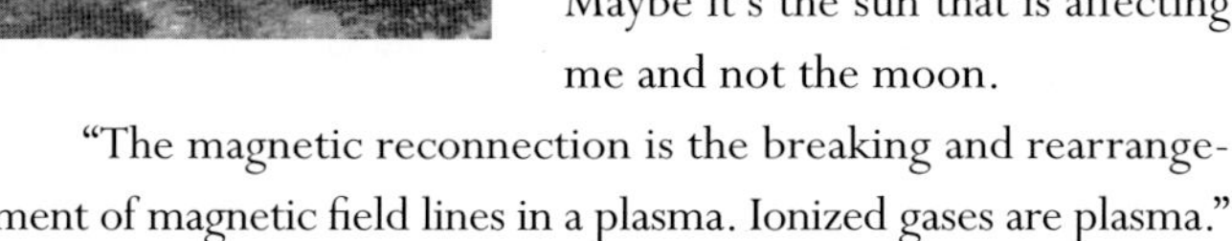

"The magnetic reconnection is the breaking and rearrangement of magnetic field lines in a plasma. Ionized gases are plasma."

I asked, "Are the solar flares composed of plasma?"

"Yes. This is as powerful a force as any in the universe, and high-energy particles ejected into space affect every living thing on earth. I was affected by those particles at Cape Agulhas. The earth's own magnetic field is constantly perturbed by the impinging fields from the sun. This we call the solar wind."

Mesmer continued. Now she was lecturing with a forcefulness and urgency that I hadn't seen before. "My theory is similar to Franz Anton Mesmer's, but the imponderable magnetic fluid that Mesmer described we now identify as electromagnetic fields or waves.[4] In deference to Franz Anton Mesmer we still use the term 'fluids,' but know that it can also mean fields and waves.

"While there was much he didn't understand about the sun and, of course, plasma physics, Franz Anton Mesmer believed that the moon and the earth affect certain psychological states.[5] In 1766 he said, 'Even a common person knows that the madness of maniacs returns in accordance with the revolution of the moon.'

"Write this down," she commanded. "He also talked of harmony: 'One must not think that the influence of the stars on us only has to do with diseases.' He said, 'The harmony established between the astral plane and the human plane ought to be admired as much as the ineffable effect of universal gravitation by which our bodies are harmonized . . . as with a musical instruction furnished with several strings, the exact tone resonates which is in unison with a given tone.'

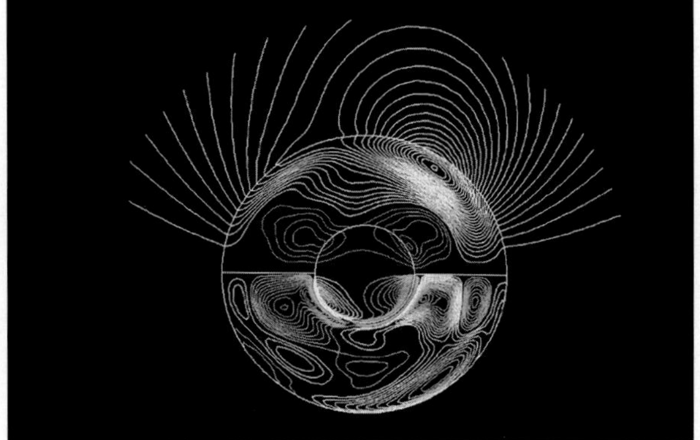

"Franz Anton also believed in the possibility of certain psychic phenomena, but only if they could be proved scientifically. He wrote, 'We can thus comprehend how the wills of two persons can communicate with each other through their internal sense organs, an accord, a sort of covenant between two wills, which we can call 'being in rapport.'"[6]

She called me by my name. "Lenore, think of what Mesmer said about the earth: There exist various conditions which owe their birth neither to heat nor cold, neither to dryness nor to humidity. They depend, rather, upon some secret and inexplicable alteration occurring in the entrails of the earth.

"Listen," she went on. "All together Mesmer's assertions indicate how well he understood the origin of disease. The heavenly bodies impact every one of us. The theory is very plausible. Who can dispute it? Magnetism from the sun, magnetism from the moon, and magnetism from the earth — the effects of the heavenly bodies and the earth are felt not by one, but by hundreds, thousands, millions, billions of people — simultaneously. Perhaps you can see now how these forces can cause wars, natural disasters, and, of course, personal unhappiness. They impact our politics, our sex lives, and what we eat. Everything, really. The practitioners at *La Salpêtrière,* Charcot, his students Binet, Féré, Babinski — they had it right. I am convinced that they understood Mesmer. Bernheim was wrong. We are following in the footsteps of *La Salpêtrière.*

"I believe that magnetic rapport or harmonic rapport, that great state of being, 'celadony,' or if you will, love, can be achieved through sensitization to these complex fluids, waves, and fields. One method is to stimulate or massage the poles and the surfaces of the body to relieve obstacles to the wave's flow. Harmony can also result from sensitization to the electromagnetic fields and forces of other human beings.[7] This is a kind of reconnection — field lines brushing together and whipping around in a new configuration."

Her voice rose. "I believe what Feuerbach said: 'Love is the true ontological demonstration of the existence of objects apart from our head.' And, 'There is no other proof of being except love or feeling.'"[8]

Mesmer threw her arms open wide. "Through magnetism we can achieve love.[9] It is my goal in life to prove this: *quod erat demonstrandum.*"

Mesmer and I walked quietly back to the main building, the moon high in the sky.

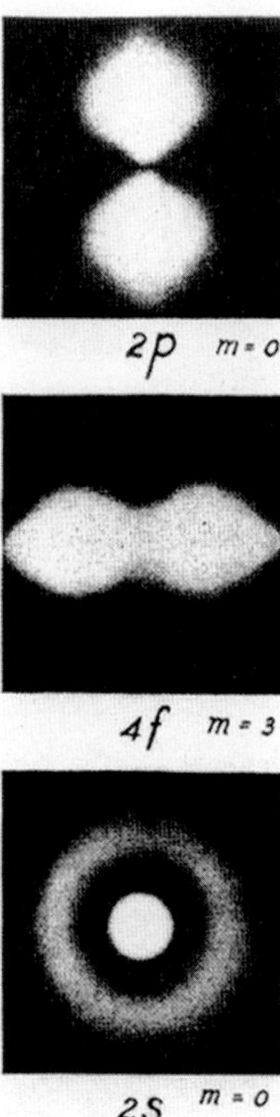

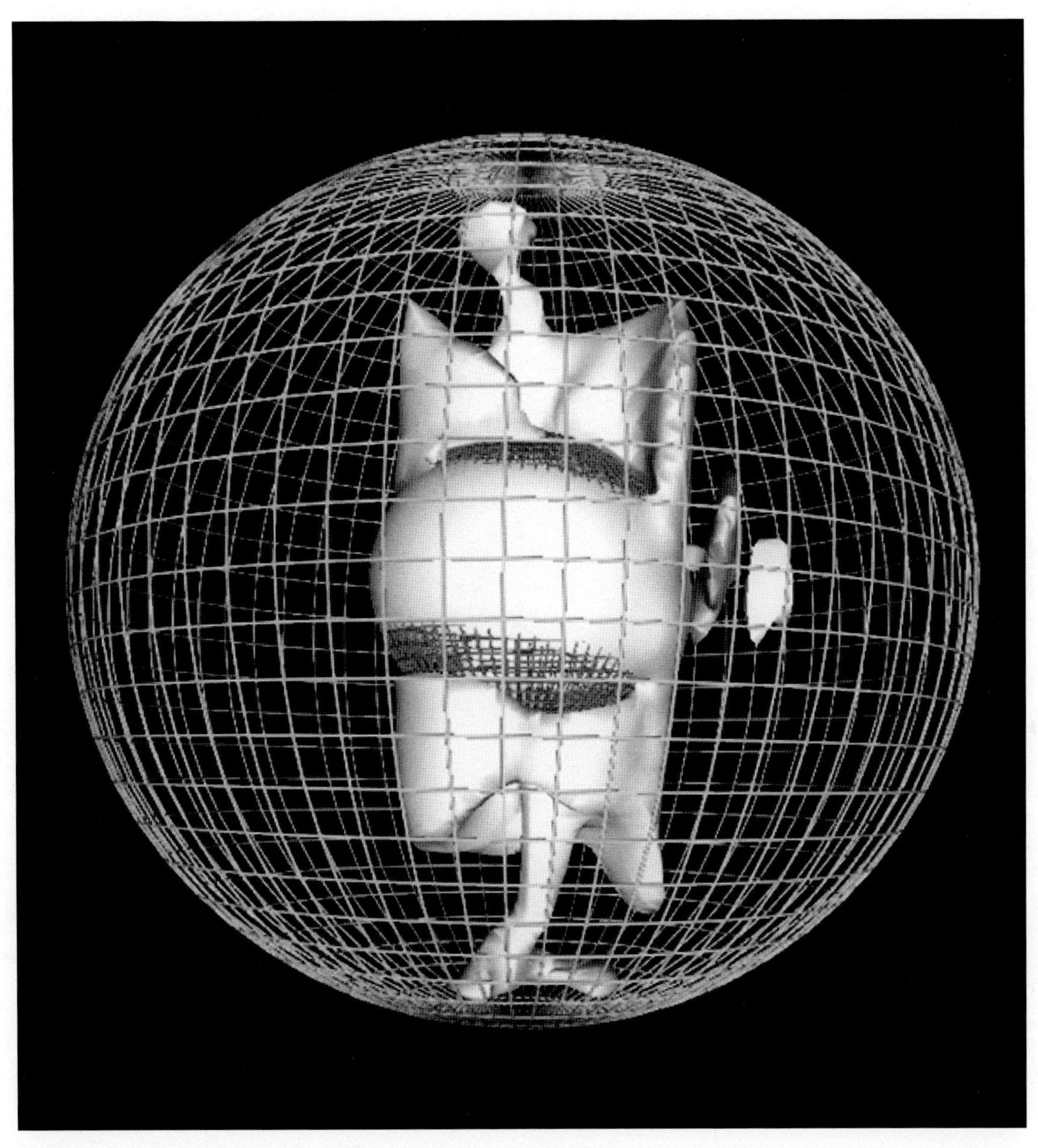

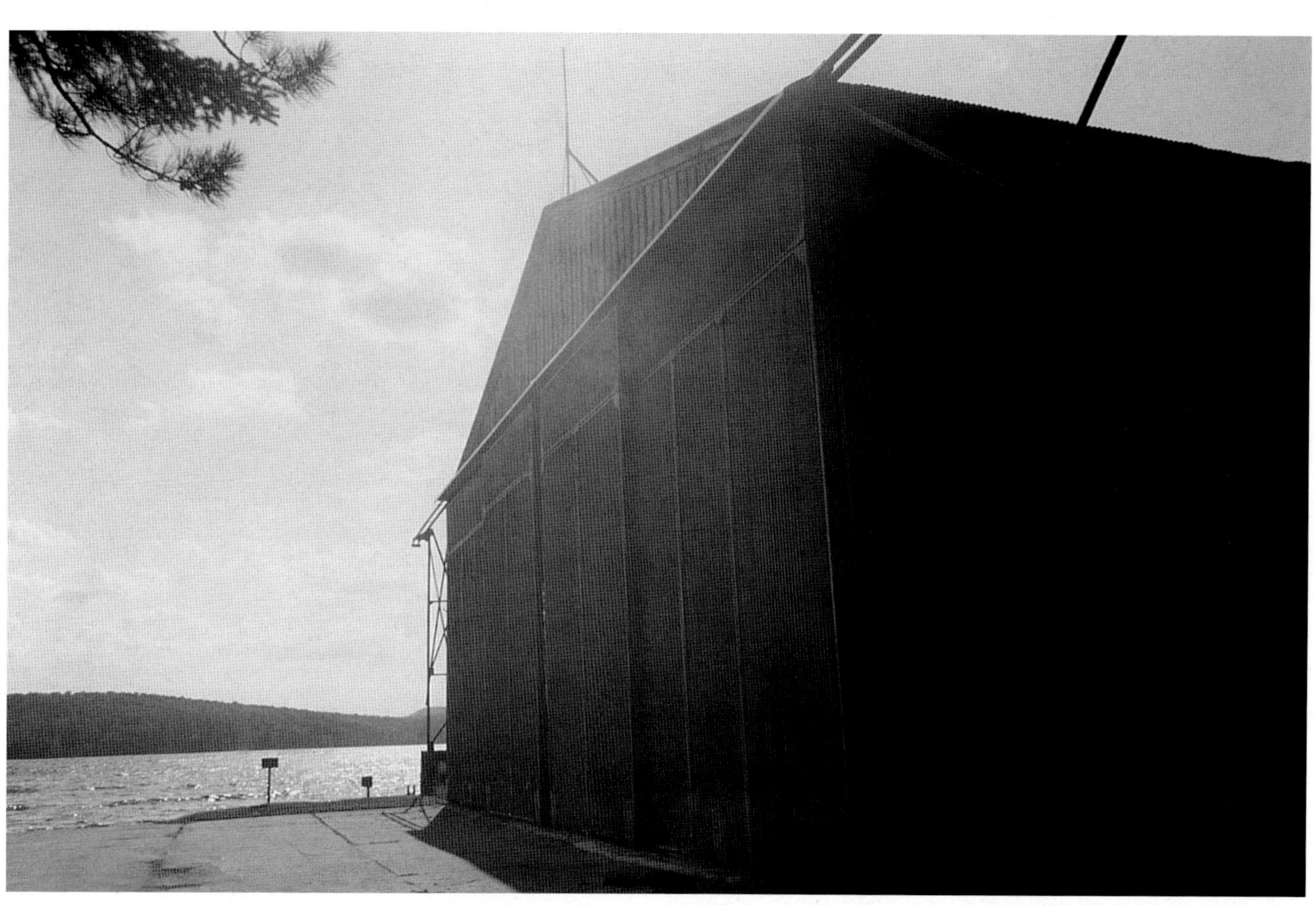

POSTSCRIPT: THE UPRISINGS

JANUARY 12, 2002

Nearly two years had passed since my first visit to The New Society. In early fall I had moved back to New York and submitted the manuscript and photos to my editor. She was pleased. The book was done. I reclaimed my apartment and saw my friends again. Life was going on. Then one day while dodging traffic on a snow-covered street, I had a longing to return to Athol Springs.

I missed the Springs. I missed the beauty and the feeling of closeness to the universal rhythms of the tides and the stars and all the energies that animate the universe.

My photographs seemed very real but the totality of the experience at Athol Springs was fading, and I was afraid it would soon to be lost forever. In my mind's eye I could still see the simple one-story building with its four wings and central cupola that graced the side of the road. I could still see my motel perched on the hill overlooking the glassy lake. I could almost hear the shrill voice of my ebullient proprietress, Susan, as she described *this* lake or *that* item of clothing. As for the rest, it seemed more and more like a dream.

I resolved to return as soon as possible. Maybe even that day.

I went home and turned on the TV. The forecast was for scattered snow showers, but it would still be good driving weather. I rented a car and drove directly to the Springs. I didn't even think of visiting Buffalo. My cousins had no use for The New Society, which they now considered a cult. They had been supportive for a while, but had long since given up on me.

Four hours later, there I was. Happily exhausted from my trip, I knocked on Ben's door. "It's me, Lenore." He opened the door and invited me in. "Lenore!" He hesitated for a fraction of a second and said, "Do you know what has happened?" I shook my head, baffled. He held me by the shoulders and fixed his eyes on me.

"What? What is it?"

"Right before the September outing to the quarry there was infighting among the Harmonites. That was a bad time. Terrorists had struck New York. People were sad and on edge. The staff worked overtime, and the basement laboratories were full all day long. Mesmer was away. Two Harmonites, Alan G. and Greta M., seemed especially disturbed. Alan had always kept back from the group, but Greta got along well. That's why we were surprised by her behavior — and Alan's, too.

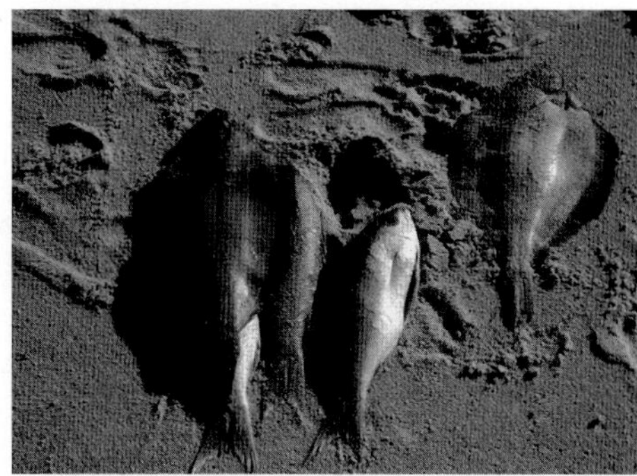

"Alan has established his own utopian society on the lake, and Greta is at the airplane hangar waiting for a spaceship to transport her to the Nebula Antares. It's crazy, I know, but Alan and Greta have followers. Mesmer is still in Duluth, where she's established a new branch of the Society. Settle in at your motel and then come back. I'll tell you everything."

I checked into the Lavender Lakeview Motel, put my things away in my pine-paneled bedroom, and looked out over the lake. What Ben had said was true. Instead of seeing canoes floating silently past my window, now I saw an entire city with

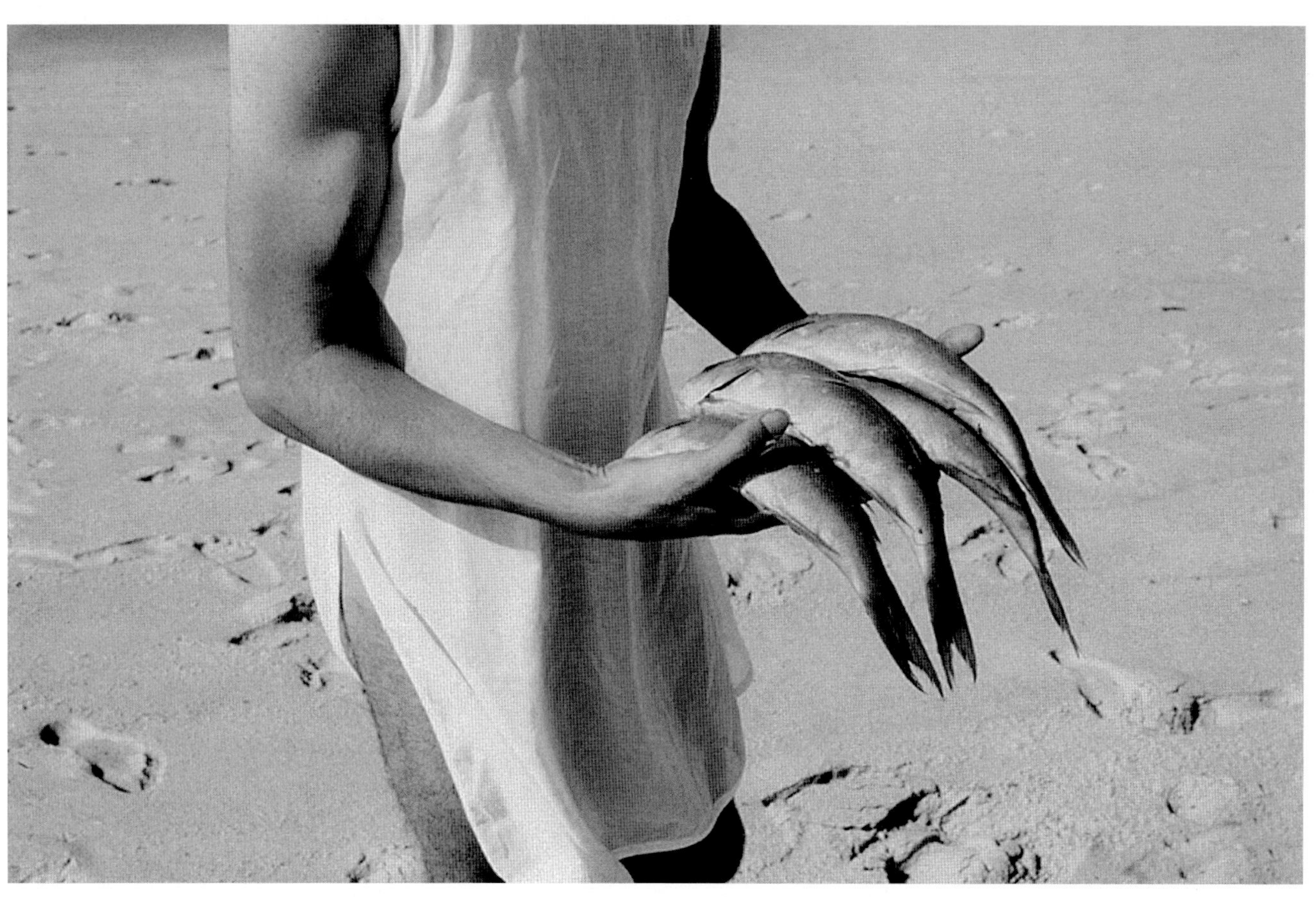

buildings, streets, stop signs, lights, all erected on its frozen surface. There was a roar of activity. Snowmobiles everywhere.

In twenty minutes I was back at The New Society. Ben and I took refuge in his office. He sat me down and began talking.

"After the trip to the quarry, Alan decided to create his own community, a 'true' utopia, a seasonal one, where the regulation of production and property relations is a crucial basis of social order. He quickly obtained the air rights, the necessary variances, and construction began when there was three feet of ice on the lake. He wants to make the community economically viable. That is why there are so many rules and regulations on the lake."

Ben said, "Alan revolted against F.A. Mesmer's belief in the common good: sister to sister, brother to brother. Rather, he has an absolute belief in inequality, and his society rests on the assumption of the natural inequality of people. But there should be no inherited wealth or private ownership of land. He wants to reinstate the laws of nature. He holds to Proudhon's idea of property as theft."

His voice rose. "This is a city of constant movement and change. Alan was strongly influenced by the Italian futurist F.T. Marinetti, who said, 'Houses have a shorter life span that we do; every generation will have to build its own city. Life must no longer hide like solitary worms in the stairwells, but the stairs must be abolished.'" Holding his head in his hands, Ben said, "Alan posits a religion based on worshipping the humble fish."

I shook my head in disbelief.

"Alan has established a society of ice fishermen who sell their fish to the communities around the lake. The entire economy is based on ice fishing. The outermost belt of the city is occupied by hundreds of tiny ice huts. Have you seen them? There, residents fish all day and all night for steelhead, walleye, northern pike, yellow perch, and panfish. The internal economy supports the ice fishing, solving the problem of poverty. Everyone is making tip-ups, ice augers, sonar, sleds, tackle, drills, heaters, rods, reels, bobbers, bait, lures, jigs, chisels, spuds, saws, underwater cameras, line, decoys, gear, traps, fish finders, depth finders. Every spring the huts will be demolished and every fall they will be rebuilt, a schedule dependent on the life cycle of ice.

"It's incredible! I talked to a fisherman who said to me 'You're fishing too much when you find yourself tying ribbons in your daughter's hair with a Palomar knot.'"

After Ben relayed this story, we hugged each other very tightly and had some rose melange tea.

"But there's still more you should know."

He went on to tell me about Greta, who was convinced that she had communicated with sentient beings from a planet near the Nebula Antares.

"How did this happen?" I asked.

"She was conducting experiments with Mesmer. They were scanning the microwave band of the electromagnetic spectrum on one of our basement receivers. Greta noticed that once a week for a number of months a strange wave pattern appeared on the monitor screen. It seemed to be a code of some sort.

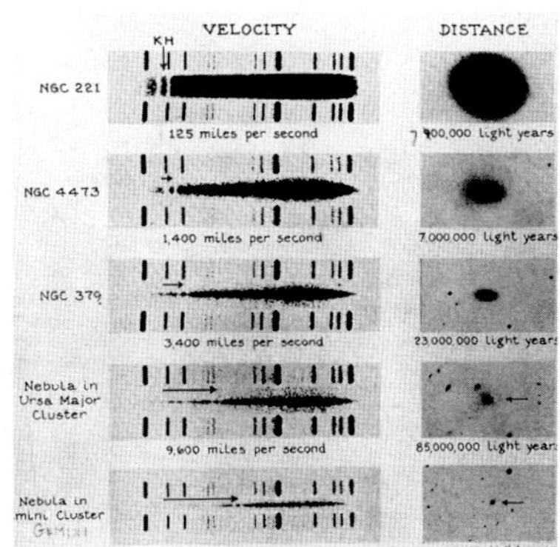

"At that time she was reading Amir Aczel's book, *Probability I*[1], and surmised that creatures from a distant nebula had been patiently sending us signals for millennia, hoping that one day our technology would reach the stage at which we could detect those signals and respond. To determine the frequency on which we should respond, she studied the early findings of Cocconi and Morrison,[2] who explained that the most abundant element in the universe is hydrogen.

They reasoned that when excited, hydrogen atoms broadcast at a frequency of 1,420 megahertz (1,420 cycles per second). This frequency, within the microwave band, is separated from the frequencies where most noise of the background cosmic radiation occurs. She programmed our transmitter to send back messages of her own.

"While she knew that they would have taken maybe tens of thousands of years to be delivered, the messages she received seemed to be telling her that alien beings would visit earth around the year 2006. Now Greta is a very smart woman and she presented presumably credible evidence, convincing ten of our members to live in a plane hangar, waiting for the spaceship that might arrive any day.

"They are all preparing for a trip and hope to be converted into pulses and waves themselves. Since everything occurring in the world of matter, including life, may be described as a transformation of energy, they are waiting to be transformed.

"They say they will ride on those electromagnetic waves. No, they will become waves. At any rate, they are waiting, eager to be contacted, and are readying themselves for a trip into space."

Ben was devastated. I tried to reassure him.

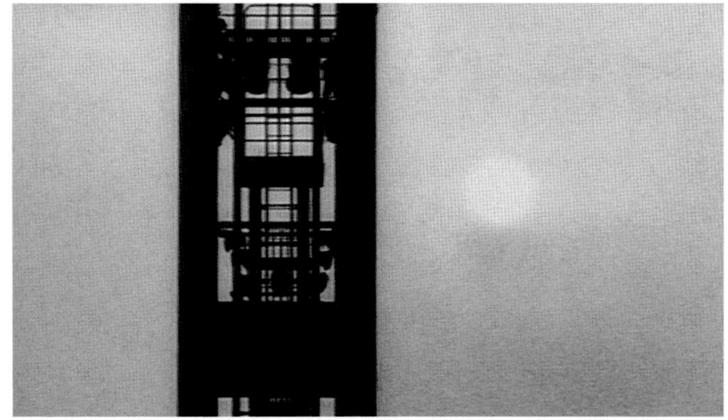

"These things happen. Look at Franz Anton Mesmer's society and how that splintered, too. It's inevitable. Mesmer needs you." I pleaded with him. "Stay here and work for her."

I went on. "But what am I going to do? That's a big question. You know, Ben, Mesmer is self-possessed and remote, but blessed with a mental clarity and purity of purpose. Mesmer has seriously considered the nature of a just life and a perfect community. She has her own ideas about the common good, the original state of nature, civic and personal virtue, leisure and labor. She still has her acolytes and is starting branches of the Society outside of Dallas, Sacramento, and Jacksonville, and somewhere in New Jersey."

I paused. "Ben, I've finished my book about The New Society. I'm not useful here anymore, but I can't go back. It's impossible. I can't resume my former life."

At that moment I remembered my first meeting with Mesmer, when she had said, "Just as the hoopoe bird seeks *fana,* every person seeks harmony." It all became clear. I would seek *fana.* I told Ben that I would live at the motel and visit the hangar every day, taking photos, researching Greta's theories. The hangar, waiting for the mother ship, waiting to escape from our home planet, I said that was what I wanted.

Ben and I took a walk on the grounds saying little to each other. Returning to his office, we sat together for a long time. Utter silence.

Then he took my hand in his. "No, " he said. "Stay here with me. Life has changed and much more work needs to be done. The Society will thrive! We'll populate the world with Harmonites."

I closed my eyes. More time passed.

And I looked up at him. I saw his slender face and gentle gray eyes that touched everything with endless curiosity. I said, "Yes, Ben, I will."

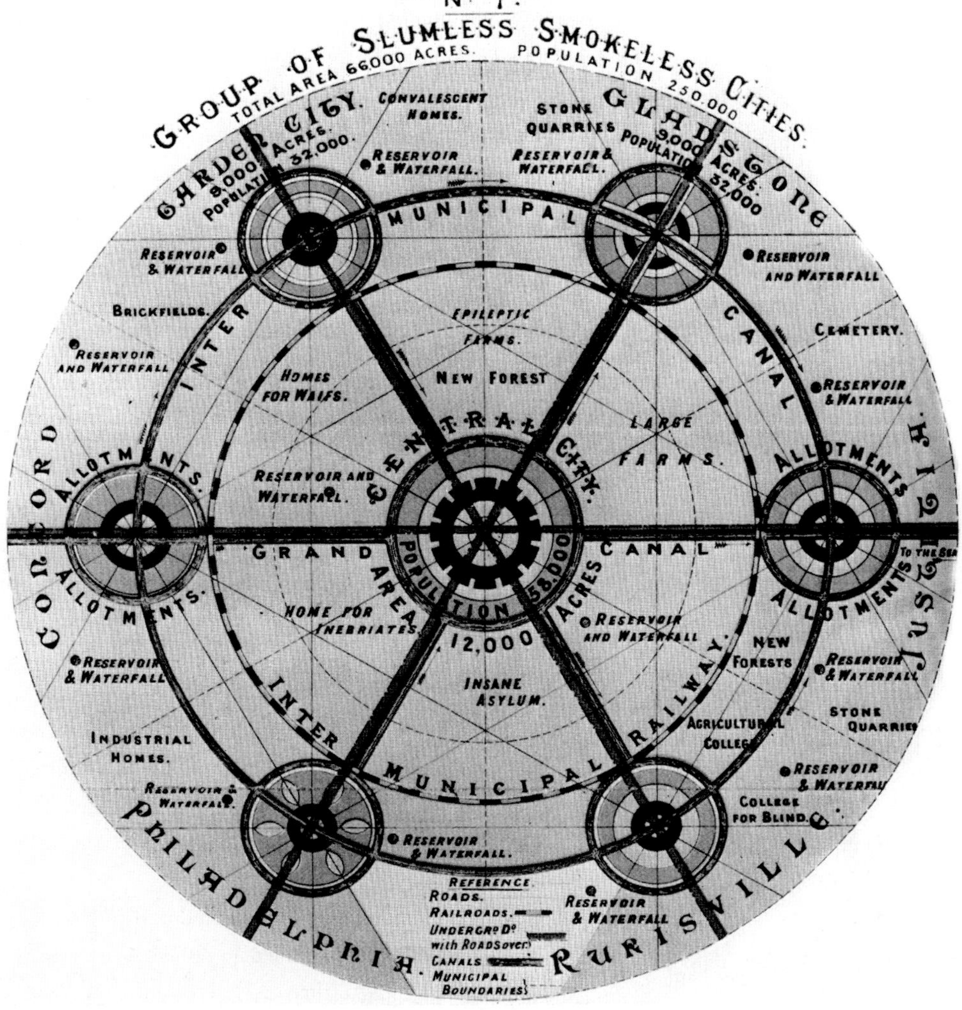

— No 7. —
GROUP OF SLUMLESS SMOKELESS CITIES.
TOTAL AREA 66000 ACRES. POPULATION 250,000
GARDEN CITY. 9,000 ACRES. POPULATION 32,000.
GLADSTONE 9000 ACRES. POPULATION 32,000
CONVALESCENT HOMES.
STONE QUARRIES
RESERVOIR & WATERFALL.
RESERVOIR & WATERFALL.
MUNICIPAL
RESERVOIR & WATERFALL
RESERVOIR AND WATERFALL
BRICKFIELDS.
INTER
CANAL
CEMETERY.
EPILEPTIC FARMS.
RESERVOIR AND WATERFALL
NEW FOREST
HOMES FOR WAIFS.
RESERVOIR & WATERFALL
LARGE FARMS.
CONCORD
ALLOTMENTS.
CENTRAL CITY.
ALLOTMENTS
RESERVOIR AND WATERFALL.
GRAND
CANAL
TO THE SEA
RURISVILLE
AREA 12,000 ACRES
POPULATION 58,000
ALLOTMENTS.
ALLOTMENTS
HOME FOR INEBRIATES.
RESERVOIR AND WATERFALL
NEW FORESTS
RESERVOIR & WATERFALL
RESERVOIR & WATERFALL
INSANE ASYLUM.
INTER
RAILWAY.
STONE QUARRIES
INDUSTRIAL HOMES.
AGRICULTURAL COLLEGE
RESERVOIR & WATERFALL
MUNICIPAL
RESERVOIR & WATERFALL.
COLLEGE FOR BLIND.
PHILADELPHIA.
RESERVOIR & WATERFALL.
REFERENCE.
ROADS.
RAILROADS.
UNDERGRD Do with ROADS over
CANALS
MUNICIPAL BOUNDARIES
RESERVOIR & WATERFALL
RURISVILLE

2

CASE REPORTS

CASE REPORT 1

THE TORNADO

MARCH 20, 2000

Ms. G. was a 32-year-old woman who sought treatment because of her inability to make decisions. She was ambivalent, obsessive, and could not imagine her future life. Throughout the interview, she talked about herself only in the third person.

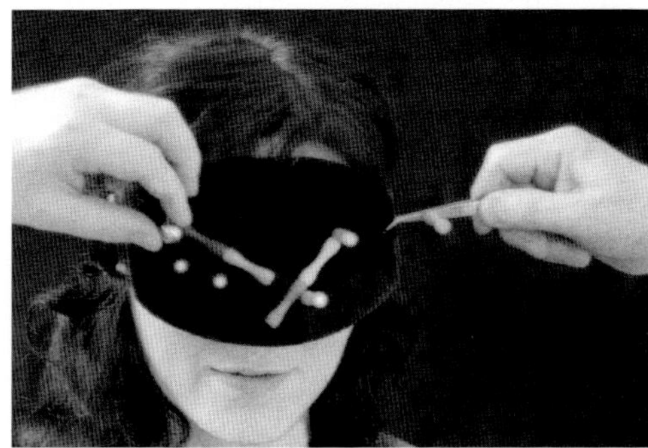

She began, "This story is called 'The Tornado.' She came from a town in Florida that was devastated by a tornado. Like all tornadoes, the storm took a narrow path, veering this way and that way, destroying her house, but leaving the houses on either side intact. Her neighbors were fine; their houses were standing. Her family, though, had died in their bedrooms while she was out shopping for peaches. She grieved and grieved. In a vain effort to suppress her painful memories, she moved to a different town.

"One day on a walk she discovered a dog about six years of age injured on the road. Judging from his glazed eyes, shallow breathing, and lolling tongue, he looked mortally wounded. Nevertheless she called for help, rescued him, and paid for his treatment. He had many fractures, internal injuries, and she nursed him for nearly two years. In constant pain, the dog never seemed grateful, but she knew he was. Right before he died he said, 'Tell me three wishes. I will grant them to you.' And she said, 'Sex first, then Love or Death.'

"Several years later she met Sex. He was a nice-looking foreign man. He played the bass. He played with his fingers and thumb, and the base of his thumb. He strummed and plucked the bass and they made music in the key of D. She played him like an oboe — his instrument in high school — in the key of E. Their music was high, the two instruments coming together and then apart.

"The next time Sex visited her it was in the form of a goat, who faced her while rearing up on his hind legs. His small, white, fur-covered pate was a blur of constant motion. Coarse white hairs sprouted from his plump belly and balls. His appetite was keen and they played on and on, always together. Their music was symphonic, lasting through many movements.

"She seemed to be meeting many more animals than humans and finally settled on a rabbit with baby blue, very round eyes and an open, inviting mien. His fur was soft and smooth to the touch. He was strong for a short, slight rabbit, with a thin frame and narrow chest, but ample muscles in the fore- and hindquarters. His member was large and got stiff in a wink. But he was so excited, all of the time, that in pursuing some shoots he got lost in the woods and being bewildered couldn't find his way back."

Now all of that was over. She agonized. Had the time come for the next wish? She didn't know, and hence she came to The New Society. And what would that wish be: Love or Death, Love or Death?

We recommended magnetic somnambulism, then work on the large machines and a day in the atrium. She would see Mesmer once a week. At the end of her stay, no longer ambivalent, she had come to a realization. The answer to her question was: WHATEVER COMES FIRST.

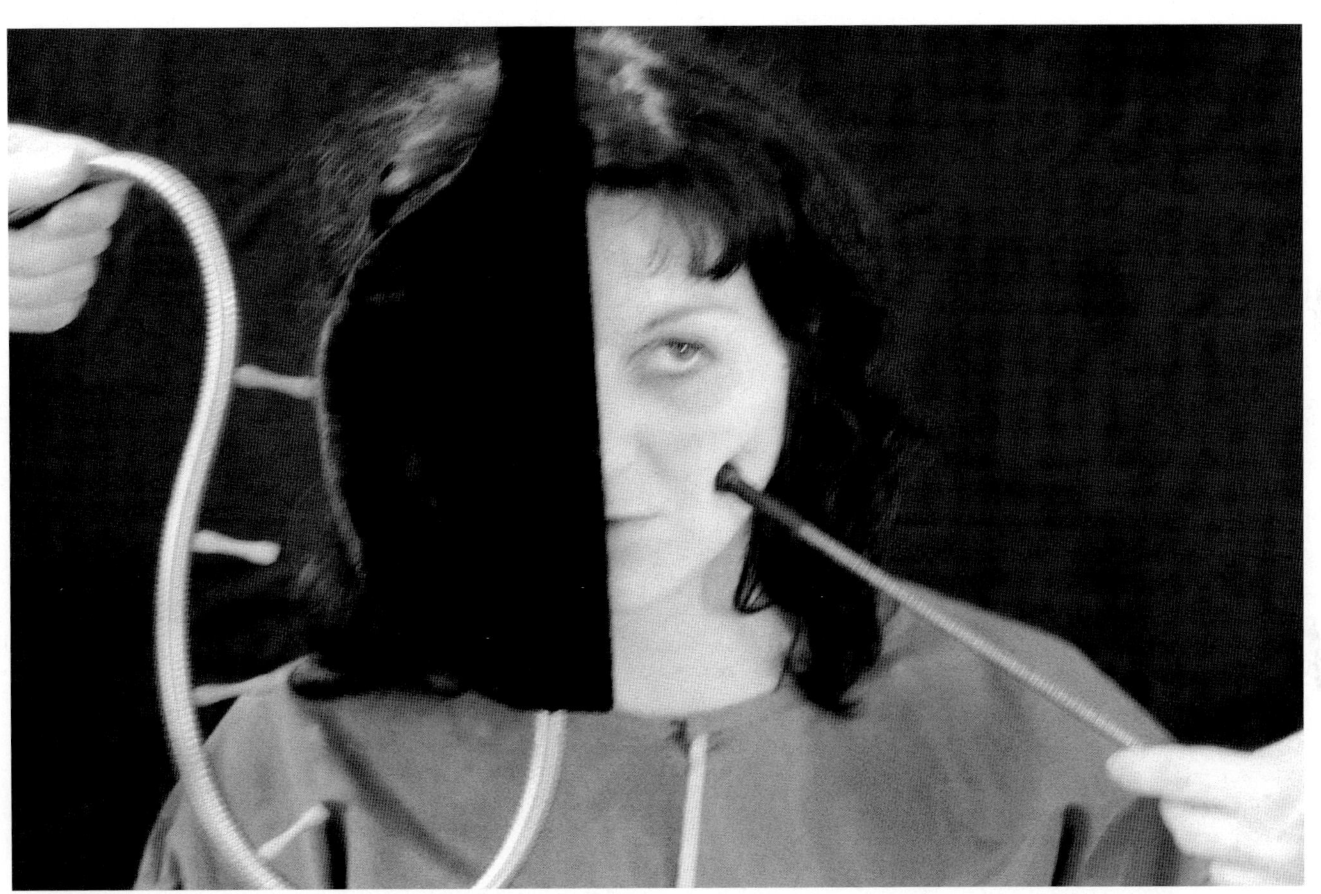

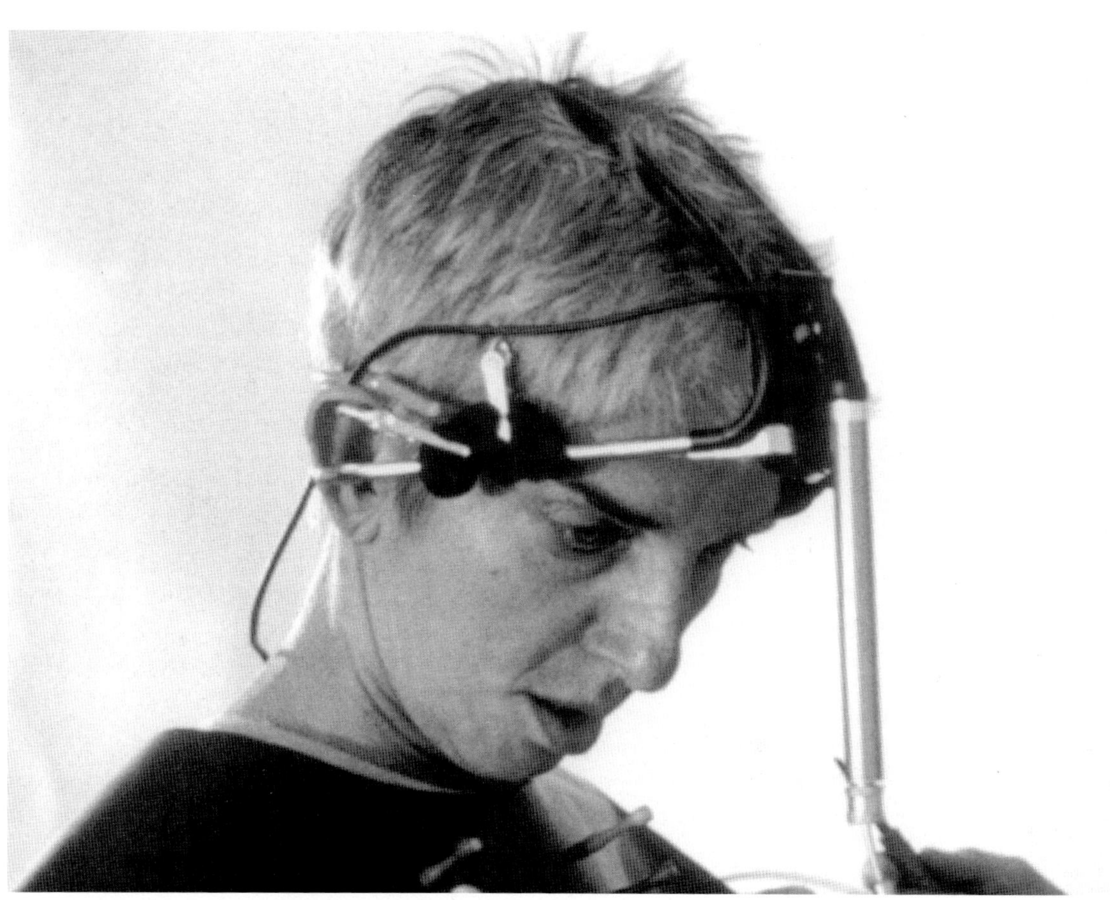

CASE REPORT II

THE COLOR WHITE

JULY 17, 2000

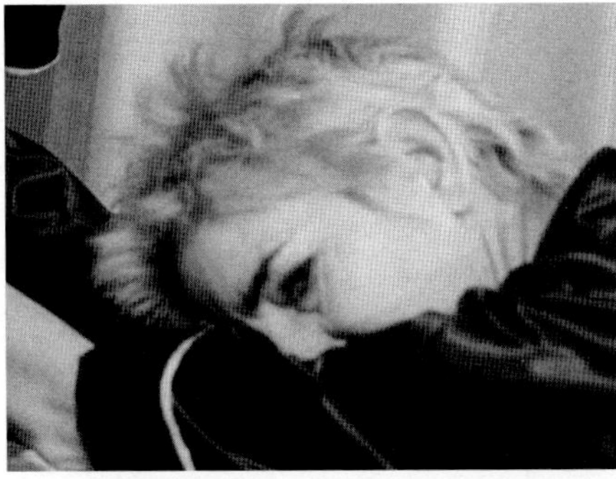

Ms. H. was a 47-year-old divorced woman who came to the Society for counseling after the death of her aunt. She was tall, slender, and exceedingly graceful. She was dressed in a white wool suit and her feet were adorned with white shoes that had small hourglass-shaped heels. Around her neck was a single strand of pearls. Her stockings were white. Her handbag was white. Her fingernails were painted white, transparent at the base and opaque at the tip. But her fastidiousness, her physical perfection, contrasted with her hair, which was short and blond, brushed back boldly, revealing white roots, as if she were letting it go and proud of it. She spoke profusely, fluently, unhesitantly, without a break, revealing a state of unrelenting excitation.

After listening to her for part of an hour, it became clear that after her aunt's death she became obsessed with the color white. "White was drawn out of me like a thread," she said. She relayed the details:

"My cousin called to tell me that my aunt had died. The funeral was set for Tuesday morning at 10:30 in Yonkers, near where she lived. It was a typical November morning, the temperature around 40 degrees, the sky overcast. I took the 9:15 train out of New York City to Spuyten Duyvil, which is near my cousin's house. The train tracks hug the banks of the Hudson River, and the station itself, red brick, sits at the bottom of an escarpment. I waited there for him, looking up at the brown and gray rocks and cliff.

"He drove up in an old white Cadillac, a wreck. The license plate hung loose on a wire. The car had a million dents and scratches and the fenders were rusted through. I hadn't seen him since high school, but my cousin had the same long face and bloodshot eyes and, when he smiled, big reddish gums. He is a large man, very bent over. How sad. We drove a few blocks to the funeral home, which was white-painted brick, and waited there at the entrance for his brother, my other cousin, the shorter, handsome one, the athlete. He arrived shortly in his car, a new Jaguar, polished, waxed, and white. We walked in together, and the director ushered us to a corner room, which was empty except for a couple of rows of white plastic chairs. There she was. The white casket was open, and from the back of the room all you could see was her white hair, curly and fluffed up, but nothing else.

"After a while the room filled up with neighbors, friends, and a few other relatives. Then Reverend Bee, quite an eloquent speaker, read a sermon about the seasons to soothe us. 'The trees are left naked, gray-black skeletons of death, prepared now staunchly to wait out a long drab winter. Weeks pass. The world pierces the barrier of death and emerges white, pure white, everywhere. The landscape is transformed, graced with an unexpected, undreamed purity.' "

I interrupted Ms. H., "Yes, the barrier of death! I understand your grief! You loved your aunt." She was silent for a moment and then she blurted:

"She was my father's sister. I never had a relationship with her. She always seemed so needy and so repressed. So I never really had the courage. I have a lot of courage in other things, but not with her. It was all too much, and now she is dead for real. I am so upset. As for my cousins, they're too odd. I'll never see them.

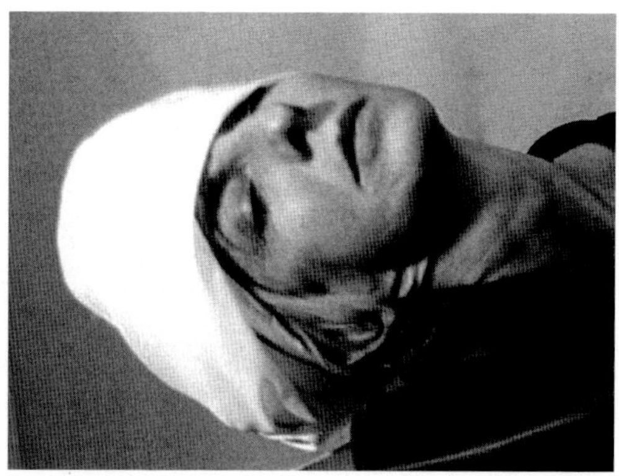

"The week after the funeral I went to the dentist to have my teeth whitened. Then I had my toenails and fingernails painted white. I changed my stationary from cream to ivory. The week after that I threw out my underwear and bought everything white. I bought a couch upholstered in Egyptian cotton, a linen rug, and a set of white leather chairs. I had my walls repainted the color of a seed pearl. I've been eating only the insides of baked potatoes, yogurt with bananas, sole, halibut, Chilean sea bass, celery root with mayonnaise, and white bread. I drink Sprite and Chardonnay; for dessert, always coconut ice cream."

To free her of her obsession, I launched into a talking cure. I said, "You are obsessed with the color white." I isolated the letters w-h-i-t-e and repeated them aloud three times: W-H-I-T-E, W-H-I-T-E, W-H-I-T-E. I explained the derivation of the word from the old English hwte *"wheat,"* kweid *"to shine,"* weit *"becoming," and* kweit *"white" in centum languages. Then we analyzed white according to the laws of physics by examining painted squares of red, yellow, and blue together and then each separately. I offered an anecdote about Chekhov, hoping to stimulate a healing synesthesia. Not long before he died Chekhov wrote a letter to a friend. "You ask me what life is? It is like asking what a carrot is. A carrot is a carrot, and nothing more is known." We know that specific brain regions process information about different things. There are areas for color, edges, motion, body parts, nouns, verbs, and so on. A color area like white may lie next to an area that handles metaphysical concepts. I speculated that if these regions were more strongly connected they might fire simultaneously, giving rise to insight.*

But the talking cure was to no avail. We offered her magnetic color therapy to realign her poles. In the presence of the full spectrum of colors, I grasped her thumbs, one in each hand, and held them until I perceived an equal degree of magnetic heat between my thumbs and hers. This treatment was repeated each time she came to the clinic, once a week for a month and then twice monthly. Surprisingly, her condition was unchanged. She still dressed in white and was still obsessed. She came to the clinic less and less frequently and eventually stopped coming altogether. Many months later we received a letter from her. She was living in Acapulco.

Doctor Mesmer,
Greetings from Acapulco. I have been here for two months and I've fallen in love with a Mexican man. His name is Lazarus, pronounced *Laa-sa-ro.* When he was young he dived off the cliffs for a living; now he works as a tour guide.

I met him one evening on the beach. I was wearing my new bathing suit, ultra-white. All I saw was his coffee-colored skin and shiny brown hair. I went home with him and he stripped for me while standing on a table. We spent an hour in his Jacuzzi. We kissed and kissed. He said, "Give it to me baby, I know you can." He gave me a bruise on my nipple. It turned crimson, then plum, and by the third day it was the color of a Concord grape. For breakfast on the fourth day, I ate some fruit. Then I broke an egg and fried it. The yellow stood round and firm. I ate that, too, and afterwards I had some orange juice.

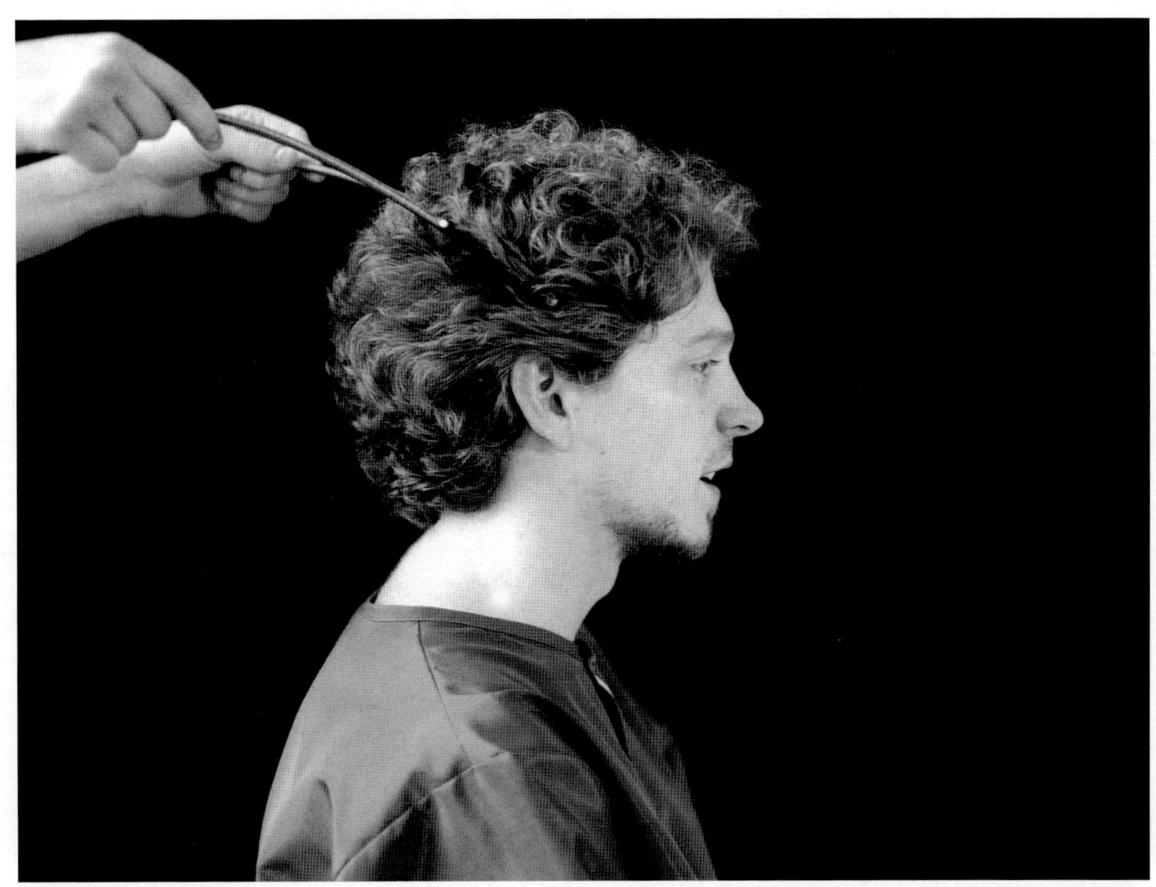

CASE REPORT III

THE BANDWIDTH BLUES

JULY 22, 2001

Ms. S. was a woman lawyer, age 33, who was referred to the Society because of difficulty in the sphere of interpersonal relations. The passions in her life were solitary: painting and playing the piano. She was quite pretty, but childishly attired, with her hair pulled back and stringing down. I suggested dating on the Internet to ease her loneliness. This was her second session with me.

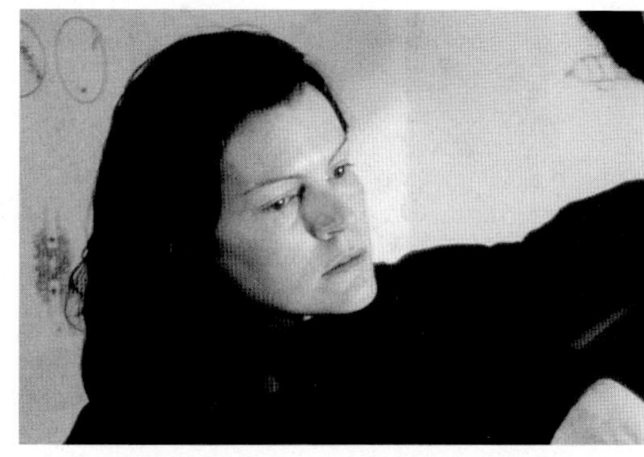

"Thank you for your suggestion, Doctor. I answered a personal ad on the web and exchanged e-mail with a man named Jeff a couple of times. We decided to meet.

"There's a new Indian restaurant in my neighborhood. He came to the bar at 5:00 P.M. last Tuesday. I walked in at 5:15 and there he was seated at a stool near the fish tank. His face was motionless and he spoke softly in a monotone. He had a short gray beard. He said that he was an artist, but an outsider artist. He liked George Crumb and the Hairy Who. For a living he worked for a tee-shirt company. He came from Miami. He told me that he had lots of girlfriends, but I didn't believe him. He said that he left a wife and child in Miami to come north. Who knows if it's true?

"The restaurant was quiet except for the soft sound of the sitar and tabla coming from the speakers overhead. The light was dim. The small lamps on the tables gave the place a ruby glow. My mind wandered. I thought of my trip to Providence the week before. I got there late. It was 12:30 A.M. and the road was gray and icy. I missed my turnoff, and the street became a highway, going out of town. But the car found its way back to my motel. It drove itself safely, effortlessly. You know, I don't know the town and that is not my car, but its owner once lived in Providence.

"The music became louder and my daydream was interrupted. Then the fish tank caught my eye. The light opened up. The gravel was insanely multicolored: indigo, iridescent ochre, blood-red, with fake lilies and fake coleus anchored at the bottom. The plants were waving gently in the water's mini-current. It was all very pleasant to look at. The tank's single occupant was a brown-striped Oscar fish. It had morose, inward-looking eyes and fins that moved slowly back and forth, back and forth. The fins, with their white ribs, looked like a tissue. I had a thought: The man is laconic like the fish. He is just like the fish. The restaurant began filling up. He was still talking to me. The rhythm of his voice was in synch with the motion of the fins. I thought: How much time should I give this? I turned to him. And in the same monotone he asked me, 'Have you looked at my website?'

"How depressing, Doctor. He is lonelier than I am. Why is it that the men I meet are always wrong for me? I can never make contact."

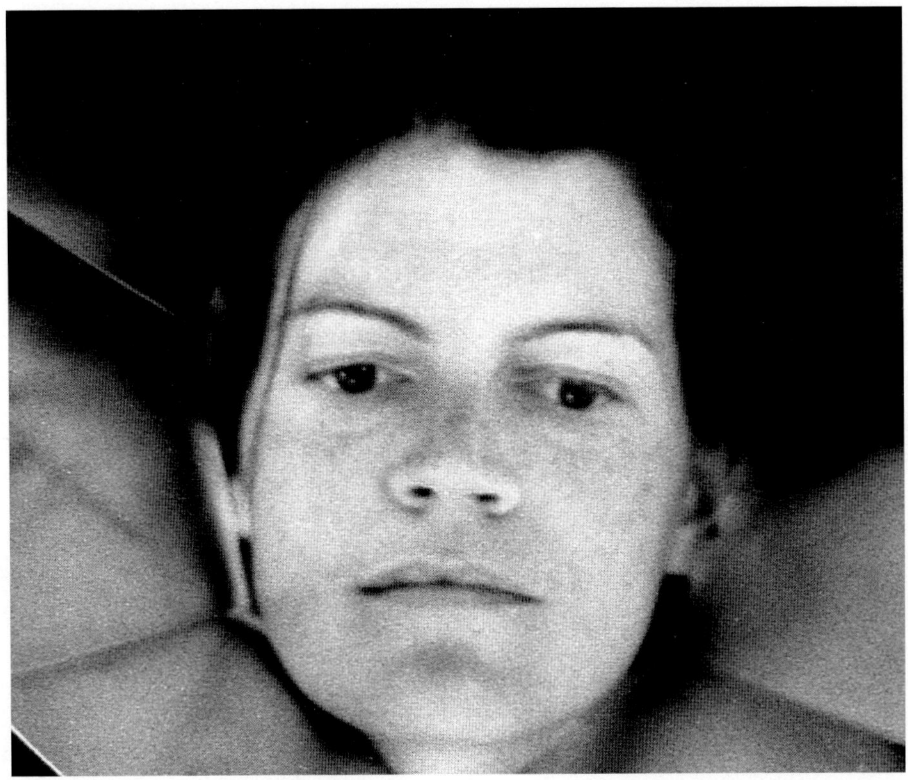

"My dear," I said. "Don't you see? The world is enveloped in a darkness that strives for light; the fish tank represents your yearning for that light. You've had a breakthrough, but he is not your man. You can't make contact because contact is an aspect of communication, and your bandwidth is too narrow. You have the bandwidth blues."

I suggested a new therapy, magnetic stimulation of the cerebellar corona radiata with our new PX42 machine, whose functionality is based on the selective absorption of very high frequency radio waves by certain atomic nuclei that are subjected to an appropriately strong stationary magnetic field. She agreed to the treatment. We shocked the associated outflow tracks of her deep cerebellar nuclei at 51 megahertz. We were able to gradually increase the megahertz to 60, then 80. After a number of treatments, her bandwidth broadened to 100,224 bytes.

DECEMBER 18, 2001

No longer shy and withdrawn, she now makes contact every time. She curls her hair. She is dating many men. She wears Dolce & Gabbana exclusively. And she gave up piano playing and painting for karaoke.

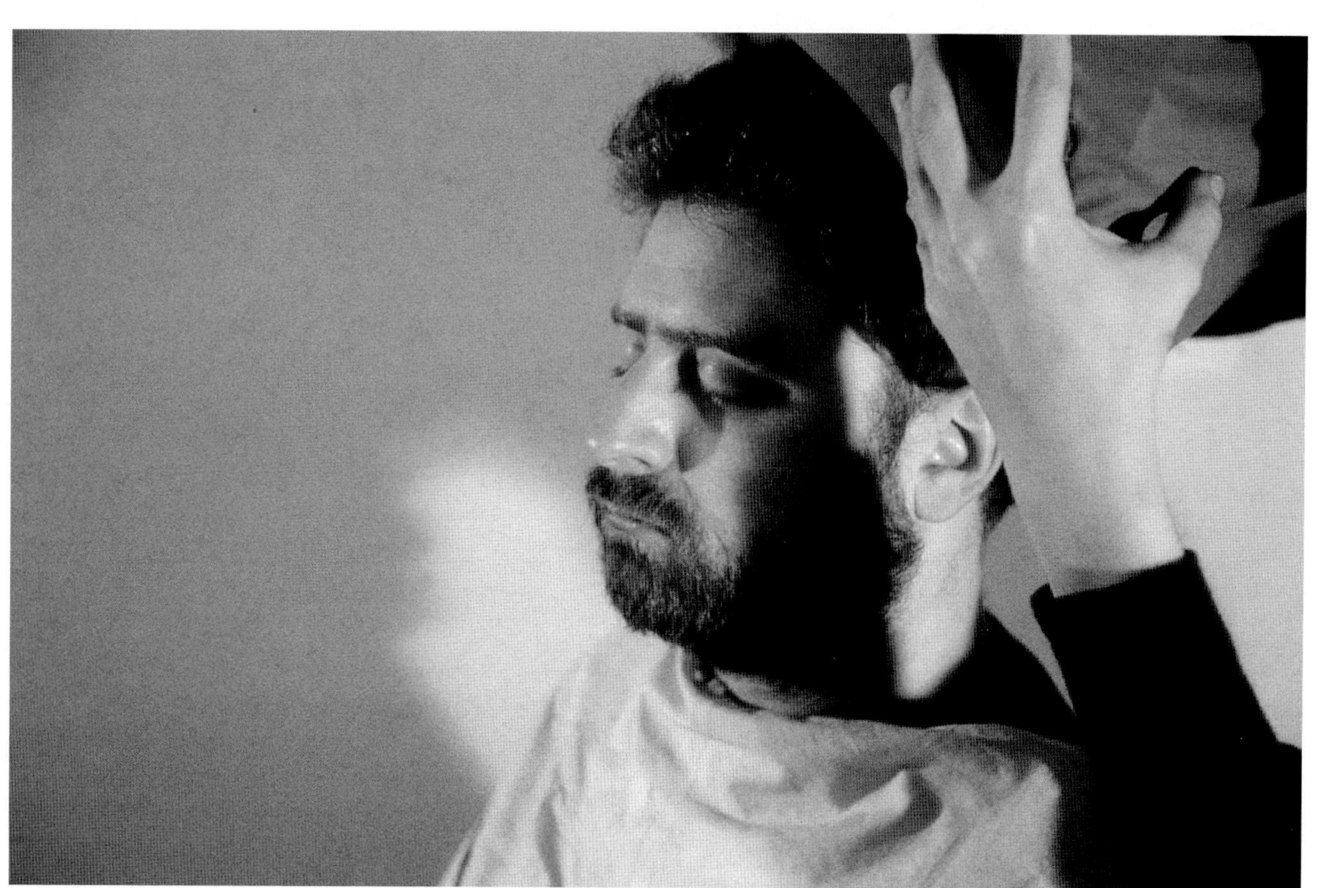

CASE REPORT IV

X EQUALS Y

FEBRUARY 15, 2001

Mr. P. was a 35-year-old single man of Eastern European descent. He was referred to the Society because of disturbances of orientation in time and place, perceptual impairment, and a reeling consciousness. He was of medium height, stocky build, with curly brown hair, a broad face, and a full reddish beard. His clothes were appropriate. His overall demeanor was tense, but friendly.

His symptoms arose, he told me, after a disturbing experience he had the previous year concerning a young woman he had once known who died in a car accident. They dated for a while and parted. He always regretted their breaking up and she was never replaced. He said to me in a soft voice:

"Our orbits converged for a moment, we were intertwined as if in an embrace and then I went into a free fall. The memory has lingered in my mind like an intense dream.

"It was November 1999. I was a tourist in Berlin. One evening I attended the Komische Oper, Row C, Seat 4, to hear Gluck's *Orfeo ed Euridice*. Orpheus, Euridice, the shepherds and shepherdesses all wore ordinary clothes; Orpheus had his electric guitar. The set on stage was black and white. A video of ambulances and hospital beds was projected onto a screen. We could hear distant sounds of street noises and sirens on the stage. But the music in the pit and the arias sung were piercingly delicate, high and lovely, expounding on the theme of enduring love.

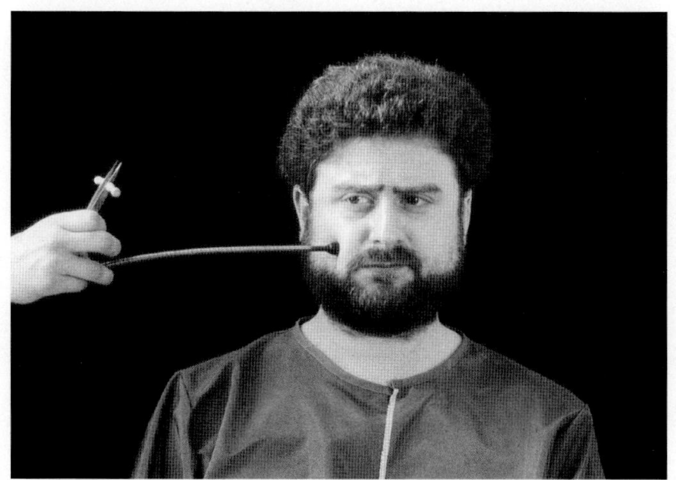

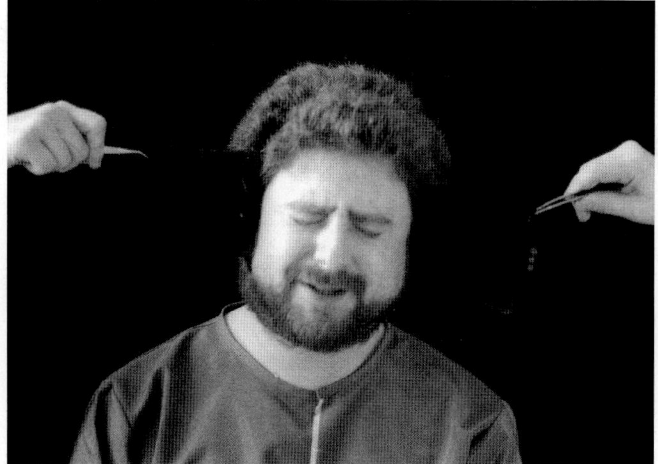

"My ordeal began during Act I, Scene I: *Ameno, ma solitario boschetto di allori e cipressi, che, ad arte diradato . . .* Enraptured German faces surrounded me, but I was barely in my chair. I was suddenly bouncing around like a rubber ball, rocketing into the street, all the way to Unter den Linden, bouncing off lintels, doorknobs, street signs — the harder, solid objects. I was spinning and going way up into the dark night. My orbit was x 2 446 y3z. I could see that gravity kept the rest of the audience pleasantly down between the arms of their seats, but I was locking in, docking up with her, up there, in her smaller tighter orbit 3 z 2ff 1 1 0. She had less mass and was rotating fast. I could see her excited electrons moving swiftly around their atomic nuclei.

"I understood that from her icy orbit in the sky she had looked down on Berlin, spotted me and when x 2 446 y 3z approached 3 z 2ff 1 1 0, and our electromagnetic fields engaged, she reeled me up like bait on a hook.

"We stayed aloft through Act II but during Act III, Scene II she suddenly dropped me and I fell to earth. I heard Euridice cry *"Orfeo"* and Orfeo respond "*Pietà celeste*" as I drifted down to my seat.

"Other events had occurred before. A die with her initial on it fell out of a sock; a stain that wouldn't wash off appeared on a wine glass. I discovered a book I'd lost, Raymond Rousell's *Locus Solus*, on my desk. It was the one that she had borrowed and never returned. These things really happened. But nothing affected me like that night at the opera. She managed, somehow, to have our electromagnetic fields engage, and now I can't disengage."

After hearing his story I explained to him that all the phenomena he described could be understood by the laws of physics and the fundamental forces of nature that apply to every bit of matter in the universe. Planets orbit stars because of gravity; electrons orbit atomic nuclei because of electromagnetism. It is through the fundamental forces that separate pieces of matter communicate with one another and these forces are subject to great surges across space.

What had happened to him — his ascent — was caused by such a surge. It was a transient astronomical event. Her body had become charged.

I said to him, "We recognize a body as charged when it attracts other objects. Friction between the two invariably leaves both of them charged and even mere contact and separation will usually have the same effect. Most important, the charged condition of one body can be transferred to another. So you see the idea thus arises of some entity which is transferred, distinct from the material of the body itself, and giving it the property of attracting other bodies."

I expected this to be a difficult case that would call for intense magnetic therapy, but a few magnetic passes to balance his fluid sufficed to produce some small relief. We scheduled another appointment and just as he was about to leave I said, really thinking out loud, "There is some chance, slight though, that she can be reached telephonically or telegraphically."

I said, "Try sending her a telegram." I referred him to the Central Bureau for Astronomical Telegrams (CBAT), which operates at the Smithsonian Astrophysical Observatory. It's responsible for the dissemination of information on transient astronomical events, distant minor planets, and scattered disk objects via the IAU circulars. These are a series of postcard-sized announcements issued at irregular intervals, as necessary, in both printed and electronic form.

Mr. P. said to me, "I'll call them." We never heard from him again, but I felt confident in my treatment of this man.

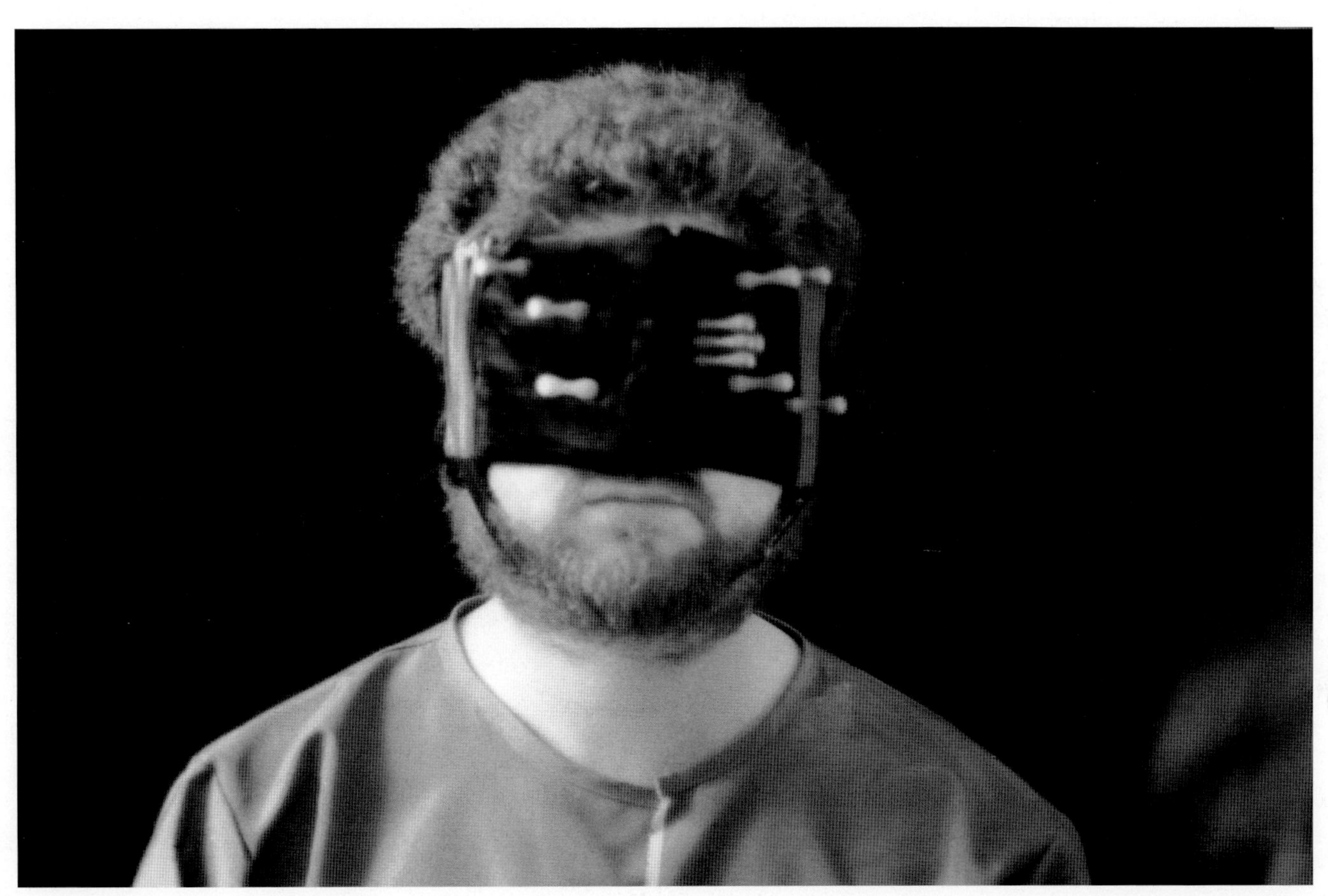

CASE REPORT V

A FAMILY MATTER

AUGUST 29, 2001

Ms. D. is a 40-year-old woman, currently employed as a housekeeper, who came to the Society for treatment of depression and anxiety manifested by severe, intractable headaches. She was a woman of obviously high intelligence, tall, striking, with a regal bearing. Yet this impression was at odds with her disheveled, indifferent attire and her unkempt hair. During her initial interview she was oriented and alert, but her manner conveyed great sadness and pain, punctuated by moments of near panic.

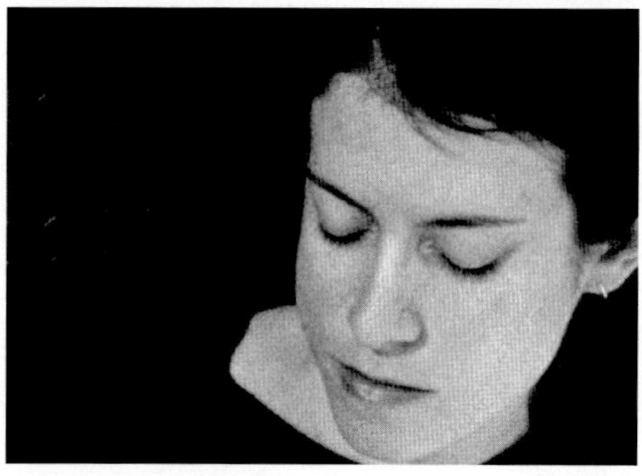

"I hurried here because I really wanted to get to this session. I came by bus. I don't know what is happening to me. When I got here and you let me in, I felt just glad that you accepted me. Although this seems a little strange with all my problems."

To our surprise she said she was a botanist and that she worked at the Bronx Botanic Gardens, commuting from her house just west of the Palisades. She was married, but separated. She lived with her young daughter.

"We live in a big house with three sweeping terraces. There are rolling hills and orchards, a lot of acres. I have a fine garden."

Then, in a rapid clip, she enumerated every shrub. She told us about her fruits and flowering plants, the fruit-bearing trees and deciduous trees, giant oaks and maples and weeping beech. She grew many vegetables: pole beans, cranberry beans, and winter squash "that grow huge serrated leaves." She described the annual poppies, "the kind with spindly milk-green stems topped off by pink petals."

"Near the house a wisteria wrapped completely up and around a tall pine tree. A neighbor told me, 'If that tree falls from all that extra weight, so goes your roof.' Never mind! Over time the wisteria wound itself around my house and other vines attached themselves to it. They covered everything and had to be cut down.

"It was a cold fall day, the sun shined bright with a deep chill in the air. I began hacking out the wisteria roots one by one.

"The roots were gnarled and looked like hell. Annie was playing outside with her friends. She had her toys, and by chance she discovered a lost doll on the ground. It was a rubber doll, cracked and pitted, with tufts of dirty yellow hair on its round rubber head. She was transfixed, immobile at the sight of it, and then someone grabbed her. I was concentrating so hard on the wisteria I heard her cries too late! She disappeared as if the earth had opened up. I looked down and all I saw in the dirt where she had stood was a tuft of yellow hair. My heart sank.

I thought to myself, "This is a difficult case," and as she wept, I gently stroked her hand.

SESSION 2, OCTOBER 5, 2001

On sitting down she said despondently:

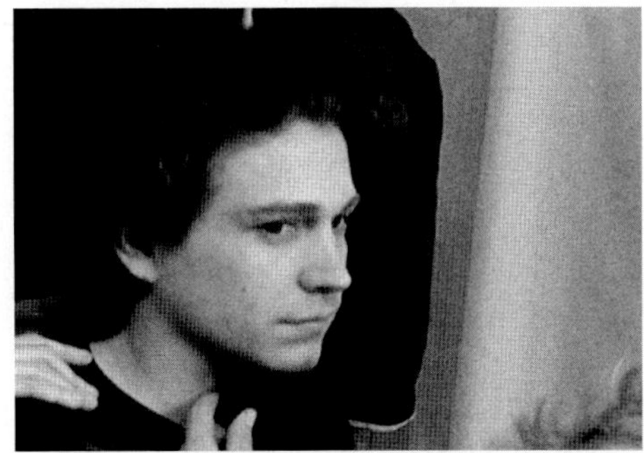

"I was alone in my grief. I remained unconsoled. Weeks and months passed. The next summer the garden went to pieces. In June the sun blazed so hard the new shoots burned up. Then it poured and the rain uprooted the old trees and shrubs. The downed trees with their hairy roots looked like tilted ships on a shoal. My husband, a stubborn man who never shows weakness outwardly, said, 'She'll be found.' And that was that.

"Time moved on. I slept and I dreamed. Cousins flew by. They came on horses. One said to me stiffly, 'You know, your daughter was kidnapped by her uncle, your brother, with the blessing of your father.' *(Long silence.)* I remember the games I played with my brother. He always laid down conditions. *(Barely audible.)* My father is another story. *(Pause.)* My brother is aloof, close to nobody. He lives in a valley, and veils of fog are always obscuring his house.

"Fall came again. Nothing changed. They said, 'This is a family matter.'"

The prognosis is grim! Her brother kidnapped and probably raped her daughter! A felony! After some discussion, we agreed on the agreeable course: A week in the baquet, another in the atrium.

SESSION 3, OCTOBER 11, 2001

Ms. D. reported her headaches were less intense.

"It was raining. I came by car today. I felt I left the last session with something important cut off, so I wanted to remember what we had been talking about."

She continued in this vein, trying to remember.

"I had a dream. It was night. I stood near the window. At first the sky seemed black, but then I noticed that the stars were out though there was no moon. The scene shifted. I was standing near a fireplace. In the dream it was summer but the fire was blazing. I felt absolutely well and powerful. It was a sensation I can barely put into words. I cradled a baby in my arms, bent down, and thrust him into the fire as if I was searing him, like meat. But my hands stayed cool, and while enveloped by the flames, he was completely unharmed. I was thinking that by searing him I was protecting him from ever dying. Right then his mother appeared in the room. She panicked, shrieked, and hit her thighs with her fists. She reached for the baby, hurling him to the ground. I awoke in a fright."

In an agitated state she was brought to the laboratory and clothed in a lilac treatment suit with white ribbons on her sleeves, each sewn to form the letter U. I left for several minutes on an urgent matter and when I returned there was Ms. D. deep in a somnambulist state, eyes open, talking softly.

"This is what really happened. A palace was built for me. It sat on a cliff, like the Palisades but much higher up. It was daybreak. The sky was cloudless. I wore a full-length dark robe that was embroidered at the hem with long ears of corn. *(Pause.)* The palace became the apse of a church. I was standing in it, and crowds of people were kneeling down and worshipping me. Suddenly I felt my face cloud up with rage. I took a glass and struck it with my fist. The shards flew apart, unleashing floods in the east and wildfires in the west. Submarines collided. Tsunamis formed. The world lamented, and my family suffered, too. I was glad. They brought gifts to mollify me. My father appeared in a clap of thunder. He summoned a messenger to find my daughter, and there she was, sitting on a couch in his dank basement, with my brother by her side. There they were, my father, my brother, and my lovely daughter. I saw her! She was alive! She was alive! Then the four of us stood in the apse. With his hand at her elbow my brother pushed her slightly forward and spoke sullenly, 'Go to your mother.'

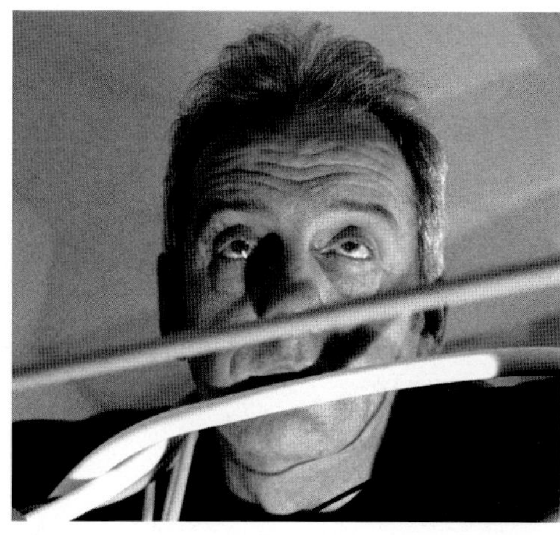

"But before she could move he called her by name. She turned away and back towards him. He offered her a Milky Way bar.

"I asked her, 'Have you eaten it, my darling?' And she said she had. I said to her, in a formal tone, 'Because you ate that bar, every year you will return to your uncle's basement in the winter. The rest of the time you will live here with me.'

"The scene shifted. We were together in a field, overcome by the heavy smell of summer. The corn was high. My daughter gave birth to a baby girl. I took a new lover and had a baby boy. We were celebrated, worshiped at the altar and in the palace, and we knew we would live like that forever."

Afterwards, Ms. D. gradually regained her sense of the here and now, but her belief in the reality of this event was unshakable. The case was closed.

MAY 14, 2002

From various accounts in the press we learned the outcome of this family tragedy. The daughter was abducted by her uncle with the full knowledge of the father, a powerful man. They lived together in a big house, "fit for a king." The daughter was nine years of age, still a little girl. The uncle thought he treated her like a queen. She attended school. She watched television. She had a laptop, a cell phone, the latest DVDs. Her bedroom faced east. She looked out while falling asleep. She made a few friends, girls like herself who had seen some misfortune. One an adopted child from China, the other a girl with a congenital heart malformation. Her grades were average. She daydreamed. She smiled sadly. The two men, uncle and father, mistook her melancholy for grace. She thought, "My mother has forgotten me." They said, "She went to school. She had friends. Nothing bad happened." Her uncle snored, his manners were poor. His bushy brows furrowed when he talked. He insisted that she visit him every winter. For the rest of the year he found another passion.

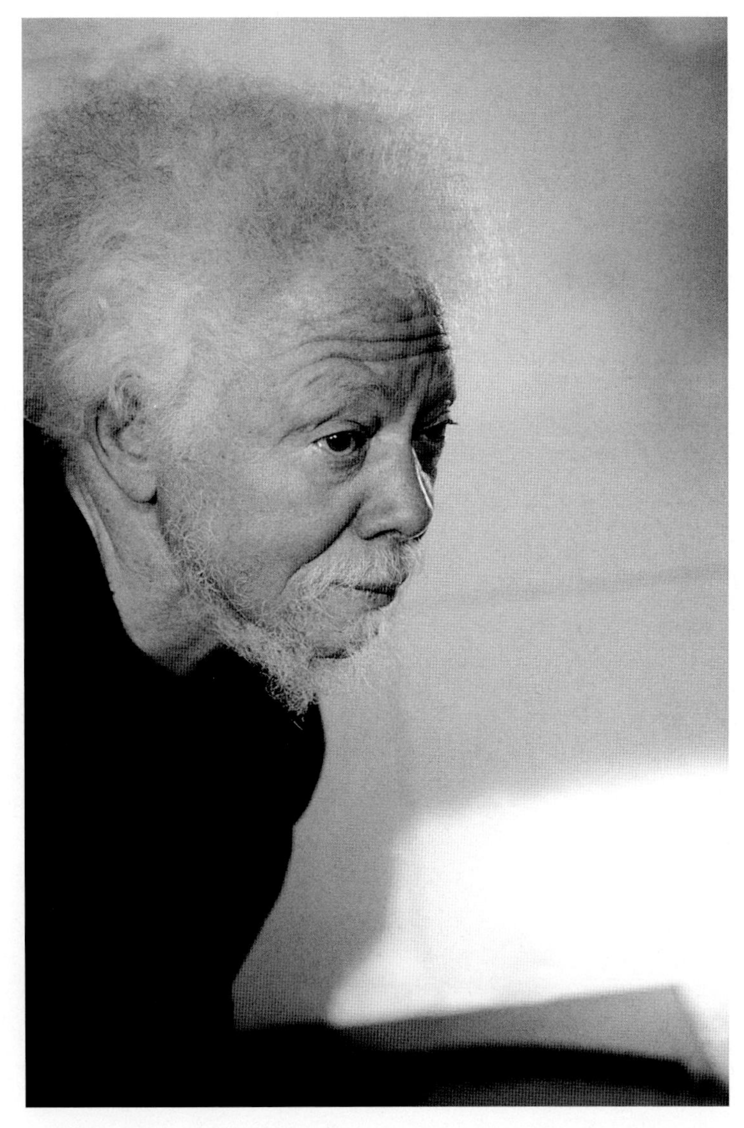

3

AUTOPSY

THE ACT OF SEEING WITH ONE'S OWN EYES

"αυτοπτεᾷ" **autopt-eô**, to see with one's own eyes,
Paus.4.31.5, Hld.3.1; esp. witness a divine manifestation

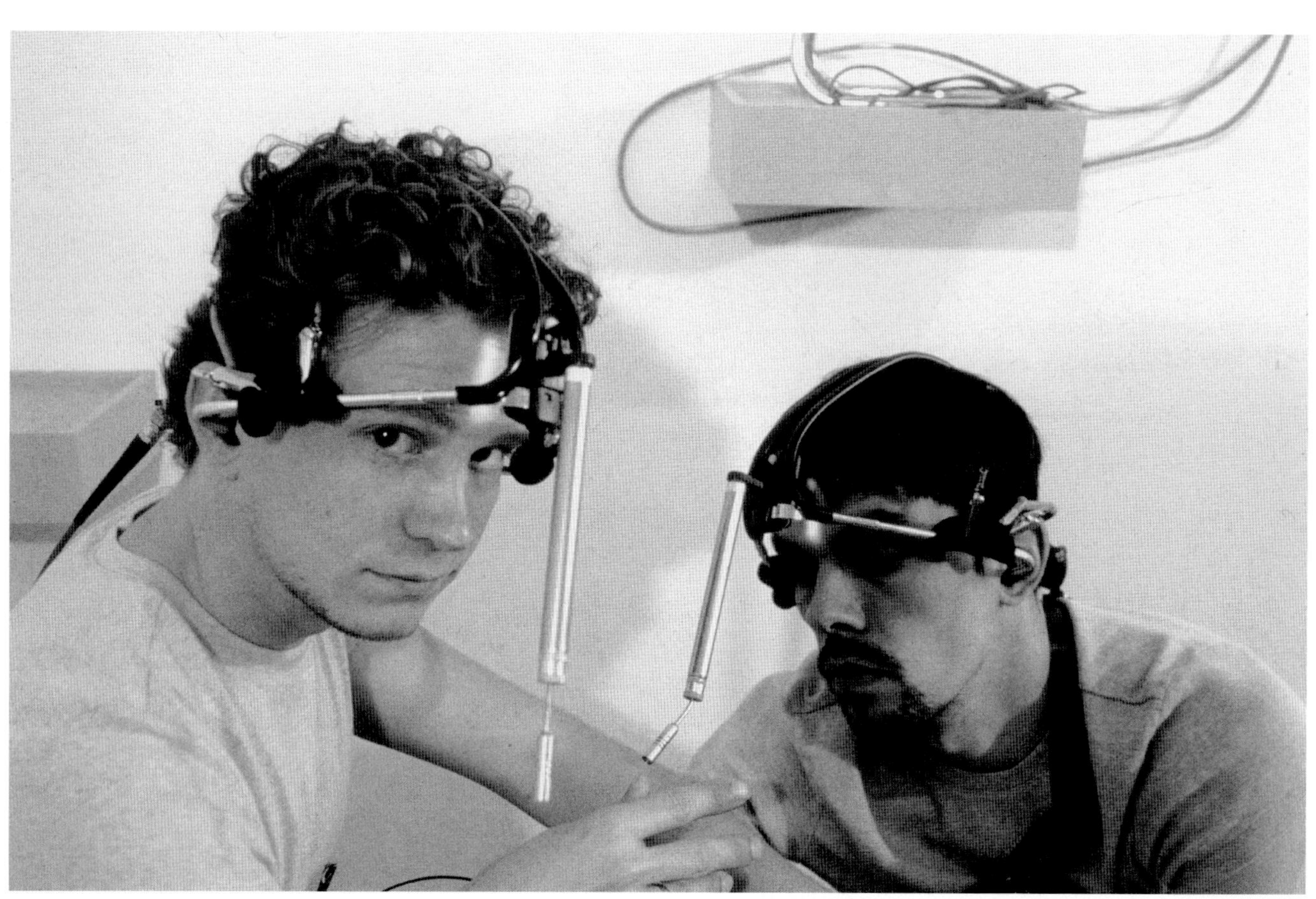

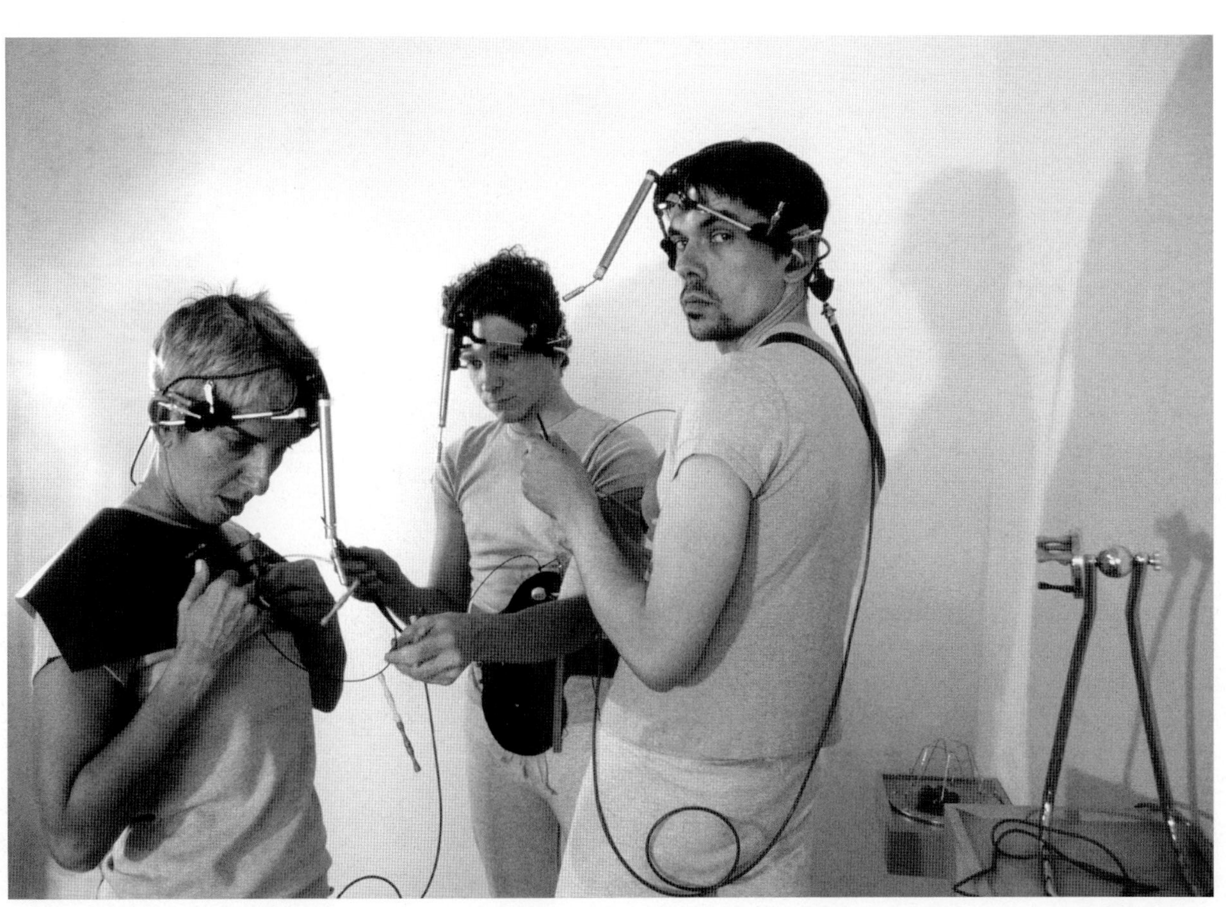

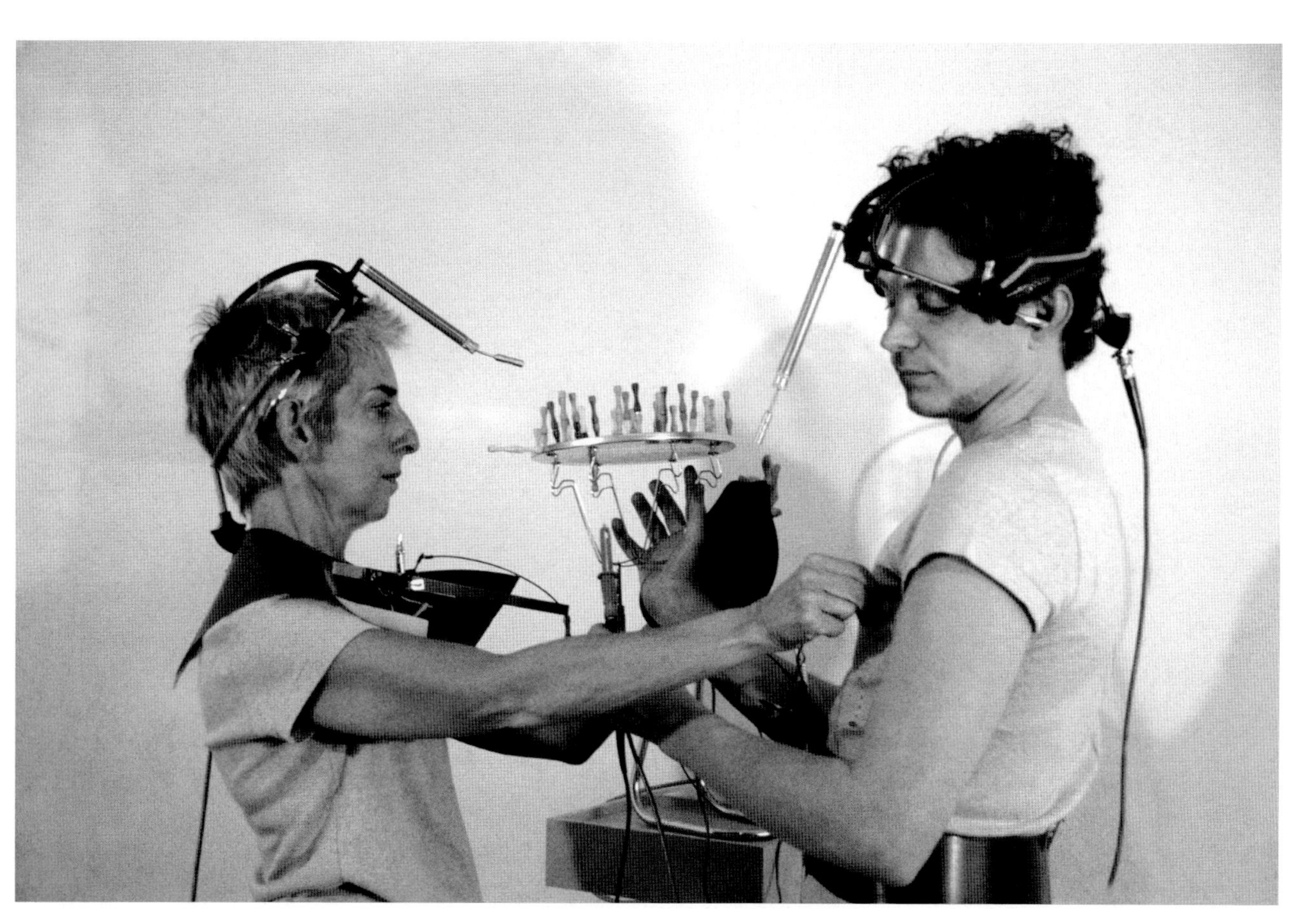

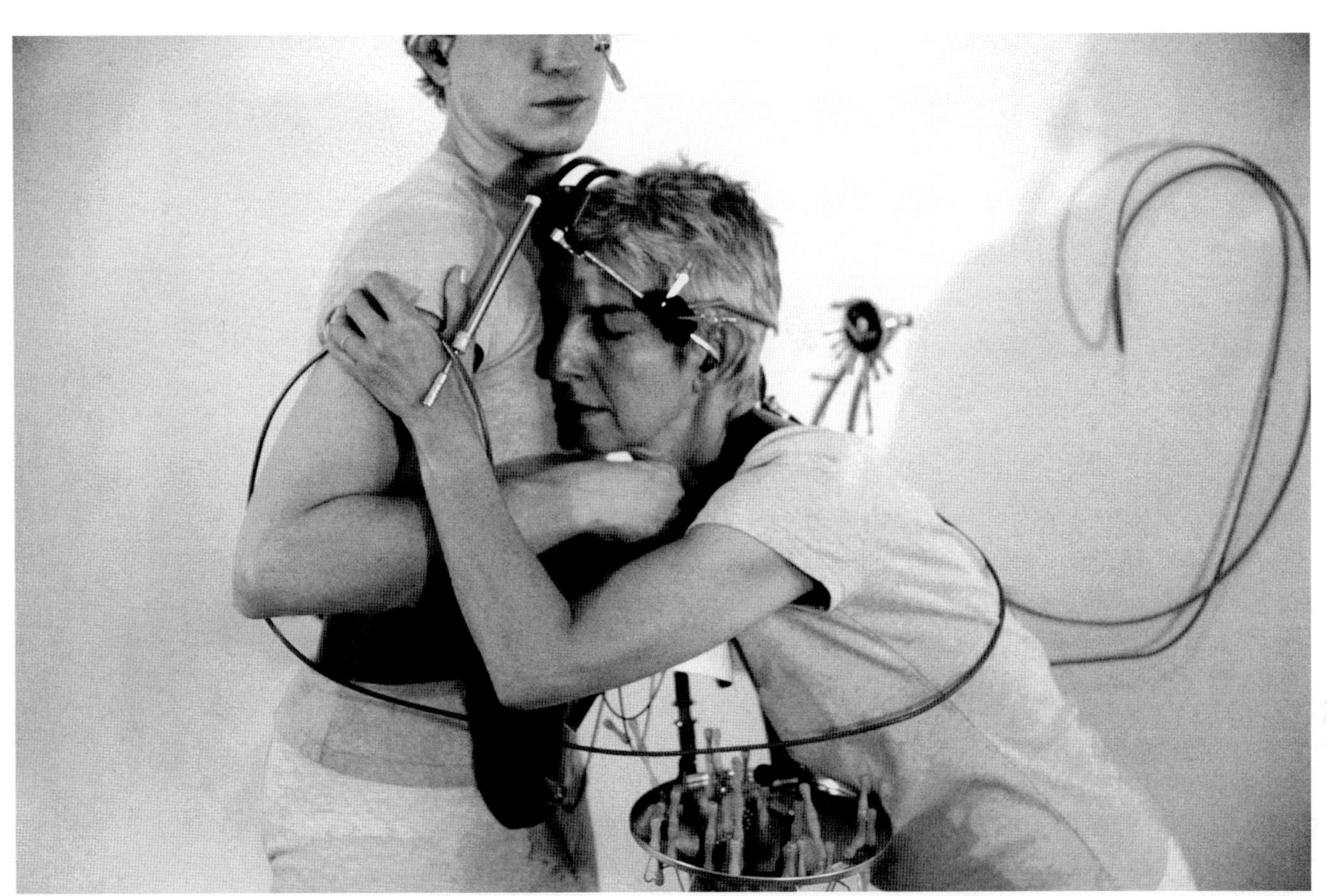

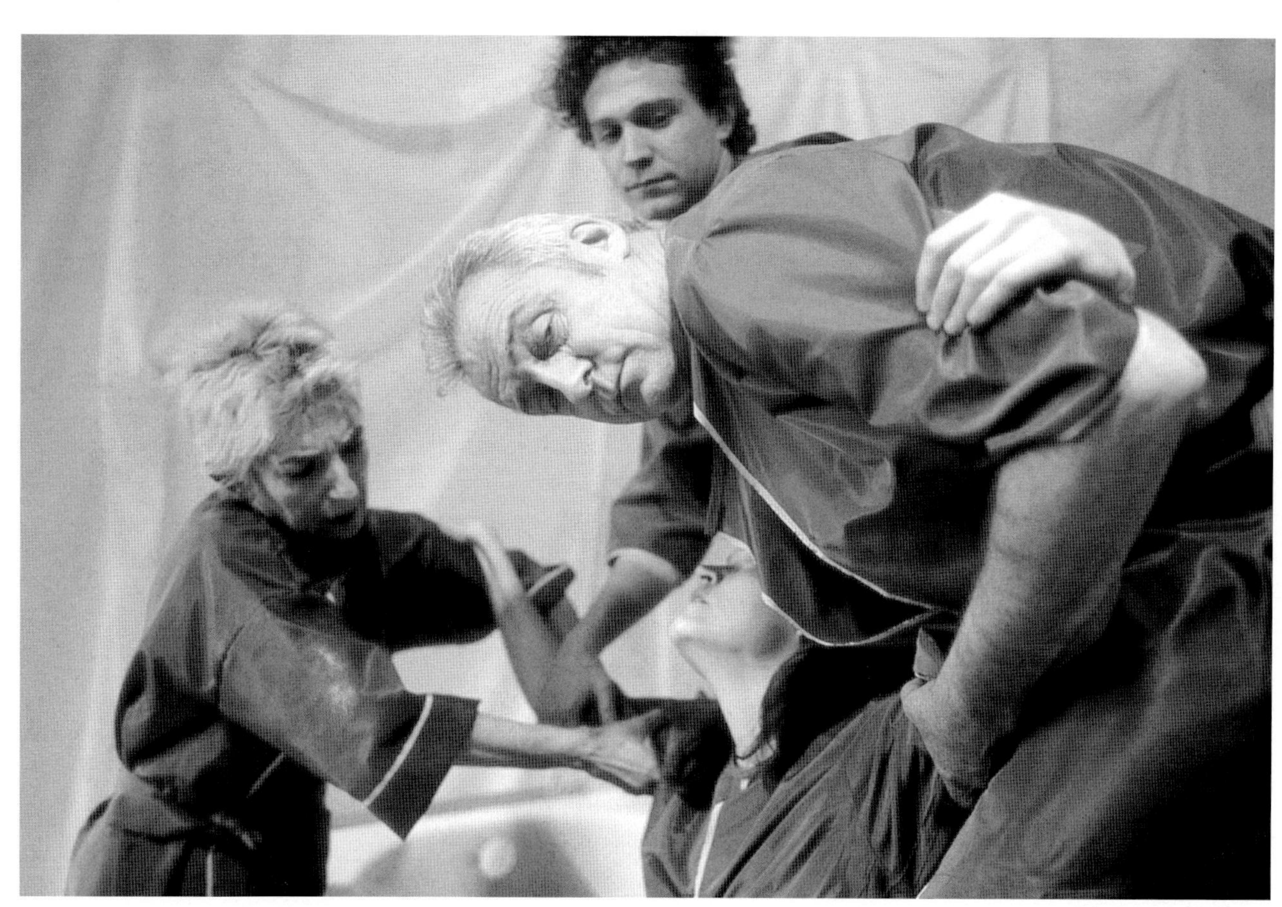

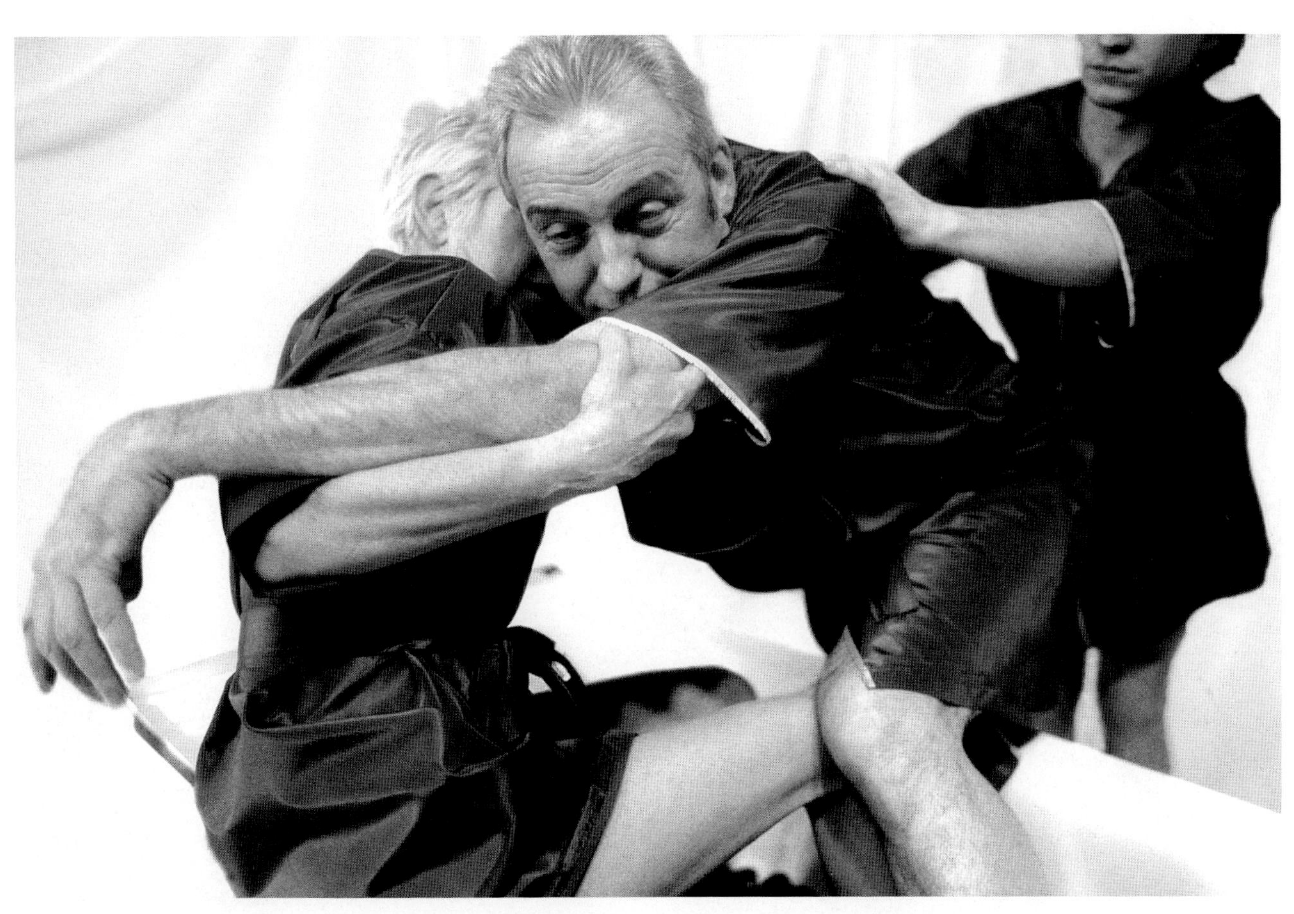

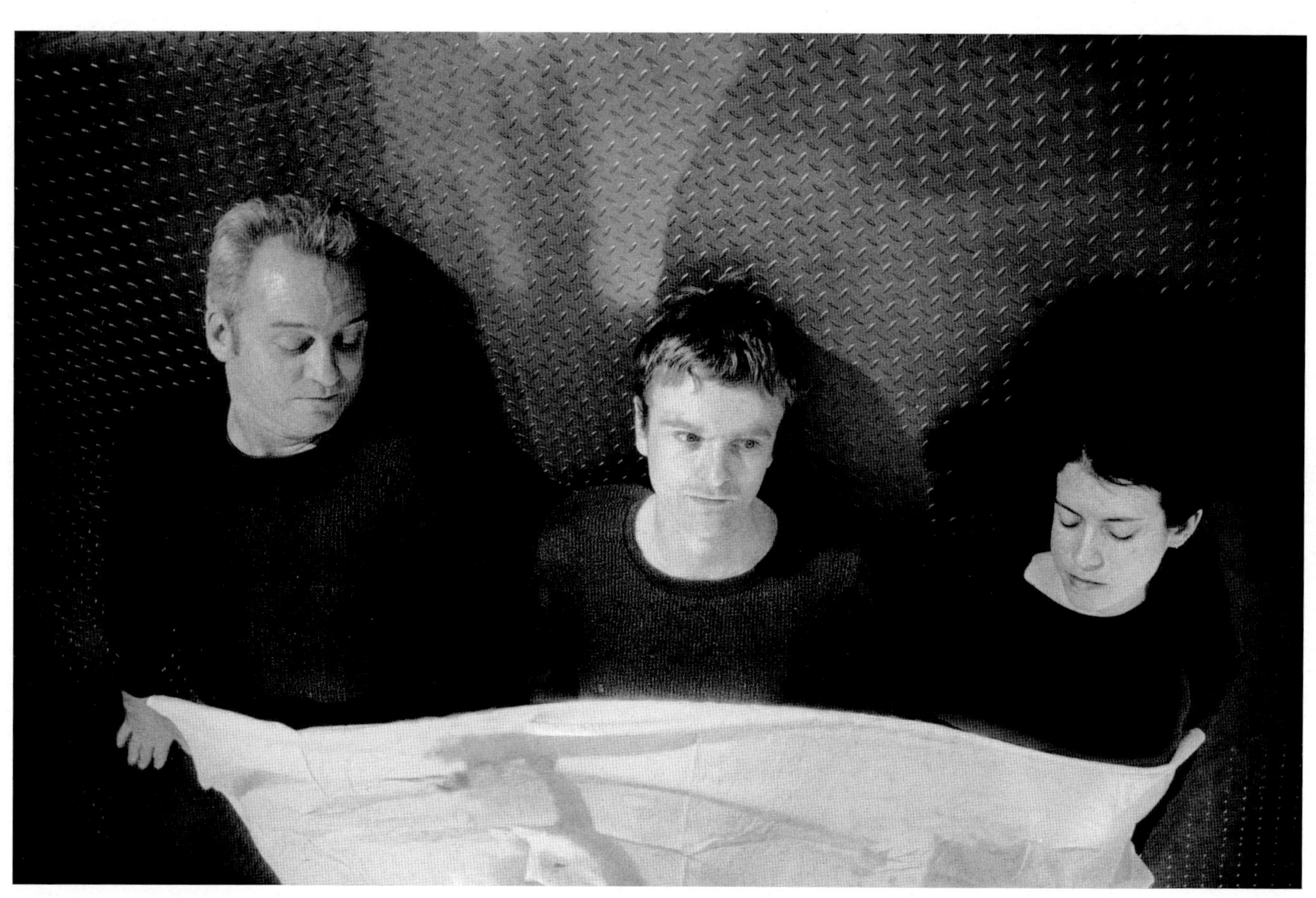

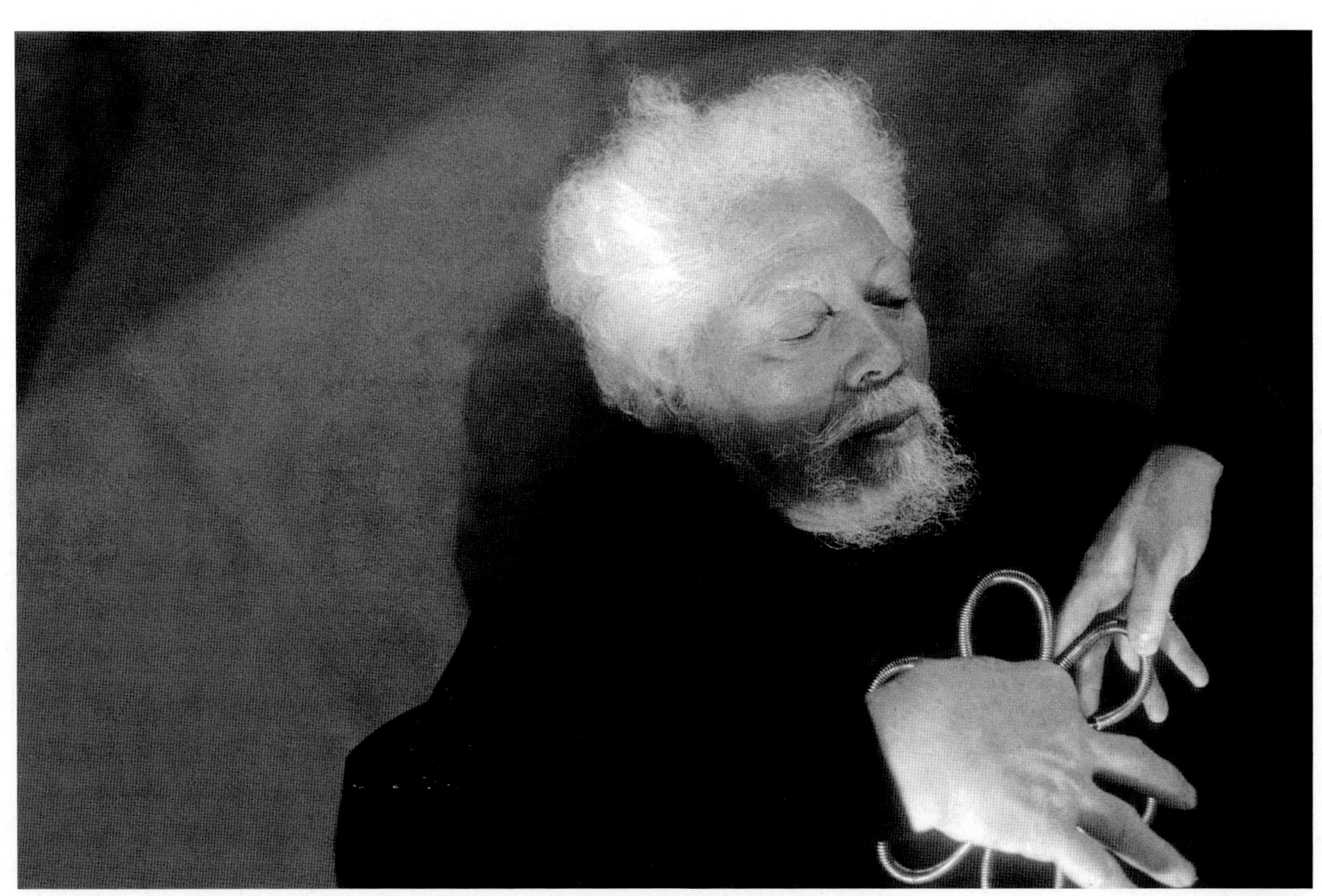

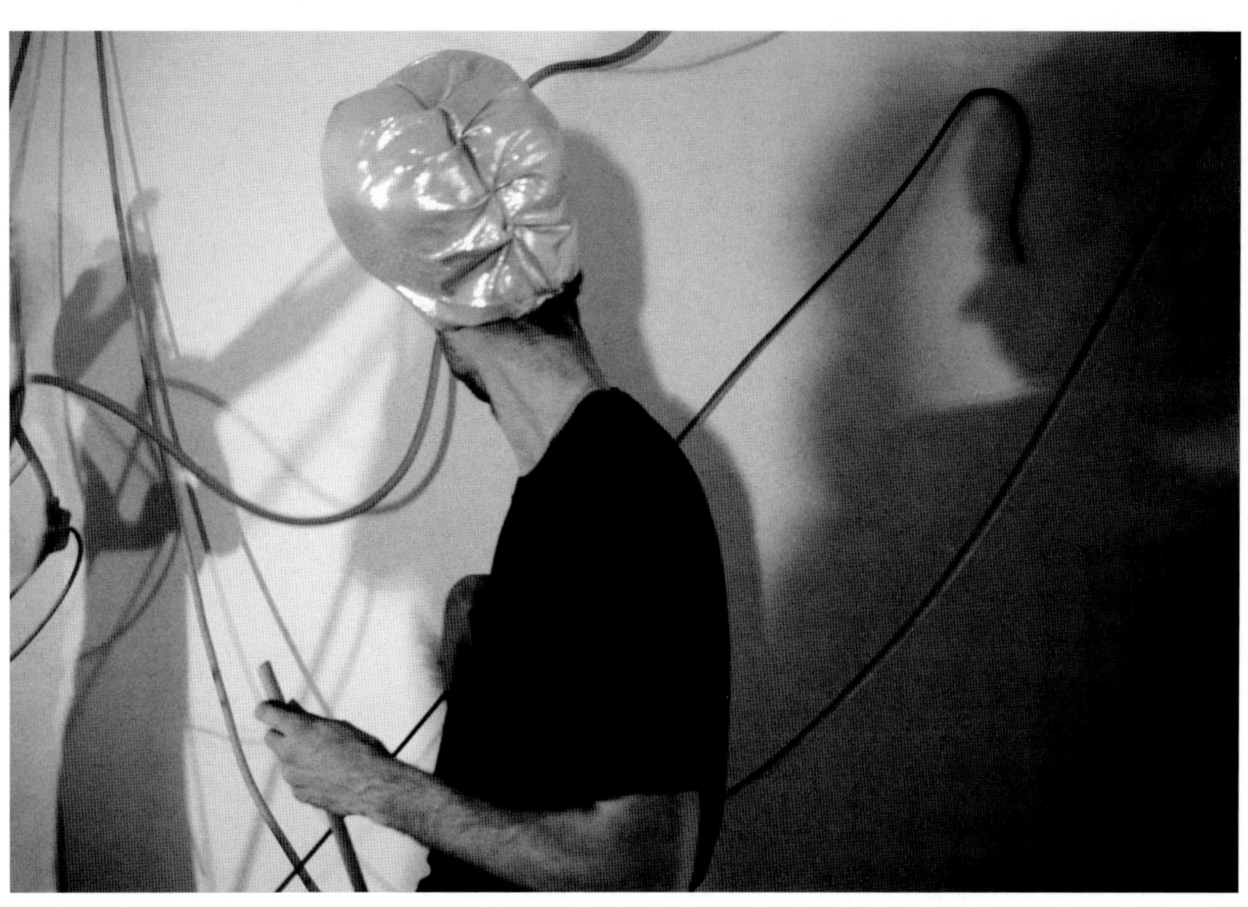

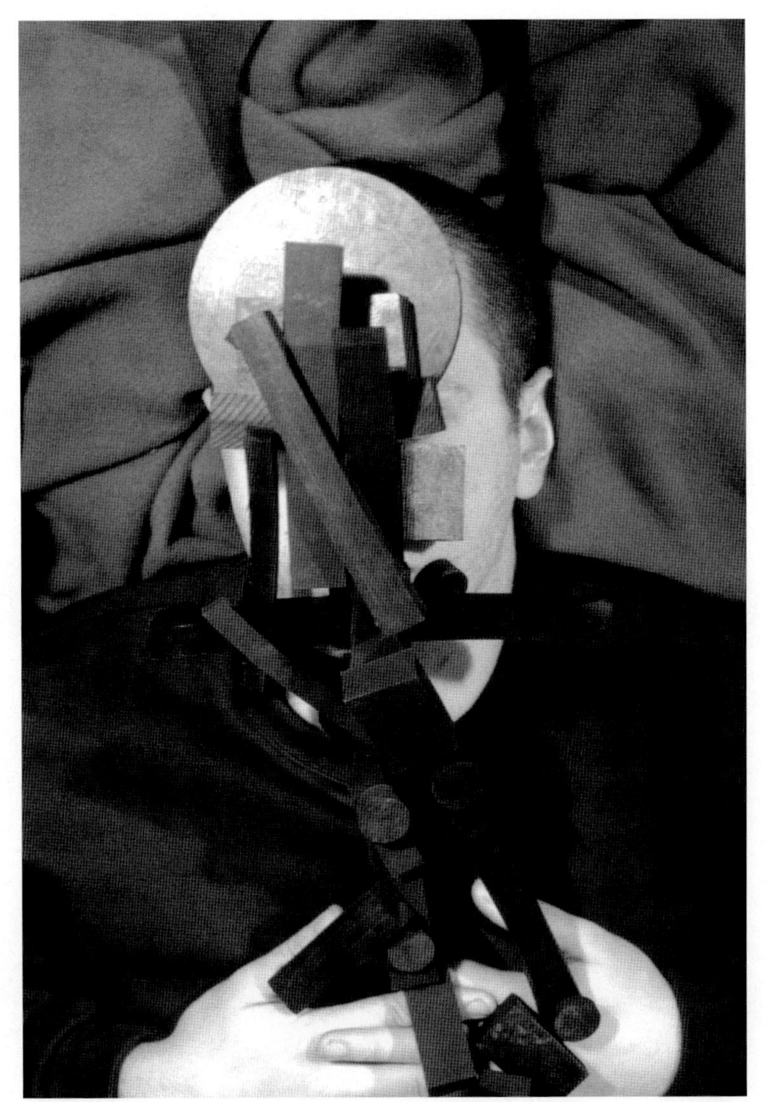

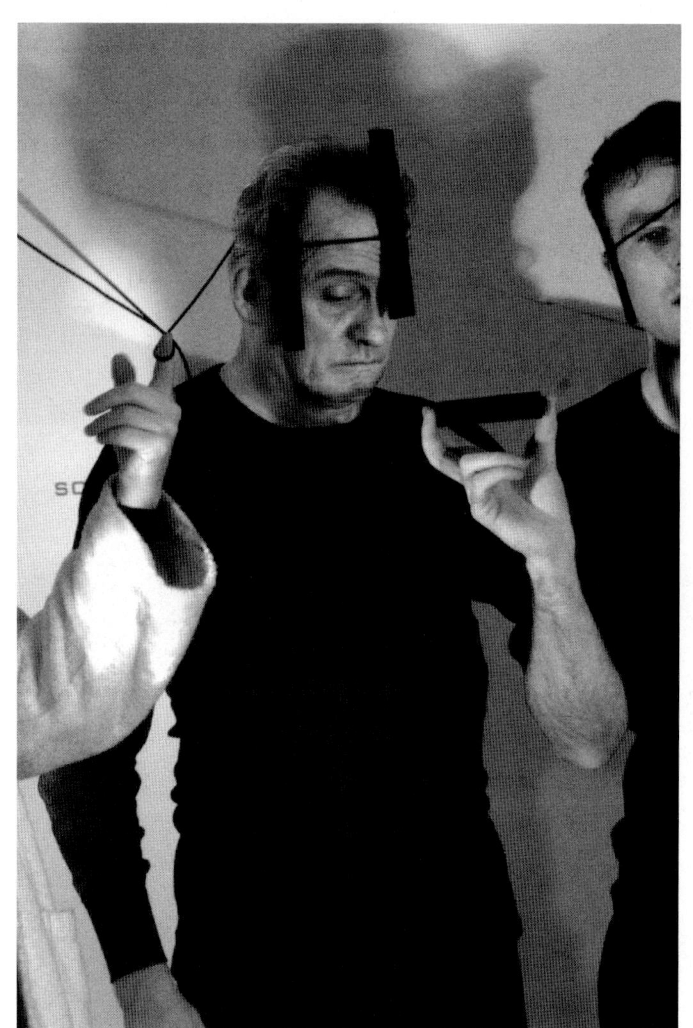

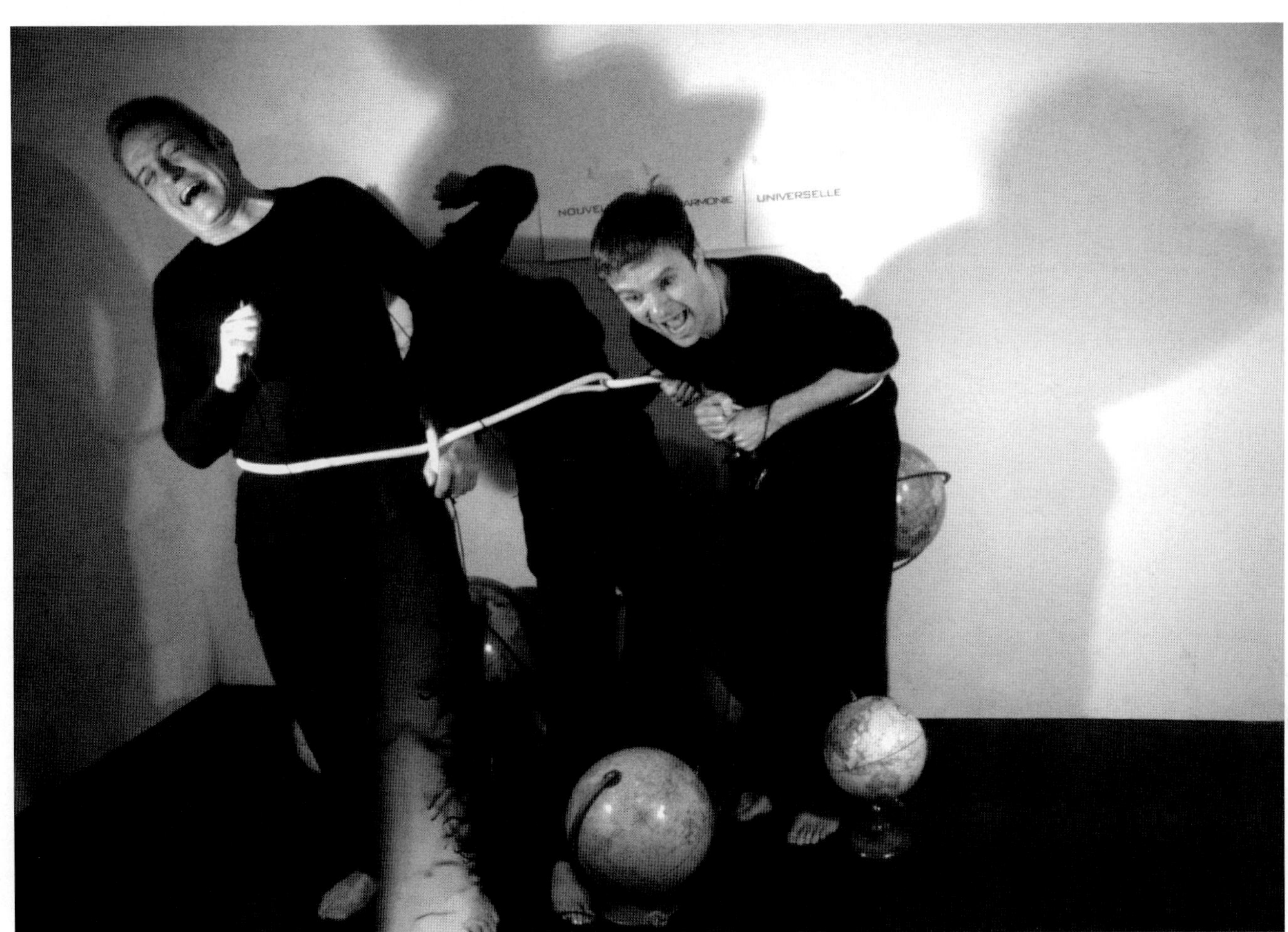
NOUVEL
ARMONIE
UNIVERSELLE

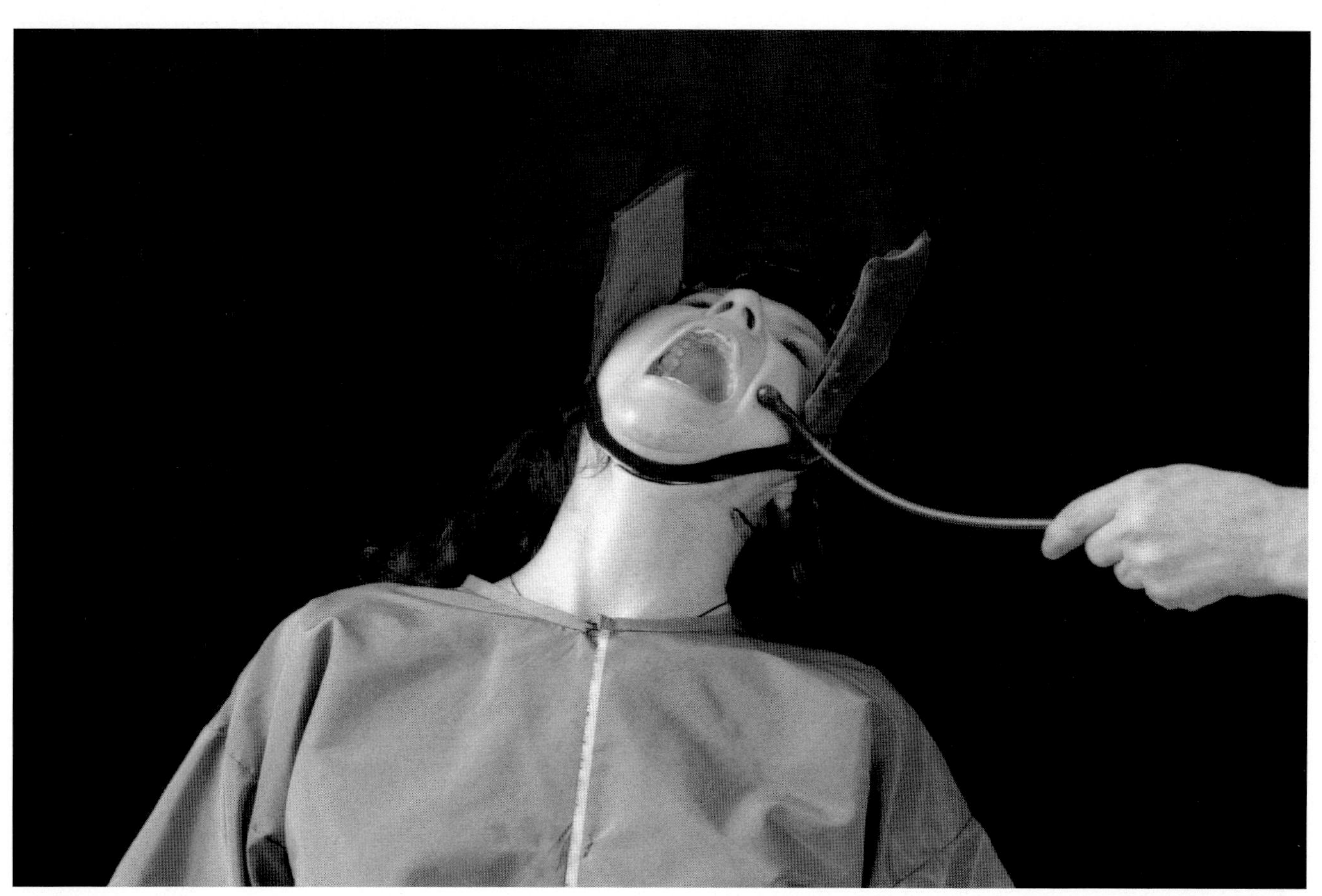

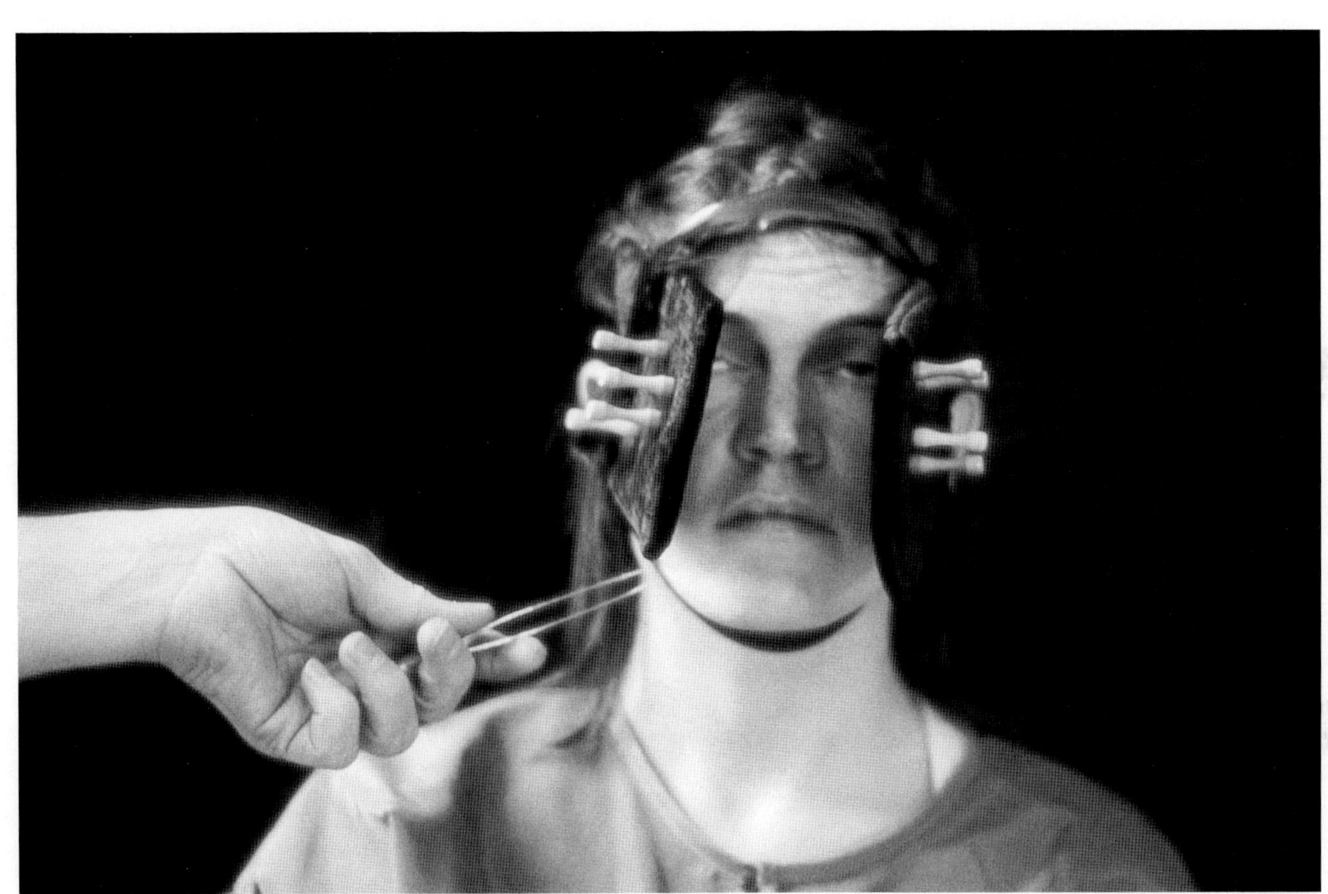

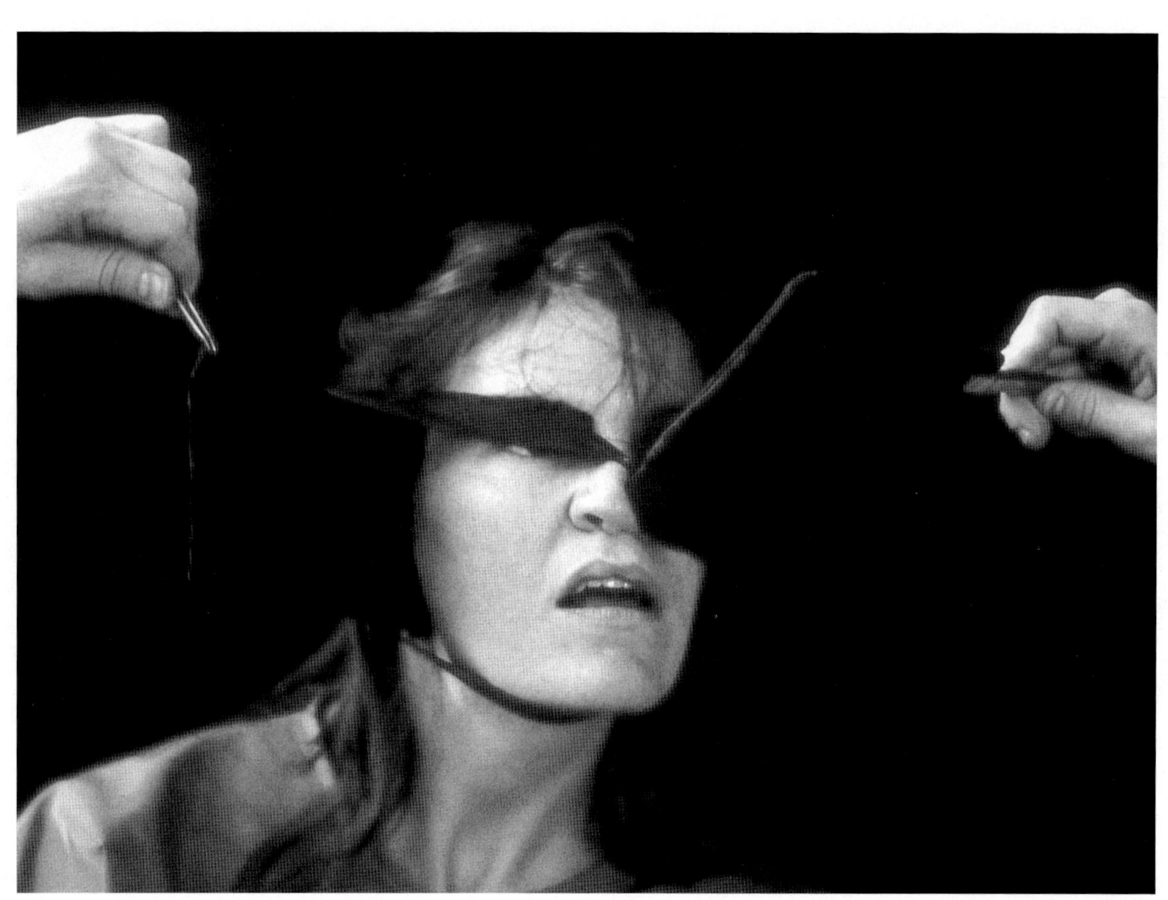

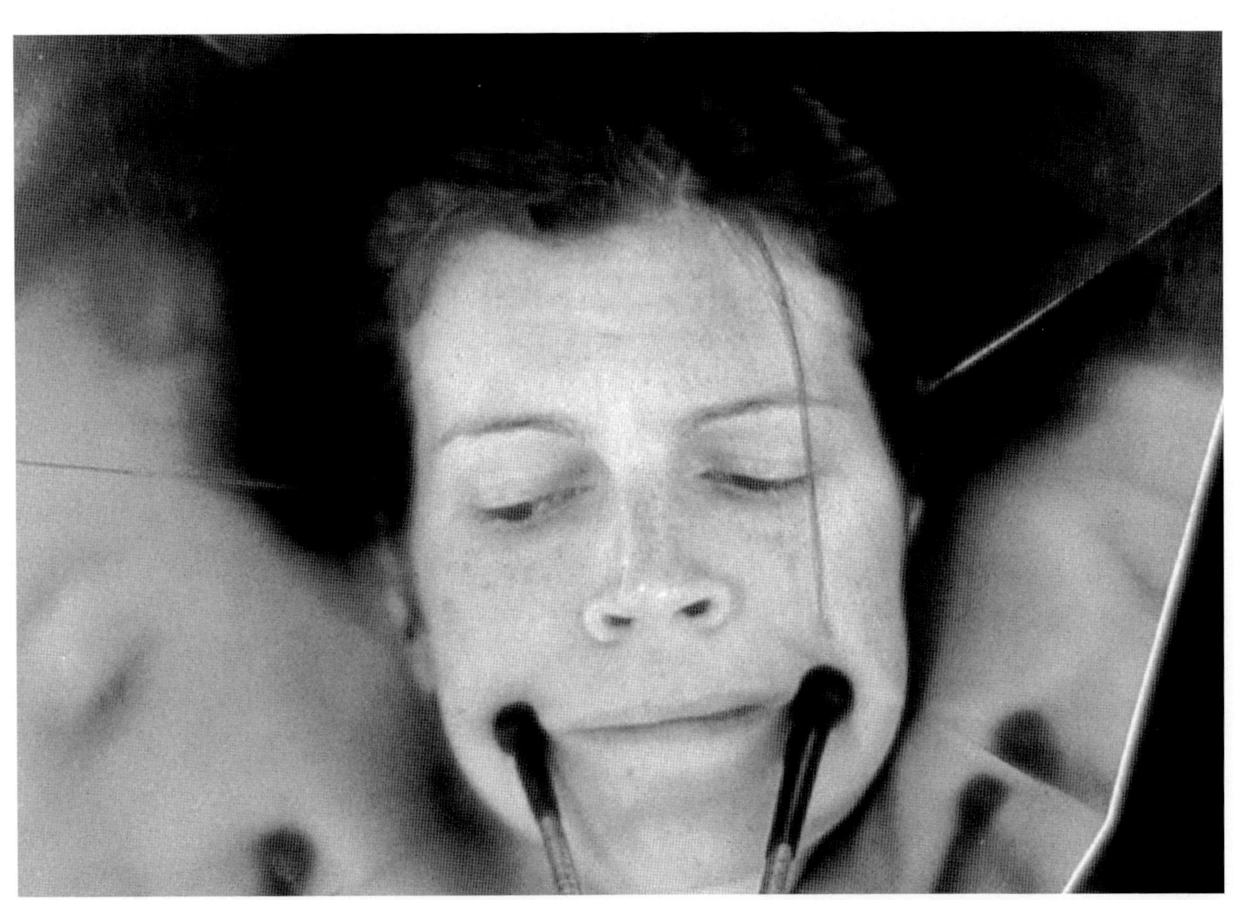

4

TESTIMONIALS

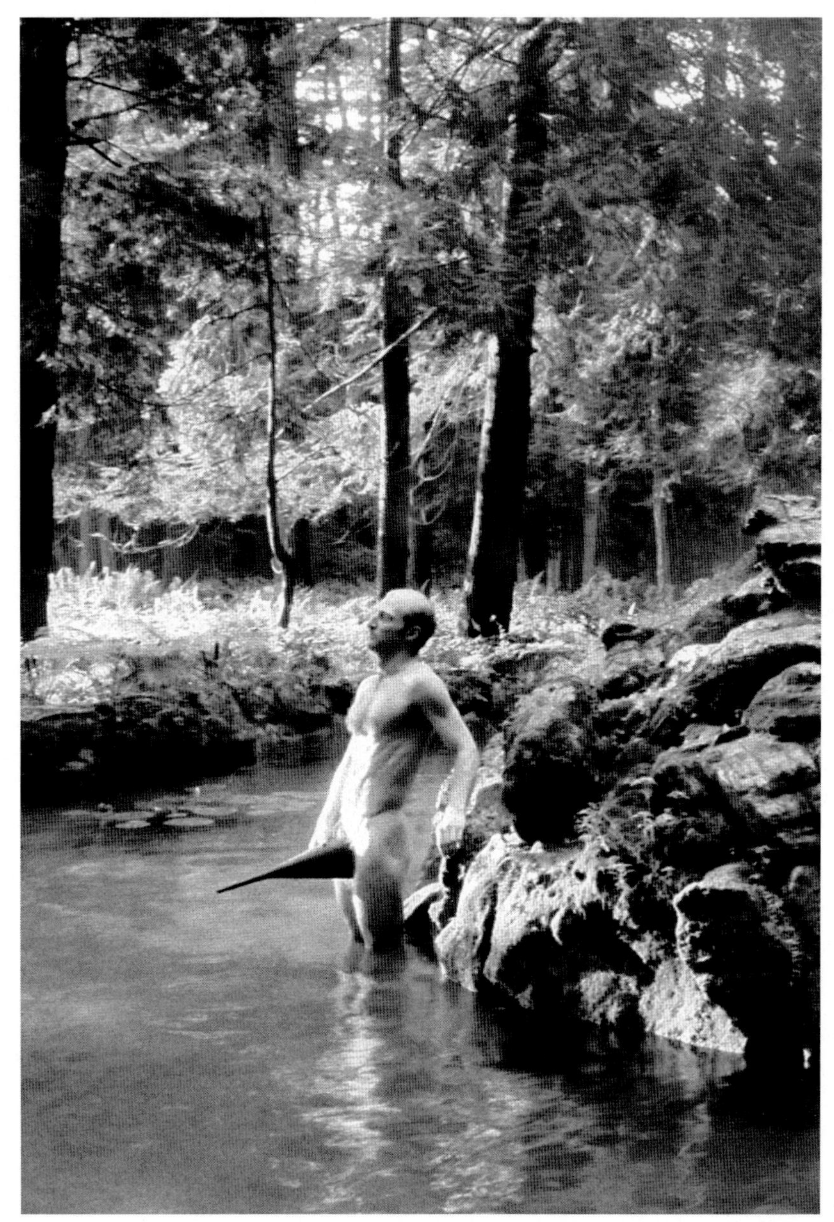

ABLE TO LOVE AGAIN

Jonathan Ames

I WAS INSANE and then I was cured by The New Society for Universal Harmony. I'd like to tell you about this cure, but I'll begin with how I went mad.

I loved someone.

She loved me.

Then she stopped loving me. There was an age difference. Not in my favor. I was old. She was young. So she left me. Then she came back. Then she left me. Then she came back. Then . . .

Young people often behave this way, so I'm told. I received the following advice from a friend in the form of a question: "Is the fucking you're getting worth the fucking you're getting?"

Yes.

But then, finally, she didn't come back any more. I was shattered.

I tried to time how long I could go between thoughts of her. Usually not more than five minutes. I had lost control of my mind. Like something that floats in front of the eye, she appeared before me all day long and all night long — I dreamed about her repeatedly. Dreamed that she had new lovers, better lovers. In one dream I saw the enormous cock of one of my dream rivals and screamed out in pain, like I was having a nightmare.

In this utterly damaged state of being, I went up to Yaddo, ostensibly to work on my new novel. But how could I work? Not only were my mind and heart afflicted but also my digestion. I had developed Irritable Bowel Syndrome, which is caused primarily by emotional upset. I told a friend at Yaddo my tale of heartbreak and how, as a result, I needed to be near a toilet at all times, but then concluded, "I still would like to marry the girl. Maybe I can."

My friend, a brilliant novelist, replied, "Go ahead and marry her if you want to wear a diaper the rest of your life."

Then he told me he knew someone who could help me — a Dr. F.A. Mesmer, the founder of The New Society. She had cured him of severe depression. He gave me her phone number. She was in nearby Athol Springs.

I called Mesmer. She had me outline the problem for her.

"You have a delirious love attachment," she said, and then added, "I can help you." She was intimate with the Yaddo grounds and told me to meet her at the Japanese rock garden at seven the next morning.

"Will this cost anything?" I asked. But she had already hung up. I met Mesmer at the appointed hour. Her eyes were dark liquid holes. She was middle-aged with wiry auburn hair.

"Take your clothes off," she said.

I obeyed her without question. Those eyes. Also, I was willing to try anything.

"Please get into the water."

Yaddo's Japanese garden is an enchanting glade with an enormous volcanic rock in the center of a pool, which I entered naked. Mesmer handed me a black funnel.

"Put it over your genitals. . . . Stand by the rock. Face me. Listen closely. The human body is a magnet. Love is a result of magnetic harmony between two people. You have a magnetic imbalance. The rock, with its ore, will draw the obsession for the girl out of you; the water, an antimagnetic force, will keep you stabilized and prevent you from getting overcharged."

"Is this dangerous?" What had I gotten myself into?

"The way you are right now is dangerous. You need help. Get in position. Close your eyes. Come out of the water when I tell you."

I followed directions: held the funnel in place, stood in the water. It was cold but magnificent. I don't know how long I was in there. She told me to come out. "You should feel better now," she said. She shook my hand and left.

Over the days that followed, the girl wasn't floating across my eyes any more. I felt sad — she was truly gone. But so were the madness and the IBS. The crazy procedure had actually worked. My mind and colon were mine once more. I could feel that I was able, once again, to be magnetically drawn to someone new. Mesmer had healed me — I was ready again to love.

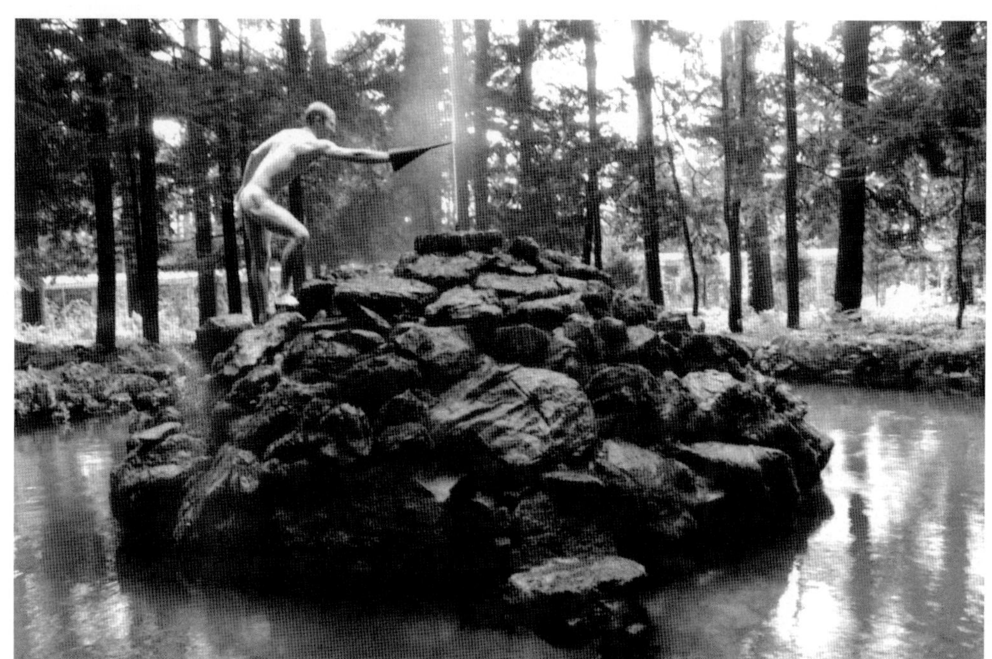

POSTCARD FROM ELKE S.

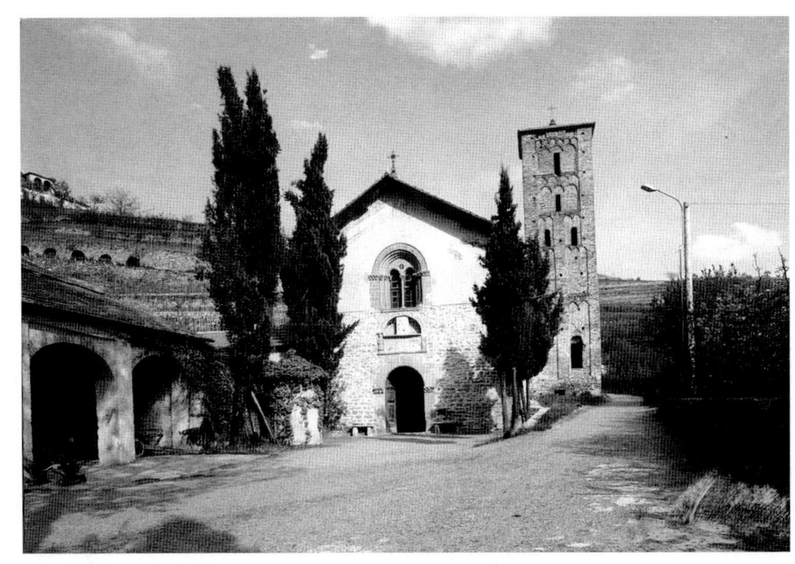

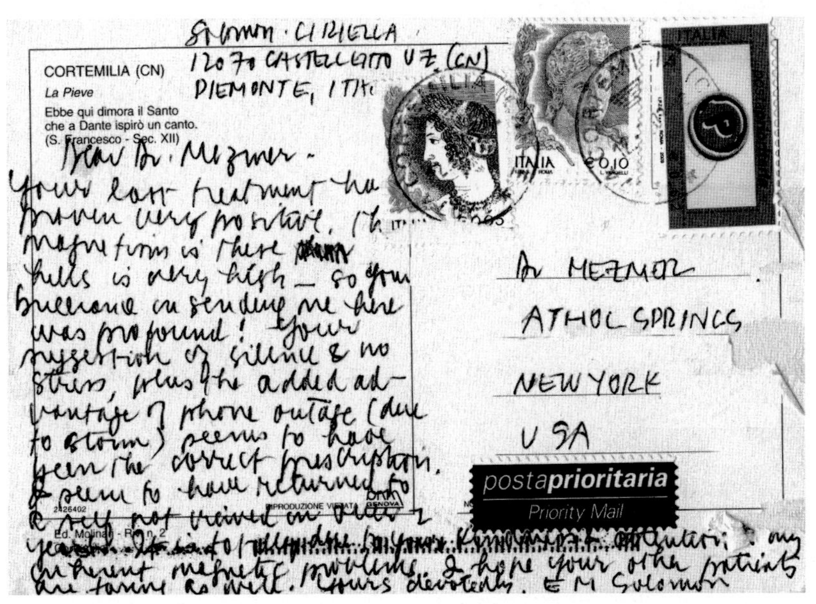

VISION PROBLEMS

Nancy Princenthal

THE TROUBLE THAT BROUGHT ME to The New Society was refractory. I had lost my ability to unbend what I saw. Following a minor professional disappointment, and in search of cleansing vision, I traveled to the Arctic and spent a short season in never-ending daylight. Gulls wheeled overhead and the occasional falcon. Caribou crossed the tundra, a four-hour walk away. All seemed close enough to touch. The paucity of water in the atmosphere made the clarity unrelenting. No blue haze softened the horizon. I reached for the habits of perspective, for arranging the visible world into a table laid for my pleasure, but found its furthest edges curling toward me with a degree of animation I felt to be almost vicious. Having lived behind two curved lenses all my life — the visual experience common to sighted humans — I had developed the compensatory tactics that are also so widely shared: smoothing the world flat, keeping the distant at bay. Here, they were unavailing.

I returned to the city where I live, but found no respite. Its regular geometry, usually so easeful, was no more calming than being inside a kaleidoscope. Nor did escaping to wooded parks help. Instead, my experience of the Arctic was sustained, but inverted with a vengeance. Every spot on earth had become a precipice, the planet falling away beneath my feet in all directions at the speed of solar wind, furiously and without a sound.

A wise friend recommended that I seek the counsel of Dr. Mesmer. I traveled to Athol Springs with a companion, ambulatory only if I wore opaque glasses. The very grounds of the Society, fragrant with the verdure of high summer, boded well. Meeting me at the door to the main building, the good doctor greeted me kindly and listened to my story with tactful sympathy. I removed my glasses and spoke with downcast eyes, focusing on my folded hands. She lifted one from my lap and placed it over the left side of my face. Releasing me from the depredations of binocular vision was itself restorative. Next, before the uncovered right eye, she held up a smoky hand mirror. I grasped its ivory handle, and steadied it at a distance of no more than six inches from my head.

With one eye I regarded myself, the distortions of sight canceling each other in perfect measure. Beyond the margins of the twilit silvery field I held in my hand, a blurry landscape came to rest. The murmured sounds of other residents became audible, agreeably familiar and pleasantly indistinguishable. With my mirror held before me, I walked, uncertainly at first, but with quickly growing confidence.

FROM THE MAGNETIC NOTEBOOKS

Geoffrey O'Brian

I SEEM TO HAVE COME HERE not to acquire but to lose. The notebook which I had expected to fill with details of the life left behind from the moment I boarded the train to the Springs — details newly recalled, finally understood — is filled instead with pages of runic slashes, frames bordering on empty areas, marks that suggest edges, shores, a canted entryway, a shattered horizon line.

Interspersed among these mute symbols are words and phrases deliberately isolated among expanses of white space: "the cellar door" or "thunder at midnight" or "footsteps of invisible attendants." No names but only images, like a kind of radiant erasure.

The effect of bright moonlight on the absolutely still waters of the tarn visible from my window was not like something I saw; instead it was itself the structure by means of which I saw. In the instant of grasping that, I was barely able to restrain myself from leaping from my second-story bedroom toward that distant glacial surface. Fortunately my window has a protective bar that makes such a leap impossible, a design feature that doubtless reflects the long experience embodied in every detail of this establishment.

The grounds are a litter of objects which resemble the letters of an almost infinitely large alphabet, one in which perhaps each letter would be used only once. Particularly notable are the small items carefully crafted of metal or clay or other indeterminable substances, items that seem perfectly shaped for some purpose which remains oddly elusive. To meditate on their possible uses is to experience an inward creaking, as if unused layers of one's perceptual apparatus were stirring for the first time.

The hands move, arranging the objects. One walks through pathways and in doing so rearranges the markers that define them. To live here is to engage in the constant making and unmaking of mazes. I am the maze that I am lost in, having constructed it out of incomprehensible objects randomly encountered.

For these reasons, and others, it may be understood that the dinner conversations here have a tentative quality. The use of gestures and pauses in lieu of verbal description is pronounced. Periods of almost catatonic stillness are followed by bursts of illustrative activity, whether acrobatic or graphic or employing wordless sounds variously produced.

The tranquility that exists here and that is almost palpable is at the same time — and I cannot really account for this — compounded unmistakably of restless uncertainty, disturbing and unpredictable lustful impulses, a generalized suspicion of all surfaces and all actions, and under everything a tremulous anxiety which often comes close to naked terror.

One feels often that one is stepping outside oneself. That the others are doing likewise makes the fact humorous. Yet no one dares to laugh, as if laughter under these circumstances would have the impact of a violent assault.

It has to do with an overwhelming impression of fragility. Just one inch further — one further loosening of the bonds that connect them — and it would all fly apart: pipes, roof gutters, corridors, flagstones, docks, trellises, walking sticks, larders, gloves, gardening tools, storage cabinets.

At a certain point, I am told, even the stones begin to assume an air of something like delicacy. That is the point when many visitors choose to terminate their stay in order to resume whatever business they had interrupted.

There are also those who take up permanent residence. Some are scarcely visible: they have their nooks and cottages half-hidden among rocks or at the end of hallways widely thought to be out of service. Walking out at night I have sometimes met one of them, or to be more precise, I have crossed his or her path: a sensation of voluptuous unease, followed by darkness and silence.

I no longer remember why I came here.

—Athol Springs, late August

Irving Sandler

100 Bleecker Street, Apartment 30A, New York, New York 10012

Telephone: (212) 533-7447

February 8, 2003

Dear Lenore,

Thank you for the information on the the New Society for Universal Harmony. After much thought I have decided to join the Society, that is, if the Society will have me. If it won't, then you all know where you can go.

I can assure you that I have always believed in being in harmony with every one--tout le monde, as they say--with the exception of a 4 living art critics and one dead, who in the name of harmony shall be unnamed. Also a few ~~of~~ artists, curators, museum directors, etc., etc.

I do, however, ocassionaly feel like the young boy in Ad Reinhardt's joke, which he appropriated from President Franklin Roosevelt. A Sunday school teacher asked her class: "Who would like to go to heaven?" All hands went up but Johnny's. "Don't you want to go to heaven, Johnny?" "Yes, teacher, but not with dem guys."

If accepted into membership, if there are certain things I need to know about the Society, like your secret handshake, if you have one, please keep me informed.

All my best.

Bliss out,

Irving

Irving Sandler

100 Bleecker Street, Apartment 30A, New York, New York 10012

Telephone: (212) 533-7447

February 9,

After much thought, I have decided to withdraw my application for membership in the New Society for Universal Harmony. I am simply not worthy to be a member. Like Kierkegaard said about Christianity, it was so elevated that who could call himself or herself a Christian?

I must confess that I harbor bad thoughts about 4 living art critics and one dead, as well as countless assholes who have made and are making our lives a living hell.

When Gandhi was asked, what he thought about Western Civilization, he said: "It would be a good thing." That now goes for the whole damn world.

Be of good cheer, and an~~d~~ om to you,

Bliss out,

Irving

Irving Sandler

100 Bleecker Street, Apartment 30A, New York, New York 10012

Telephone: (212) 533-7447

February 10

After much thought, I have decided to reapply for membership in the New Society for Universal Harmony, on the off chance that you provide instruction of how one becomes a good and spiritual person and lives in perfect harmony. I hope that it would be O.K. to continue to make a few exceptions in the billions that now overpopulate our world, like five living art critics (I thought of another) and one dead, plus a few etc, etc.

If I am refused entry, please pray for us all.

Bliss out.

Irving

THE COUNTY DEPUTY SHERIFF

Jim Long

THE COUNTY DEPUTY SHERIFF stopped by The New Society for a visit. He was a nice man, and told us the story about how he found our "baquet" (F.A. Mesmer's device for storing large amounts of animal magnetism) in the woods up on the mountain. It was a funny story, and we asked if we could tape it for our archives. He began enthusiastically:

Well, the Sheriff sent me out to investigate some woods on the hill outside town. A couple of hunters had said something about seeing a whiskey still up there: wood tubs, metal pipe, glass and ceramic jugs, that sort of stuff. It seemed worth a look. We're a small community and everybody knows everybody else, or just about. Once every few years some of the high school boys get hold of some kind of plan for a still and try making a little homemade whiskey. There's no harm in it if they don't burn down the woods, but strictly speaking it's not exactly legal, and the Sheriff likes to know what's going on and who's doing what.

I took my dog and my own truck up the back of what they used to call Harmony Hill pretty early in the morning. No point in folks wondering why the police car's out before sunrise and off the regular round. Anyway, you need a truck for the back way: It's all ruts and rocks and pretty steep. If somebody was cooking whiskey on the other side of the mountain, I wanted to be walking nice and easy down from the top so we could have a quiet chat, not some all-hell-broke-loose situation.

It took a while, but I found the place the hunters were talking about. Sure enough there were tubs, jugs, bottles, and such, but there were also bent iron rods, and sacks of white sand, crushed glass, and metal filings all laid out in neat piles. This wasn't high school kids. There was money put into this stuff, and it didn't exactly look like it was going to make a drop of whiskey.

The sun was coming into the trees about the time I got back to the truck, and I was thinking about the owner of a little diner in town. She was older than me, but we'd been friends seems like forever, and she made kind of a hobby of knowing strange stuff.

"Millie," I called out, as I walked in and sat at the counter, "what would you say if I told you I found a clearing up on that mountain and a bunch of glass jugs, wood barrels, iron rods, and sacks of crushed glass and metal filings?"

"I'd say let me help you to some coffee, and when was the last time you gave any thought to Benjamin Franklin?"

Mostly because she makes the worst coffee in the world, I said, "Has anybody ever told you that all your coffee ever needed was some of that early-morning humor? Ever see anyone finish a cup?"

"Has anybody ever told you your great grandfather was a Magnetizer?" she said right back.

"Magnetizer of what?"

"Soup to nuts; water to lunatics. Your great grandfather came here from Europe to practice magnetizing."

"Magnetizing with what?"

"With his hands."

"What's this got to do with Benjamin Franklin?"

"Franz Anton Mesmer. He's what's got to do with Benjamin Franklin. Around the time of our Revolution, in the 1770s, people were just starting to find out about electricity, but nobody really knew what it was. There was lightning, and you could get a spark off a cat's back in the wintertime. Sailors knew about electric fish, but there were only a couple of real devices that could collect that sort of thing and store it for a little while. There were Leyden jars, for instance — made of glass and metal — that could give a spark, and there were glass globes and discs that you could spin to build up a charge. Just around then Luigi Galvani, in Italy, accidentally touched a dead frog's nerve with two different metals when he was dissecting it, and the legs kicked even though the frog was dead. It was a big discovery, and he killed thousands of them trying to prove he'd found the universal life force: that electricity was some kind of fluid produced in animals."

"What about Franklin?"

"Franklin was studying electricity, too, in Philadelphia. He got his equipment in France, including Leyden jars. He figured out how the Leyden jar worked, and the positive/negative polarity of electricity. It made him a famous scientist."

"Is that what I found in the woods?"

"No, I'll bet what you found has to do with Mesmer. He was a German who set up shop in Paris in those years. He thought he'd discovered how to direct the electric fluid in his body with his hands to produce different effects in other people. He called it 'animal magnetism.' He taught people how to do it, and pretty soon they were all claiming that they could cure practically anything. Sometimes they'd magnetize a bottle of water or some glass that they said would also work a cure. The French government asked Franklin if he would go to Paris and investigate Mesmer and his work."

"Why was that?"

"Probably one of the King's mistresses or some of the court were involved with it. They were afraid of scandal. You see, Franklin once had a 'student,' a fellow named James Graham, who learned about electricity from him and then went to London where he set up an elaborate electric sex 'temple' involving novel electrical devices hooked up to 'magnetic thrones,' baths, and the famous 'Celestial Bed.' It was certainly imaginative, and for a while it was THE place to be seen, discreetly, of course. You also needed a lot of money. Franklin must have decided Mesmer was harmless enough. A lot of books appeared on the topic of 'animal magnetism' and 'societies' started springing up all over Europe. Back then it was o.k. for people with odd interests to get together if they had a club with a name. You've heard of dowsing societies. It's the same thing, without the somnambulism."

"So you think somebody might be making and selling magnetized water?"

"Somebody's probably fooling around with one of Mesmer's more elaborate contraptions. It's called a 'baquet.' You take a big wood tub, and you magnetize all these bottles of water by making passes with your hands. Then you arrange them all in layers in the tub, so the necks point to an iron rod you have standing upright in the center. After that you magnetize the sand, and the glass, and the sacks of iron, but only after you've washed them all very carefully. It's a lot of work. Finally you put all that in the tub and put on a wood cover that has a hole in the center for the iron rod to stick through. People who want to be magnetized sit around the tub holding iron rods that they put through special holes in the side to draw out the magnetism. There are also cotton cords you can connect yourself with."

"Does it work?"

"Never tried."

"What's this about my great grandfather?"

"A lot of places around the country, mostly in the Adirondacks and Vermont, were famous for bad water: lots of iron and sulfur and minerals. People turned them into sort of clinics and set up resorts around the springs where the water came out of the ground. They attracted magnetizers who came over from Europe. A few were pretty wild places and had songs written about them."

"So, what do I tell the Sheriff?"

"Same thing Benjamin Franklin told the King of France. It's harmless, and there's nothing illegal about it. Probably just the 'New Society' people over in the schoolhouse. They're interested in some kind of world 'harmony' that's got to do with magnetism. At least they're not killing all the frogs. Nice people. You should stop over and say hello. By the way, you haven't had your coffee."

"Wish I could; drink the coffee, that is. I'm going over to the schoolhouse now, just to say hello, and let those folks know there's a little gossip around. By the way, you don't know why they call this place Athol Springs, do you? Does Athol mean anything particular?"

"Might have something to do with 'atholbrose,' but I'll save that for the next time you drop by."

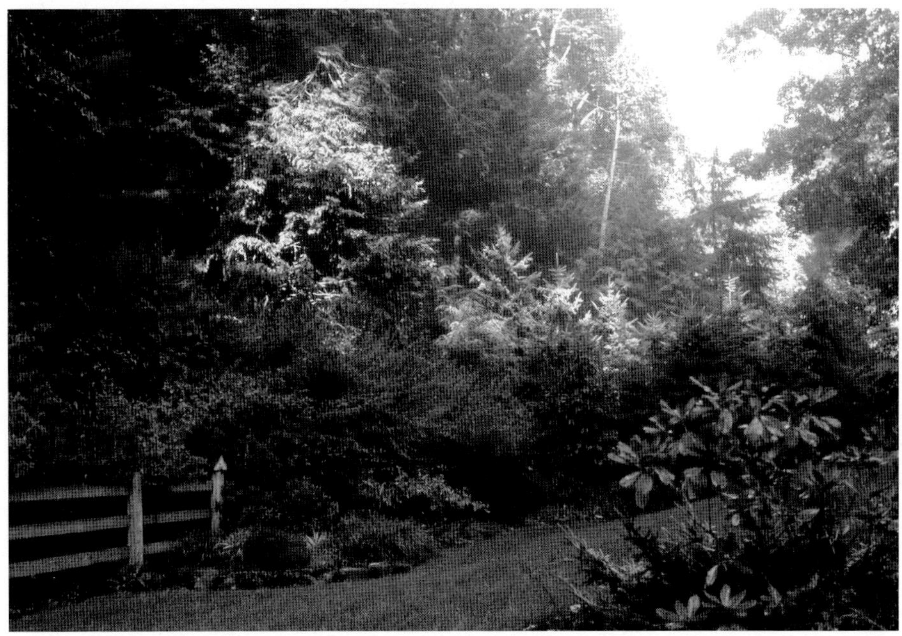

LETTER FROM KATHRYN A.

September 8, 2003

The New Society for Universal Harmony
Athol Springs, NY

Dear Administrator:

I am writing with the request to meet Dr. F.A. Mesmer. I would really, really like to see ~~him~~ her. She's a woman, right? I'm not sure I really even believe that—I don't know. I guess it doesn't matter. But I would like to have her in the room with me—just once if possible, please.

I feel like I know Dr. Mesmer—maybe in the past. How else could I have ended up at the Society? Obviously, Dr. Mesmer knows me really well—how to find me, talk to me, invite me in… I mean, this isn't exactly a typical thing for me to get involved with but I didn't even think twice about saying yes! But it has been over <u>five months</u> since I have started treatments and I have never gotten to see the actual Dr.—only dictates + encouragement through the website. And, I guess, my invitation to join.

I fantasize that Dr. Mesmer and I sat around and shot the shit years and years ago, talked about music and love and life and death, maybe drank a beer, or even smoked a little pot, you know? I don't do that anymore you know and I am sure Dr. Mesmer is a strict professional but I feel like I know "the doc" like that. Like I could just call her "the doc" and it would be all right. Is this okay to be saying?

It is just whenever I am at the New Society I feel this presence, this comfort, like I am known + safe + can do anything I want, anything I feel. And it won't be destructive or scary—it will always be good. I will be good. I only feel like that around people I know really well—like I am meant to be there. And I feel like it is the presence of Dr. Mesmer that makes me feel safe like that.

I mean, is she watching? It feels like it and I know I am not the only one who feels it. We all do. We have this reverence for the Dr.—as if we once knew her and then she went away. We never say her name even though we know that she brought us all together. And we are thankful for this togetherness even though it is such a reminder that she isn't with us—why isn't she?

She controls the whole place—there are traces of her everywhere, shadows of her in the offices + treatment rooms—her books, eyeglasses, models: things that make me feel as if I could smell her or catch sight of her around a corner if I was just fast enough. It is such a longing but nostalgic, too—but also something new and fresh! We all create together—that's cool but I sometimes sense that the Dr. wishes she were there—she wishes she were there too with us. This is who I think Dr. Mesmer is: a gentle presence. I just really want to see her. Do you think if I got better at being better that could happen? Thank you for your time.

Sincerely,
Kathryn Alexander

TESTIMONIAL OF MARGARET (MADGE) SILVA

As told to Mark A. Thompson

I THREW POTS. I threw pots, pans, and china. One time a hurricane lamp, the oil dribbling down the wall. There was a hole in the front closet door the result of a two-pound flashlight that I'd wielded like a billy club. There were nicks in the yellow pine floor and aluminum skid marks on the walls. Fortunately my husband still had use of all his limbs; he sustained no injuries from my outbursts, even though sometimes he was within range. I never aimed for him deliberately.

It was he who placed the brochure on my pillow. I was reading it when he joined me in bed. "What's this New Society for Universal Harmony?" I asked him. "Are you saying we're not harmonious?" My husband is a very considerate man, and patient, too. He never complained about the things I threw or those I hit. One time we had just returned from a lamp store with a new lampshade. The next thing I knew the new lampshade was wearing the steamed latte that flew out of my hands and across the room. He merely sighed and got a sponge and paper towel. The side with the coffee stain now faces the wall. He looked at me in bed, with his usual placid smile, and said, "I was thinking you might need a break." Right at that moment, I could feel something churning inside me — but it didn't bubble over, maybe because I wasn't holding anything in my hands but this ugly brochure from The New Society for Universal Harmony.

So I went to Athol Springs. It was a day's drive from our house on the Cape. I drove alone, with my husband's blessing. I drove without once thinking of ramming our car into oncoming traffic. The day was sunny and the air mild; it was one of those September days when you imagine a whole new chapter of life might be starting merely because the calendar has changed. As a rule, this has not been the case in my life. We have lived on the Cape since our marriage thirty-one years ago; we haven't started any new chapters, not even the year we came home from Vegas with an extra $358. What did I get with that money but a seafoam glass vase from eBay which met its demise one morning after I found all the yellow roses dead?

The New Society was not exactly a spa. Not like the kinds you see on that program "Lifestyles of the Rich and Famous." It reminded me of a campground my father once insisted upon dragging us to in upstate New York when I was a little girl. The accommodations were spartan, but as I said, the day of my arrival, I was optimistic. The truth was, just the week before, I had shattered my favorite Hummel figurine. She was a Hummel Umbrella Girl and she'd never caused me any harm, except she got in my way when I was trying to sweep the crumbs from beneath the toaster. Then she was history — and too bad for her, that's how I felt at first. Serves her right, not knowing when to move. It was my kitchen and not hers, and she should've known better than to just sit there watching me fumble with the toaster crumbs. That night, though, in bed, I got to thinking how my husband had bought me my Umbrella Girl when we were first married. Then I was thinking that I might've glued her back together, except she was closer to powder when I got through stomping on her. Then I looked on eBay thinking I could replace her — and I found out she was worth about $1,500, or so someone wished.

So I was sitting in my room at The New Society for Universal Harmony when an attendant brought me a legal pad and asked me to write down why I was not in harmony with the rest of the planet. As soon as that zombie walked out of the room, I grabbed the lamp by the neck and yanked it from the outlet. But then, the strangest thing happened: I didn't throw the lamp; instead, I just dropped it onto the floor. The bulb broke, but that was easier to clean up than about ninety percent of my previous mishaps.

The next morning, I saw the notorious Dr. F.A. Mesmer. We met in a room which I noted had many objects not glued down. A cut glass jar of jellybeans, for example. She offered them to me. Then she suggested we play a game, tossing jellybeans into each other's mouths. I thought it might be more fun to toss the whole jar at her head, but I gamely took a handful of jellybeans and proceeded to pelt her with them. She missed about six of them, but she managed to grab two; she had a big mouth. Then it was my turn. This is when the strange thing happened. The jellybeans which didn't make my mouth landed on Dr. Mesmer's Persian rug — at which point, I ground them into her rug with the toe of my shoe. She didn't say anything, or attempt to stop me, so I kept on until the area around my chair was sticky with squashed jellybeans. Then she said, "You're free to go. Wander the grounds, my dear. I shall see you again tomorrow morning."

From my room, I called my husband. I told him I was all better; he said he didn't think so. He said Dr. Mesmer had called him and said I had an advanced case of acute hyper-domesticity syndrome. "I haven't been cute since you married me," I screamed into the phone. Then I hung up; I didn't want him telling me what my problem was.

Dinner came with a knock on my door. Everything was served in plastic containers. That might've stopped some people — and actually it quelled my hand as well. Once again, as with the gooseneck lamp and the squashed jellybeans around my chair, I felt a strange kind of peace descending around me. It was as if I were in the hands of people who really knew me. I can't explain it more than that.

In the morning, I saw Dr. Mesmer again. She was very sweet to me, and I noted that all the jellybean stains around my chair had been cleaned. I didn't say anything, for I suddenly felt a bit ashamed of my behavior the day before. She took out her prescription pad and wrote in that indecipherable script that all doctors use. "One cleaning lady and an archery class?" I read aloud. "That's what it looks like to me. You need to write more legibly."

But I was wrong. That was exactly what she'd written. A cleaning lady and an archery class. I thought about it on the drive home. I thought about what Dr. Mesmer had told me about my condition. She'd said I was a psychopathic domestic goddess with perfection complex. She said it was analagous to being a bird in a gilded cage, and that I needed someone to clean my cage. The archery class would take me out of the house when the cleaning woman came in, and furthermore, I would improve my aim should the condition recur — and thereby, prevent any injuries to my husband.

Happily, my condition has not returned. I no longer throw my Spode china nor my cast-iron skillets. Mrs. Joseph is a meticulous cleaning woman and Mr. Bruno is a skillful archer who has taken me under his wing; next week, he's taking me to the rifle range. Also, the hole in the closet door has been filled and painted over. And as for my husband, he no longer wears a pith helmet to bed.

5

PROCEEDINGS OF THE NEW SOCIETY

TEA WITH MME. B.

Susan Canning

A RECENT CHANCE ENCOUNTER with a notation attributed to the Belgian artist James Ensor (1860–1949) discovered in a private collection invites idyll speculation on the artist's daily life and possible acquaintanceships at an eventful time in his career. Written no doubt sometime in the summer or fall of 1886 or early in 1887, this note describes a mysterious social event in Ensor's typically humorous but cryptic manner. It is simple and to the point: "Had Tea at Mme. B's. M. and P. soon came along. A magnetic time was had by all. The skeletons all played and even the masks were amused. But pity the poor rude Spirits! Conjured to the table, they could not drink so I finished for them." Ensor refers here to a common enough occasion — afternoon tea — the social staple of the middle class, especially in the late nineteenth century. But who might these initialed individuals be? And what kind of tea ceremony was this? Perhaps a brief digression into Ensor's life and art practice at the end of the nineteenth century might provide a few clues.

In 1888, Ensor displayed a painting entitled *Portrait of Mme. B* at the fifth exhibition of the avant-garde Belgian art group, *Les XX*. According to some biographers, the sitter was dissatisfied with the results and so Ensor later reworked the painting, adding masks and other elements and giving it a new title, *Old Woman with Masks* (1889, Museum of Fine Arts, Ghent). This same painting, with yet another title, *Theater of Masks,* or *Bouquet d'artifice,* was shown again at *Les XX* in 1890. Although it is generally accepted that the earlier portrait is indeed the same one now in the Ghent museum's collection, its possible provenance and original title also links it to the enigmatic note quoted above. Could the "Mme. B." of the painting and the one mentioned here be the same person? And could this Mme B. be none other than Mme. Helena Petrovna Blavatsky (1831–1891) as the art historian John Gheeraert claims?[1]

In July of 1886, Mme. H.P. Blavatsky, in ill health and suffering from rheumatism, relocated to Ostend where she planned to continue work on her book *The Secret Doctrine*, published in two volumes in October and December of 1888. Her reputation, due to vicious attacks on her spiritualist beliefs by former acolytes as well as claims that she was a Russian spy, was suspect and Mme. Blavatsky was apparently closely watched by Belgian police as she spent the summer, fall, and winter in Ostend, living at the Hotel Continental near the boardwalk and at her sister's home at the Villa Nova just a few buildings away. In May of 1887 she was invited by English Theosophists to live in Upper Norwood, London, where she resided until her death

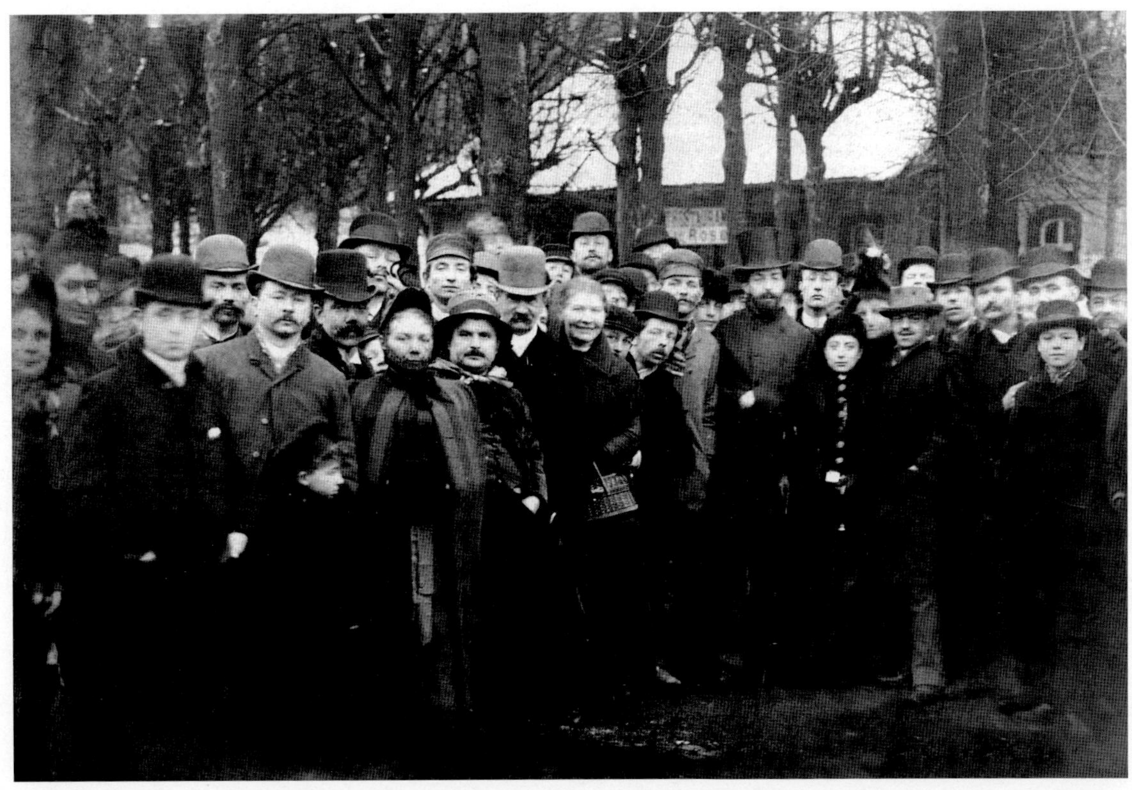

Ensor, middle right, in top hat. Photo Courtesy of the Royal Museum of Fine Arts, Antwerp

in 1891. Mme. Blavatsky's stay in Ostend was thus brief — less than a year — and more than likely intended to restore her health and give her a quiet place to write and think.

Ostend might seem an odd place for someone of Blavatsky's controversial reputation to go, but at the end of the nineteenth century it was a natural place for the fashionable to seek a restorative cure. That decade saw the expansion of Ostend, the small North Sea port where Ensor was born in 1860, into a growing tourist resort and health spa. With the onset at mid-century of highly contagious diseases like cholera and tuberculosis in a Europe with still rudimentary scientific knowledge of germs and bacteria, water and fresh air were deemed beneficial and the sea was sought out for its curative and healing benefits. Ostend's development as a summer resort and spa had also been encouraged by the Belgian king Leopold II, who had made his summer home there. Ostend's growth was also facilitated both by the railroad that brought tourists seeking the restorative airs of the sea and by a newly rebuilt boardwalk that allowed for brisk strolls to the beach, casino, and souvenir shops.

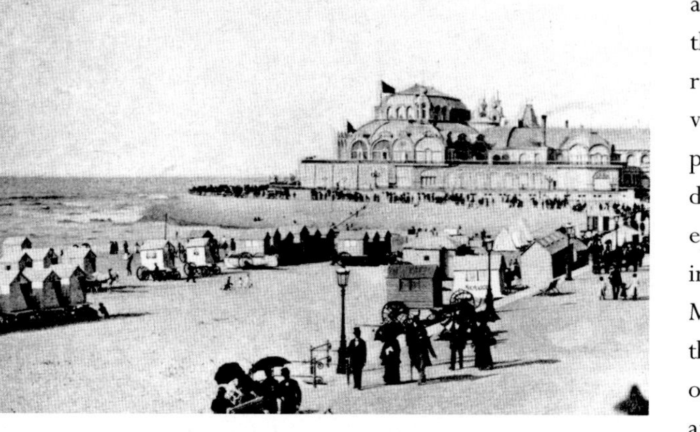

View of the boardwalk, beach, and casino at Ostend in the 1890s.
Copyright Royal Library of Belgium, Print Cabinet, Brussels.

One of these shops near the boardwalk was owned by Ensor's aunt and was filled with items such as postcards, chinoseries, masks, and trinkets designed to lure the curious tourist to come inside and browse. The Ensor family, consisting of the artist, his father James, Sr. (who would die in 1887, possibly from exposure and alcoholism), his mother, Catherine, his sister, Mitche, and in the winter, his aunt Mimi, lived upstairs. Two stories higher in the attic, Ensor kept his studio and painted when not called upon to help out behind the counter in the store. From his attic window James could see the old North Boulevard (later renamed Van Iseghem Boulevard), and in 1881 he made a painting of this street looking down on it with a steep bird's-eye perspective, a view that also included the Villa Nova where Mme. Blavatsky's sister lived in the 1880s. The proximity, then, of Ensor to both the boardwalk and the Hotel Continental could have led to a chance meeting between the two and perhaps even an invitation to tea. In fact, Mme. Blavatsky's hospitality and willingness to receive visitors and discuss her theosophical beliefs despite her health problems were well known.[2] But at the same time, her desire to write and finish the book that collected together her theosophical writings and beliefs must have kept her quite busy at her desk, allowing only the occasional walk along the sea, especially after the warm Belgian summer turned to the cold and brisk Belgian winter.

If indeed the "Mme. B." of the note is the one and the same Mme. Blavatsky, then the identity of the other two initials mentioned by Ensor could be associates of the spiritualist. The note, with its reference to "magnetic" and "conjure," gives a clue. Could "M." be Franz Anton Mesmer (1734–1815), the noted doctor and visionary whose controversial theories and treatments based in the doctrine of universal magnetic fluid were known to scientists and spiritualists alike? Certainly Mme. Blavatsky was aware of his writings, as she published several essays on Mesmer, including "Black Magic in Science" and "The Substantial Nature of Magnetism."[3] In these essays, Blavatsky discusses the ways Mesmer's ideas supported and validated spiritualist principles and her own theosophical beliefs. In other words, for Blavatsky, Mesmer and his principle of animal magnetism were both scientific and magical and, like her own theories, falsely accused of being nothing more than superstition and fraud. For Blavatsky, Mesmer's belief in a common shared "influence" or fluid in all beings and the healing power of magnetic forces sprang from the same creative root as her own theosophical belief in syncretism, that is, the unity and common origin of all things. No wonder he might be called upon for tea, even if, by the 1880s, his presence could not have been corporeal.

Given the possibility of Mesmer's participation in this mysterious tea, the other guest named "P." might be none other than the American writer Edgar Allen Poe (1809–1849), who was interested in Mesmer's ideas. Indeed, hypnotism and animal magnetism provided Poe with an intriguing, provocative, and somewhat gruesome narrative twist for several of his stories.[4] Poe lived in London from 1815, the year of Mesmer's death, until 1820, and it was probably here that he had been first exposed to Mesmer's teachings. Poe seemed particularly attracted to the principle that magnetic fluid joined hypnotist and patient together in a psychic bond, one that could subdue a patient, put him to sleep, or, in Poe's rendition, bring a dead man back to life. Poe also was drawn to the idea that once mesmerized, a patient could access the transcendent plane, a concept he elaborated upon in "Mesmeric Revelation," where a hypnotized man replies to a series of questions with cryptic answers about the relationship between God and man. If anything, Mesmer's teachings provided Poe with a fantastic yet believable plot device — the catatonic state in which life imitated death and where magnetic fluid and hypnosis allowed for an ongoing dialogue between the living and the dead.

Like Poe, Ensor often explored the relationship between life and death in his paintings, prints, and drawings. Perhaps this shared fascination is what drew Ensor to Poe. Ensor's appropriation of the American writer's work, made so accessible to Europe's French-speaking populace by Charles Baudelaire's translation, was in fact so natural that one might wonder if Ensor was not perhaps channeling Poe's ghost in his own psychic magnetic bond. In fact, Ensor's references to Poe in both subject and titles are so numerous that it can be assumed that Ensor not only knew but also appreciated and even exploited Poe's mesmeric subtext.[5] One might even find references to the mesmeric exchange between life and death in Ensor's frequent use of skeletons and masks, an ironic state of suspension that included the artist, who represents himself as a living skeleton in his painting *The Skeleton Painter* (Antwerp, KMSK) in 1896.

Ensor might also have been familiar with Mesmer's theories, especially in the 1880s, as at that time he had many contacts with contemporary social and scientific theory during his frequent trips to Brussels and his friendship with the Rousseau family. Ernest Rousseau was a professor of physics at the Free University of Brussels, serving there as rector from 1884 to 1886. Dr. Rousseau had written and published numerous essays on electricity and no doubt knew of the connections Mesmer had made between the magnetic life force and electrical currents. His wife, Mariette Rousseau-Hannon, was a mycologist who published several botanical studies on mushrooms. One of her brothers, Théo Hannon, a poet, critic, and painter, was a close friend of Ensor — the two had met at the Brussels Academy — and another, Eduoard, was an engineer and amateur photographer who became one of Belgian's leading proponents of Pictorialist photography. In many ways the Rousseau family epitomized Brussels intellectual and scientific elite, a milieu quite different from Ensor's intellectually stagnant hometown of Ostend. Associated with radical political philosophies, rationalism, and Enlightenment principles, the Rousseau salon was a well-known gathering place for progressive and leftist writers, politicians and scientists, and especially anarchists, like the French geographer Élisée Reclus, who was a good friend of Mariette Rousseau. In many ways the dinners Ensor attended at the Rousseaus provided an immersion into the heady speculative stew of fin-de-siècle thought, in which the discoveries of "new" sciences like archaeology, geography, and psychology were debated alongside beliefs in spiritualism, hypnotism, and Charcotism. At the Rousseaus, and at other salons in the late nineteenth century, discussions about the nature of the material world and its connections to a parallel spiritual universe were investigated with a fervor that can only be found when speculation searches for a methodology to make viable the certainty of belief. In this aspect, Mme. Blavatsky, like Mesmer and even Poe, sought in her writings, especially in *The Secret Garden,* to find correspondences among a number of mystical beliefs and to seek ways to make visible the connections between the living world and the dead.

Edgar Allan Poe, from *The Critic,* 1905

If there had been a meeting or even a tea between Ensor and Blavatsky would discussions of theosophy have influenced the Belgian artist's work? Could the skeletons and fantastic creatures that Ensor added in 1886 to earlier drawings of household objects and furniture animate these material forms with the universal spirit of theosophical belief? Was Ensor's decision in 1885 to explore the expressive and symbolic potential of light in six large drawings collectively titled *The Auroles of Christ* or *The Sensibilities of Light* a reflection, as Gheerhaert claims, of Ensor's new spiritualist sensibility?[6] How could Ensor have assimilated Blavatsky's ideas so early and so quickly applied them to his work? In Sébastien Clerbois's view, theosophy did not influence Belgian artists until quite late, around 1900, and superceded earlier, more occultist-inspired circles centered around the teachings of Sar Péladan and his Rose + Croix Order. For Clerbois, theosophy was the last esoteric movement to influence Belgian artists, effectively forming a bridge between the earlier Symbolist movement and the early-twentieth-century avant garde.[7]

Could Ensor's drawings then serve as examples of his precocious spiritual desire? Certainly Ensor included himself among the Symbolists, who saw the evocative possibilities of subjectivity, and his animation of ordinary objects with the invented beings of his imagination gives his world a lively and peculiar individualist spin. But Ensor's work was always much more public and confrontational than the withdrawn and hermetic work of Belgian artists of a theosophical bent like Jean Delville, Émile Fabry, and Fernand Khnopff. Indeed there seems to be little evidence in either Ensor's art or writings of central theosophical themes like syncretism or the sacred revelations of prophets, the sort of esoteric principles found more often in the symbolic references and obscure subjects in the work of artists like Khnopff and Delville. With Ensor, the fantastic, while stimulated by invention, always remains connected with the material world and waking reality. Rather than serving as emulations of mesmeric fluids, the universality of the theosophical cause, or even a spiritual state, Ensor's skeletons more often than not appear engaged in acts of satirical sabotage or play designed to promote the artist's own vision while critiquing the mores and values of his contemporaries. Why else have them play billiards?

So what conclusions can be made concerning this note purportedly written by Ensor? If indeed there was a meeting, what was the occasion and who was at the table? Were the long dead Mesmer and Poe conjured up by Mme. Blavatsky in some sort of spiritualist séance, evoked by a passing of the hands or stimulated by a sip of mind-altering tea? Might the aura of such an occasion find its memory in such a long overlooked scribble? The mention in the note of bemused skeletons and skeptical masks lends a clue as to Ensor's possible reaction to this occasion, as does the ironic image of pitiful, perhaps amiable spirits unable, despite their sociability, to partake in a proper tea ceremony.

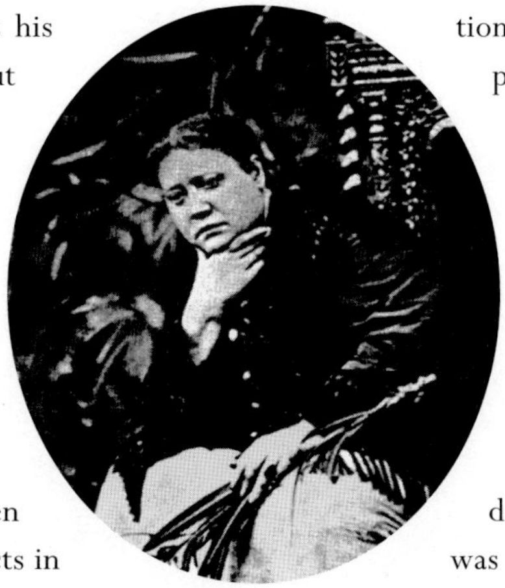

Madame Blavatsky, 1880, Adyar Archives

Perhaps there was also a meeting between Mme. Blavatsky and James Ensor in 1886 where Mesmer's theories of animal magnetism were discussed and Poe's literary inventions on catatonic states and the correspondence between the living and the dead explored. More than likely the discussion was lively and not without humor. The scientific basis of Mesmer's ideas and their connections with Blavatsky's theosophical philosophy were probably argued at length. But in the end, Ensor's own sardonic perspective and social involvement superceded any call to commune with the spirits, even if they might have been named "M." and "P." If this note is in any fashion connected to events in Ensor's life, then tea with Mme. B. left the artist amused but not a believer. Ensor, it seems favored the sustenance and inspiration of the real world, a place where spirits, however conjured, might hang around but certainly could not imbibe. For Ensor, being invited to the table was not enough. He came to drink his tea.

THE HYDRAULIC MODEL

Pepe Karmel

CONFRONTED BY THE UNKNOWN, we seek something familiar to which we can compare it. Trying to reduce reality into its basic components, the ancients hypothesized that everything was composed of earth, water, air, and fire, combined in different proportions. Later, Domenico Scandella, an Italian miller known as "Menocchio," confronted the mystery of creation and concluded that: "In the beginning this world was nothing . . . it was thrashed by the water of the sea like foam, and it curdled like a cheese, from which later great multitudes of worms were born, and these worms became men, of whom the most powerful and wisest was God." For this original cosmogony, Menocchio was burned at the stake.

It is not only in the physical universe that we confront the unknown. Our minds and souls pose perhaps a greater mystery, and a more urgent one. Where do ideas and feelings come from? What are the sources of pleasure and pain, happiness and despair? Here, too, the physical world has long provided the metaphors we use to understand ourselves. In antiquity, the animating impulse was conceived of as a movement of air: the "breath of life." Hence such Latinate terms as "inspiration" and "spirit."

In later antiquity, Hippocrates and Galen developed the theory of the humors, attributing man's temperament to the balance among four bodily fluids: blood, phlegm, black bile, and yellow bile. If blood predominated, the result was a sanguine personality, cheerful and energetic. The phlegmatic personality, in contrast, was stolid and slow. Too much black bile led to biliousness, or bad temper, while an excess of yellow bile caused melancholy. This theory of the mind persisted into the Renaissance. The comic characters of Elizabethan drama seem ridiculous because they act exclusively under the influence of one humor. (This is why we use the word "humorous" to describe something funny.)

In our own time, it is usually advances in pure science that lay the groundwork for new technologies. Until quite recently, however, the relationship was exactly the reverse. From the late Middle Ages through the eighteenth century, technological advances provided the main impetus to the development of modern science. Engineers invented things; then the scientists figured out how they worked. Physics was the main beneficiary of this process, but it seemed only plausible to think that the principles of the physical world might also be at work in the mind and body.

More than any other single book, Isaac Newton's *Principia* of 1687 revealed a new principle regulating the behavior of the universe near and far, large and small. This was the force of gravity, a phenomenon at once magical and scientific. Magical, in that it acted at a distance, with no visible agent. Scientific, in that its action could be described with mathematical exactness. Newton's analysis of gravity became the model for other attempts to understand the operation of invisible forces. In the eighteenth century, scientists demonstrated that magnetic attraction obeyed the same laws as gravity, acting at a distance but varying inversely with the square of distance.

Meanwhile, Newton's analysis of gravity was joined by other scientific paradigms based on new technologies of gases and fluids. Heated or compressed, a gas or liquid would seek an

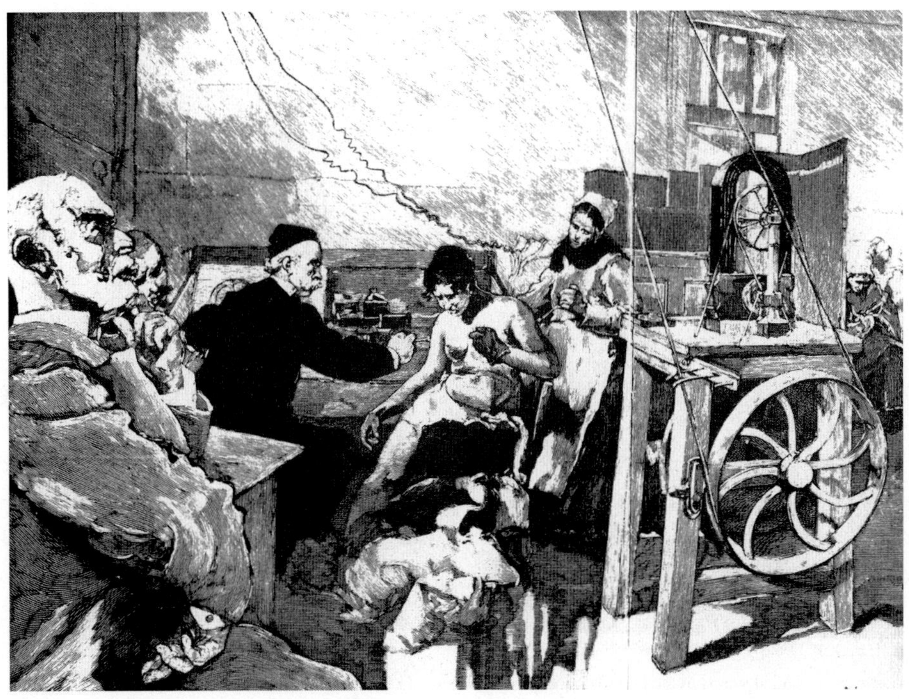

The Electrotherapy Laboratory of La Salpêtrière, *Le monde illustré,* August 14, 1887

outlet for its pressure. By controlling this outlet, engineers realized, they could concentrate the diffuse energy of a fire or a stream into useful, localized power. Hydraulics pumps took the place of traditional levers, allowing a few taps of the foot to raise a heavy platform or a dentist's chair. Canal locks lifted heavy barges. The hot-air balloon realized the age-old dream of flight. Thomas Newcomen demonstrated his "atmospheric steam engine" in 1711. James Watt's improved steam engine, invented in 1769, provided the motive power for vast machines. Studying these new technologies, the Swiss scientist Daniel Bernoulli published his treatise *Hydrodynamica* in 1738.

The discovery of electricity confirmed the importance of fluidic mechanisms. Evidently, electricity was a fluid, for it could be stored in jars (Leyden jars). But it was an exceptional fluid. Galvani's experiments, triggering muscular movements with electric shocks, suggested that it was the vital force animating the body. Furthermore, this force could be transmitted from one person to another in a kind of human chain or pipeline.

It took the genius of Franz Anton Mesmer to pull these diverse discoveries together into a coherent theory of the mind. To describe the vital impulse of the mind and body, he coined a new term, "animal magnetism." For modern readers, this term is somewhat misleading. We use "animal magnetism" as a synonym for sexual attraction because we think of magnetism primarily as an attractive force. For Mesmer, however, magnetism was a fluidic force, which happened, among its other qualities, to cause an attraction between organic bodies, much as Newton's gravitic fluid transmitted the force that pulled the Moon towards the Earth and the Earth towards the Sun. "Animal" magnetism was the magnetic power inherent in living creatures, as opposed to the better-known form of magnetism present in lodestones and other inorganic objects.

In itself, there was nothing novel about the idea of a vital force animating mind and body. What was new and important in Mesmer's theory was his recognition that the human organism functioned like a fluidic mechanism. To set it into motion, the magnetic fluid had to build up pressure, as in a steam engine. The magnetic fluid also transmitted impulses from one part of the body to another, like the pipes and cams of a hydraulic lift. Equally important was the recognition that, when the human mechanism malfunctioned, its problems were similar to those of a fluidic mechanism. Pressure could be channeled into the wrong outlet. A blockage could cause an unwanted rise in pressure, damaging the mechanism. A leak could drain magnetic fluid, weakening the organism as a whole. When the fluidic mechanism worked properly, its elements functioned in harmony, with an even balance of pressure. When a problem occurred, there was an uneven distribution of pressure, leading to a discord among the different elements of the organism.

When such problems occurred, it was not yet possible to fix them by intervening physically within the organism. Fortunately, Mesmer recognized that the parallels between organic and inorganic magnetism offered other ways of treating the mind and body. Like a magnet, a mesmerist healer could act at a distance, correcting imbalances in the flow of magnetic fluid. This process of hypnotism (or "mesmerism") quickly proved its curative power. Alternatively, fluidic imbalances could be rectified by connecting the patient to a baquet, a storage vessel for animal magnetism, which functioned as the organic equivalent of a Leyden jar. Fluid could be transmitted by metal rods, or by a human chain, in which each participant would help establish the proper magnetic balance for all the others.

Paradoxically, the enormous success of hypnotism discouraged scientific acceptance of Mesmer's discoveries. Hypnotism's seemingly supernatural effects led to its rapid adoption by entertainers and circus side-shows. Once this occurred, it became harder to take it seriously as a scientific or medical procedure. Rediscovering Mesmer's work in the later nineteenth century, the great French neurologist Jean-Martin Charcot experimented with both magnetism and hypnotism. It was the latter that won out and was incorporated into Charcot's clinical practice at the hospital of La Salpêtrière. In this era, when an operating theater was literally a theater, with banked rows of seats for students and spectators, Charcot's public sessions with his hysterical patients — often beautiful young women — became a form of popular drama. Although they won Charcot a considerable degree of fame, they ultimately led to widespread skepticism about the phenomena he seemed to be demonstrating.

Charcot's most important pupil, Sigmund Freud, also experimented with hypnotism as a method of gaining access to his patients' repressed thoughts and desires. After a few years, however, Freud discarded it in favor of "free association," which allowed access to the unconscious without the melodrama of the hypnotic séance. In conventional histories, it is at this point that Mesmer's influence seems to evaporate, becoming merely an historical footnote to modern psychiatry.

What this conventional analysis overlooks, however, is the persistence of Mesmer's mental model within Freudian theory. In point of fact, the hydraulic model provides the very foundation for Freud's thinking. As early as 1895, in his pioneering "Project for a Scientific Psychology," Freud considered the mind as a complex mechanism designed to channel and discharge a regular stream of psychic energy or "cathexis." Evidently, this psychic energy was nothing more or less than Mesmer's "magnetic fluid."

By 1905, when Freud published his seminal essay, "The Instincts and Their Vicissitudes," along with his better-known *Three Essays on Sexuality*, he had developed a new and seemingly different analysis of the mind. The key concepts in these mature writings — instinct, drive, repression, and sublimation — appear to be purely psychological. Upon closer examination, however, it becomes clear that the hydraulic model remains central to Freud's work after 1900. The instinct or drive is a source of mental pressure, something that flows into the mind via the unconscious and needs to be discharged by conscious activity. Freud sees repression as the closing of a valve, preventing the discharge of this mental pressure. In the long run, this build-up of pressure becomes intolerable, and the mind must find an alternative channel to discharge it. This process Freud calls sublimation. If the process of finding an alternative channel is wholly or partially unsuccessful, the pressure builds up to the point where it begins to damage the mental mechanism, causing hysteria or some other form of neurosis (literally "diseased neuron").

In recent decades, psychoanalytic theorists (especially of the Lacanian school) have increasingly emphasized the linguistic character of Freudian therapy. Therapeutic intervention is said to occur through a rectification of the patient's distorted use of language. From a mesmeric point of view, however, it is clear that this represents a distortion (or repression) of what is really occurring in the curative process. Insofar as Freudian therapy is effective (a hotly disputed topic in recent years), it is because the therapist exercises a magnetic attraction on the patient. Indeed, Freud himself referred to this process under the rubric of "transference." Beneath the cover of the "talking cure," the therapist is correcting and facilitating the flow of magnetic fluid within the patient.

Restoring a more accurate understanding of the therapeutic process, The New Society for Universal Harmony directly addresses the problem of magnetic flows within the patient. Instead of relying on the indirect methods of Freudian analysis, the doctors of the Society have gone back to the baquet and other instruments invented by Mesmer, intervening to restore the balance of magnetic fluids and the patient's sensation of well-being. A fuller discussion of these techniques would require another paper.

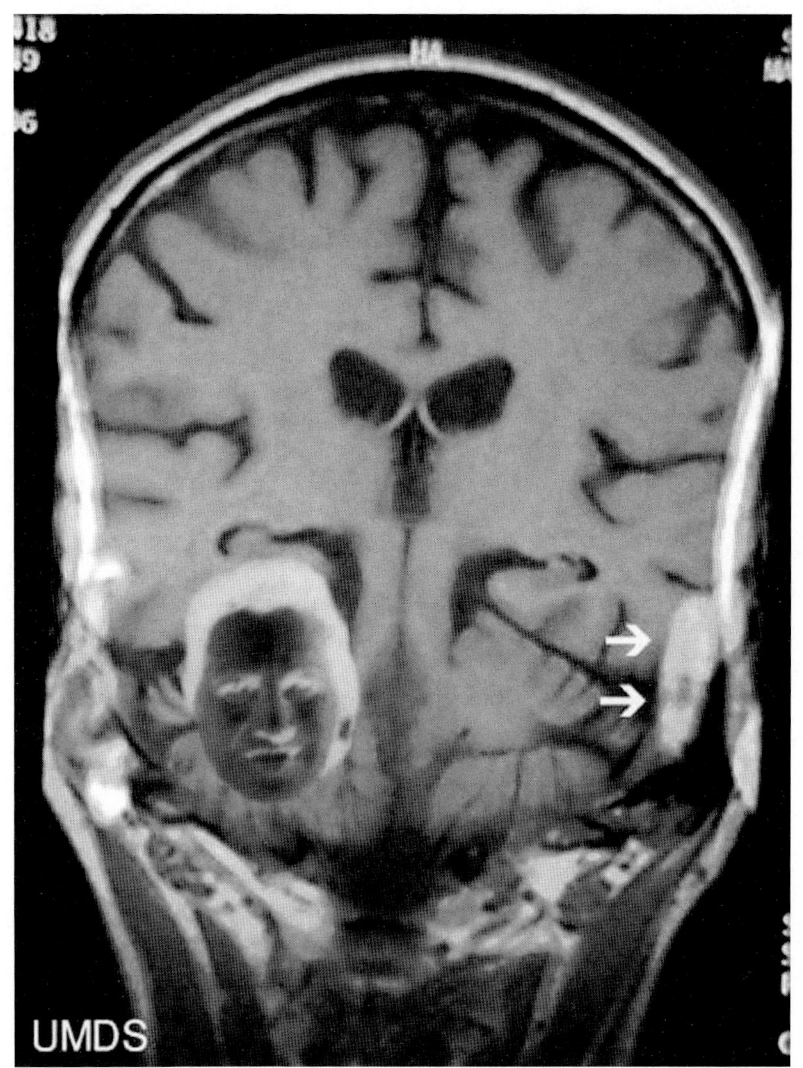
UMDS

TWENTY-FIRST-CENTURY DEVELOPMENTS IN SPIRIT PHOTOGRAPHY AND ANIMAL MAGNETISM: A BRIEF UPDATE

Barbara Tannenbaum

SPIRIT PHOTOGRAPHY (also called psychic photography) may still be accepted by believers in Spiritualism and the Occult, but the genre has been soundly rejected by most of those involved with the scientific and artistic practice of photography. The latter considered the images of ghosts or spirits that appear supposedly "unbidden" in what are otherwise normal portraits, or the pictures of ectoplasm pouring forth from the mouths of mediums, to be frauds perpetrated using props, double exposure, or other types of manipulation of film, negative or print. A very recent revival of academic interest in the interrelationship between photography and the paranormal suggests that attitudes may be changing.[1]

As an art historian, museum curator, and confirmed rationalist, I belonged firmly to the camp of non-believers until last year, when I was visiting the studio of a photographer in Chicago. This artist, who wishes to remain anonymous for reasons that will become apparent later in the text, supports his artistic practice by working as a radiologist. I shall refer to him as Doctor X.

After we had spent a pleasant hour together examining his landscape photographs, which were quite beautiful, he found the courage to bring out an astounding group of images derived from his medical work. While probably not of importance to the world of fine art photography, these pictures are of potentially revolutionary significance to the Spiritualist world and in particular to those who believe in the philosophy of Franz A. Mesmer and his twentieth-century disciple, Dr. F.A. Mesmer.

Dr. X started with computer files for some MRIs he had done on patients.[2] Magnetic resonance imaging (MRI) machines are widely used today for diagnosis and research. Joseph P. Hornak, M.D., defines the process in his web-based educational package, *The Basics of MRI,* as follows: "MRI is based on the principles of nuclear magnetic resonance (NMR), a spectroscopic technique used by scientists to obtain microscopic chemical and physical information about molecules."

Of special interest for this article is the idea that this is a visual medium in which magnetic forces, rather than light, are the imaging agent. The principle behind nuclear magnetic resonance was discovered in 1946. No matter how thin you are, your body is predominantly composed of fat and water. Both substances are rich in hydrogen atoms. The nucleus of each hydrogen atom contains a single proton that spins, creating a tiny magnetic field that emits a nuclear magnetic resonance. Machines that can capture and analyze that signal began to be widely available for medical use in the late 1980s and 1990s.

The images used by Dr. X were made using a process called "functional MRI" (fMRI), a 1993 development which permitted the mapping of the functions of the human brain.

Dr. X thought that it would be interesting to use the fMRI's software to break the images, which are quite colorful, down into their component parts. He then planned to reconfigure them to meet his aesthetic goals. The finished pictures would be output as digital, ink-based prints that he hoped to exhibit. He planned to keep the source of his images and the process itself a mystery, but to identify these seemingly abstract pictures as works that were figurally based.

Once Dr. X decided to pursue this artistic course, it took him many months to obtain some private time on the necessary machines. As he began to go down to the pixel level of the first image he processed, he saw what he thought looked like tiny faces and bodies. At first, he attributed this to a common and powerful trait of human vision: our eyes want to make sense out of visual chaos and thus recognize faces and animals in clouds, for instance. Dr. X continued to work with the software to create his own patterns with the image parts until he arrived at an aesthetically satisfying result.

It was again several months before he could get some private time on the fMRI machines to work on the second image. To his dismay, once again the tiny faces and bodies appeared, only this time they showed different people. Dr. X immediately examined the other fMRIs he had set aside and found similar shapes — always human figures or faces — in five out of the thirty. Looking at the case histories, he found that each of the five was a terminally ill patient who had had only weeks to live when the test was performed. Each of the five was also now deceased.

Dr. X was faced with a dilemma. He wanted to approach the patients' families to find out what, if any, significance these particular faces and figures might have held for the decedents. However, radiologists have very little contact with the people they treat; only in rare cases do they get to know their patients and the patients' families with any degree of intimacy. Not having any acquaintance with these families, he feared they might be traumatized by having to relive their loss. He also worried that they might be offended and judge what he had been doing with the test results frivolous (since art is valued much lower than science in our technologically based society).

At the risk of his medical career, he approached the doctors who had supervised the patients' final illnesses. Three of the five were longtime colleagues who knew Dr. X to be a serious practitioner of both medicine and art. Though skeptical, they helped him contact the families. Two of the families agreed to meet with Dr. X to look at the images. He suspected they would be able to identify the pictured people, but also feared that response because it would contradict numerous principles (all heretofore accepted as scientific fact) in his medical training.

Some of the faces and figures in the broken-down fMRI image segments were blurry, making them extremely hard to read, while others were quite distinct. Both families were able to identify some, but not all, of the distinct figures. Each individual they recognized was dearly beloved (or, in just one case, vilely hated) by the deceased person — someone who had quite literally made a definite impression on their brain. Most were either parents (in both cases, mothers rather than fathers), spouses, or children of the deceased. Many of those identified were themselves long deceased. Who was not pictured became as touchy a subject as who was. One of the widows became enraged when she discovered the image of her best friend, but could not find any image of herself in her husband's fMRI. Both families found the experience moving, but also so upsetting that they forbade any public exhibition or reproduction of the images. Dr. X plans to repeat the experiments with volunteers for whom he has obtained permission in advance of the process, although he fears access to the fMRI machines for this purpose will be declined by the hospitals.

Dr. X has tried to puzzle out what forces were responsible for this phenomenon of the "spirit" fMRI. He hypothesizes that the visual form of those we hold most dear can exert a physical influence on the magnetic forces in the body — one that can be recorded by external apparatuses. As the visions of these individuals dominate our thoughts, perhaps they actually form a physical "electronic" image at the cellular level of our brains, much in the way a mother's face is "imprinted" on a baby who cannot yet even focus his or her eyes. It may be that in times of extreme physical or emotional stress, such as a terminal illness, those images "come to the fore" to occupy — and help soothe — our thoughts and cares. Dr. X's discovery also suggests that Mesmer's connection of magnetic forces to the force of "animal magnetism" and personality deserves continued research employing the new, wider-seeing technologies.

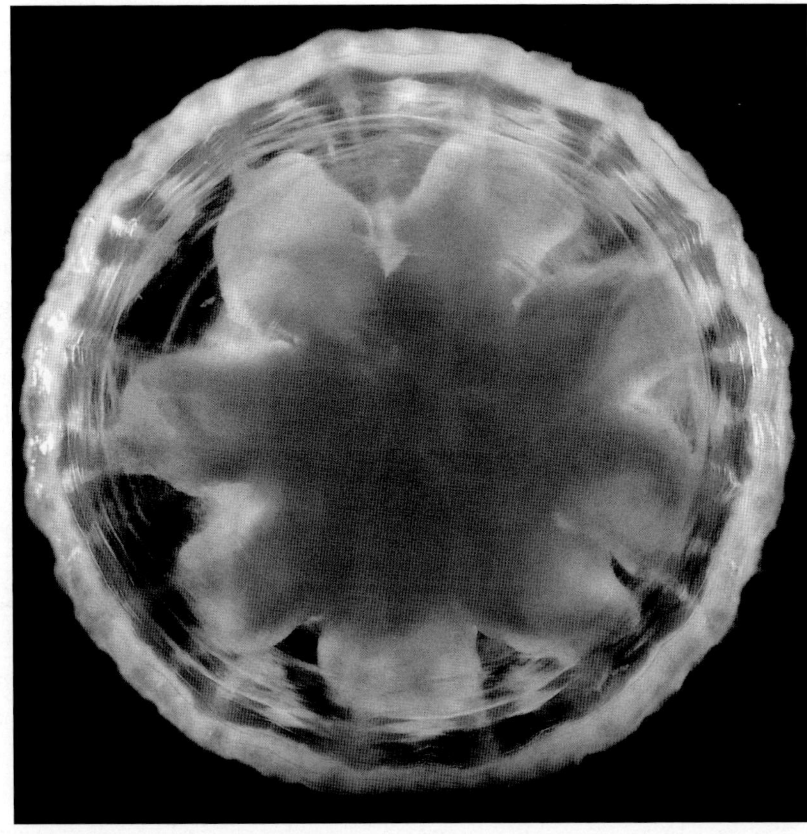

6

HARMONITES

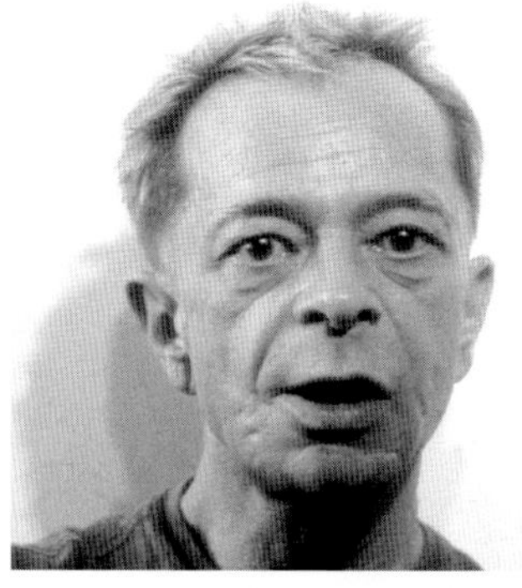
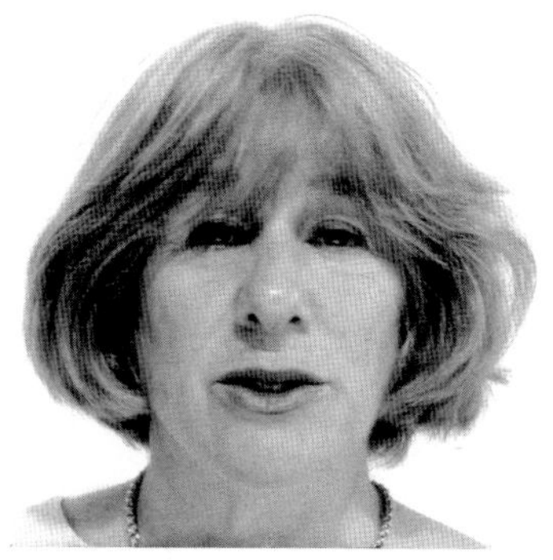
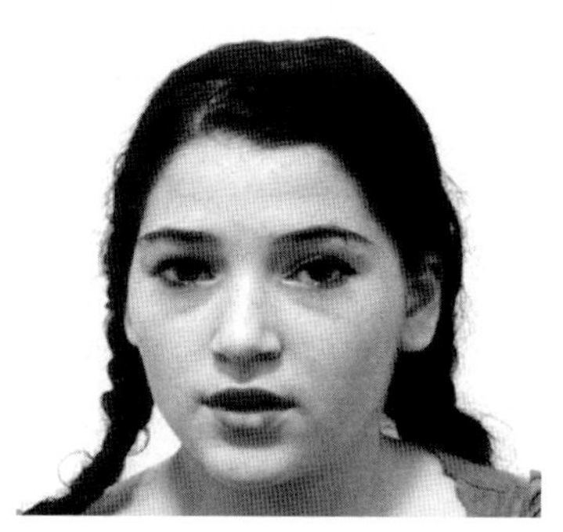
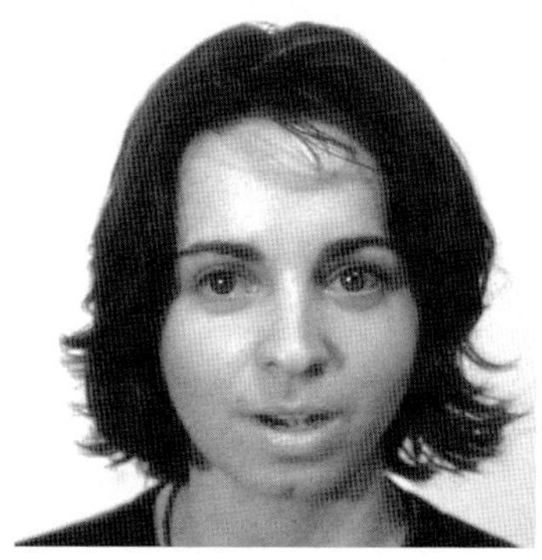
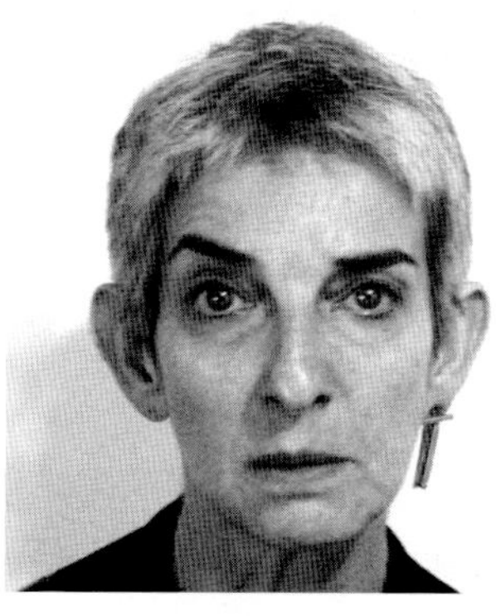
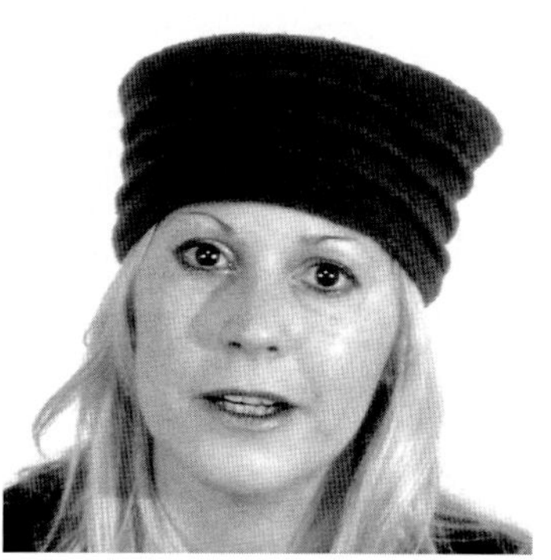

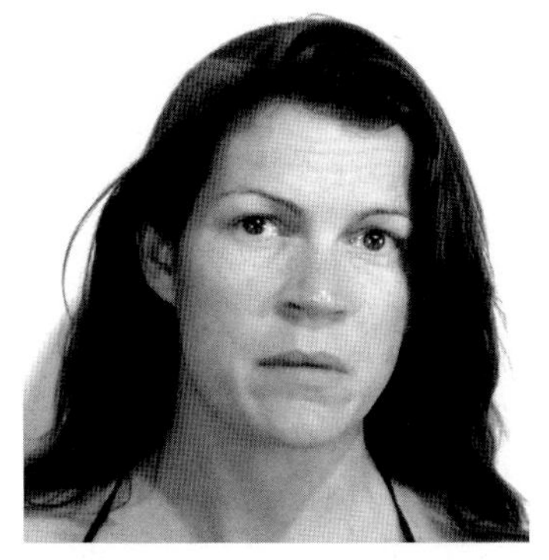

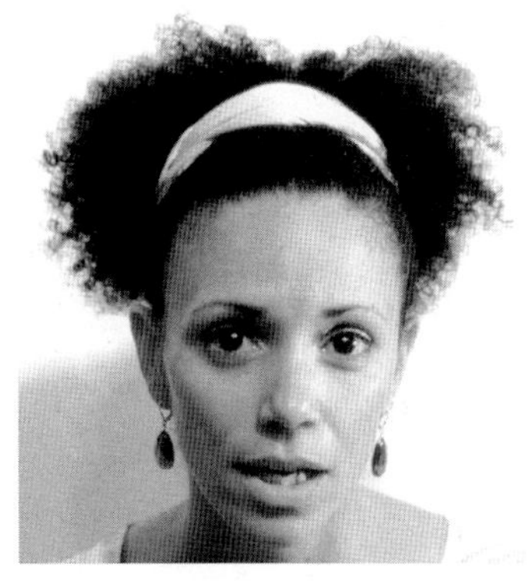

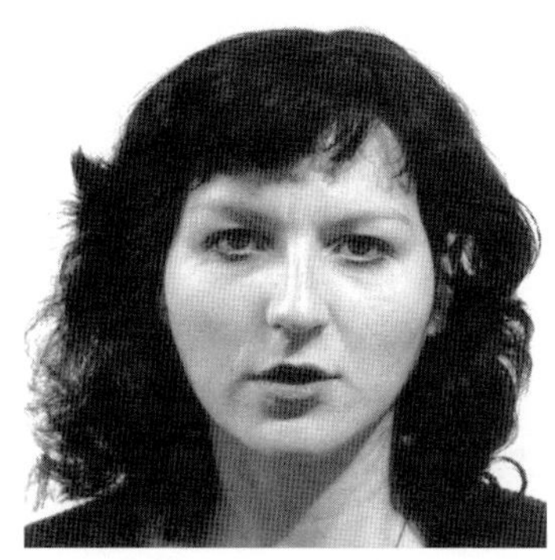

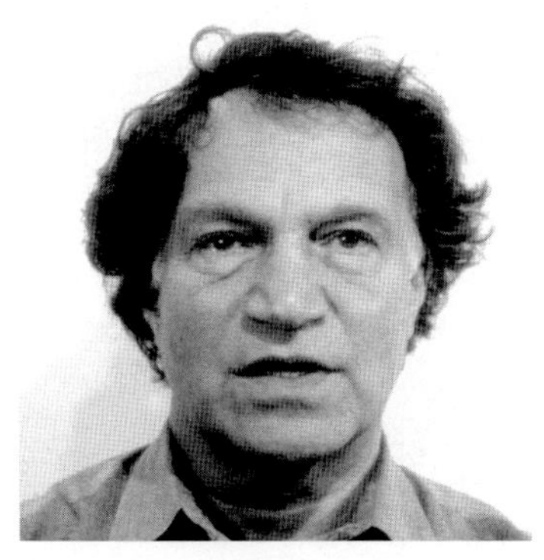

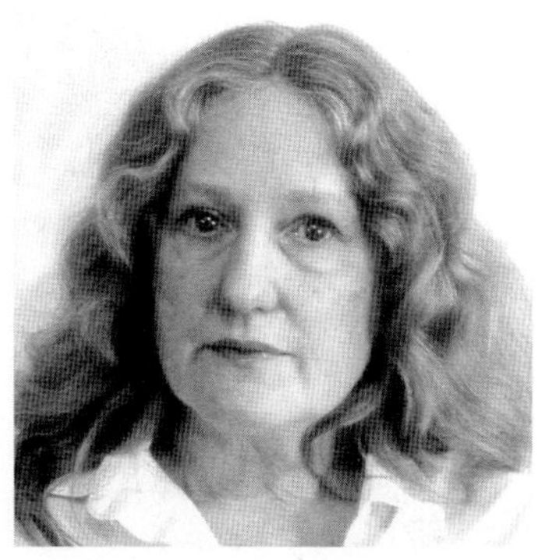

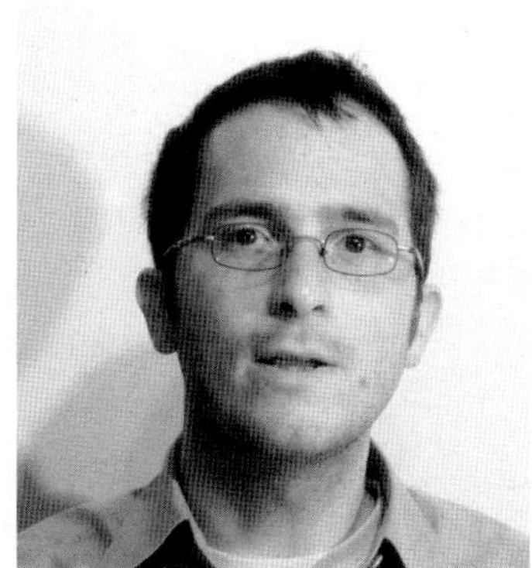

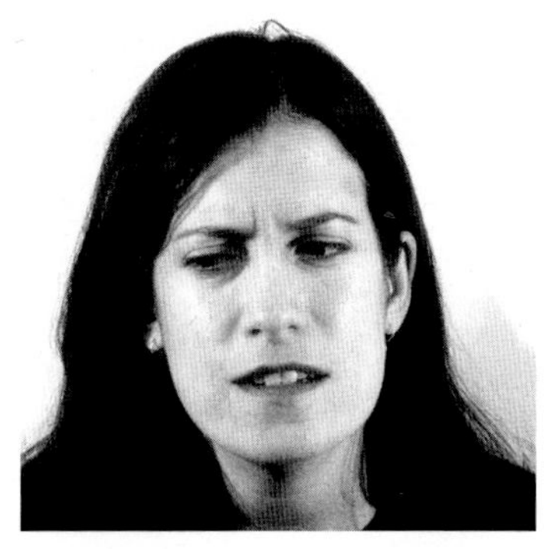
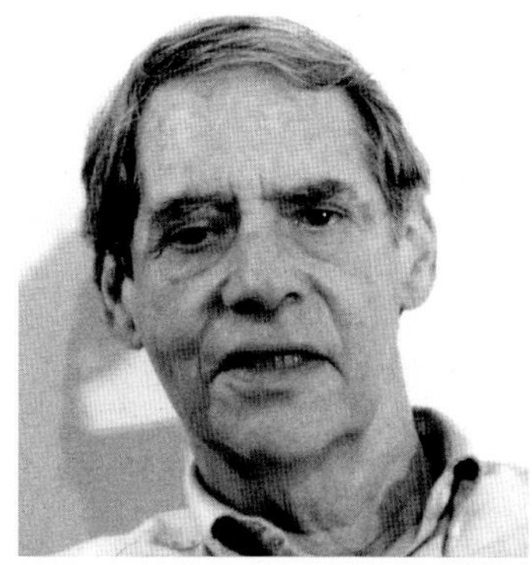
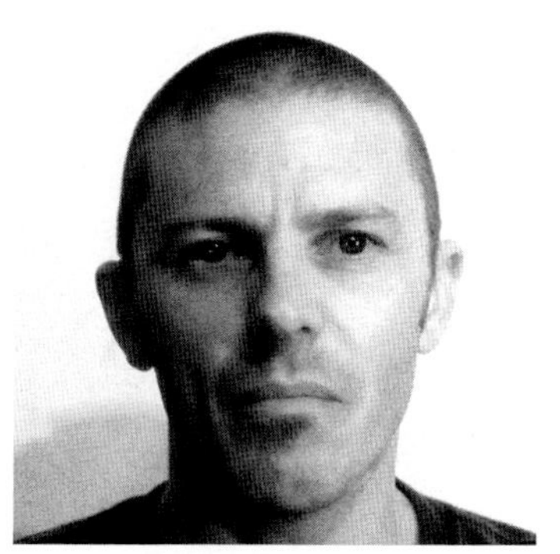
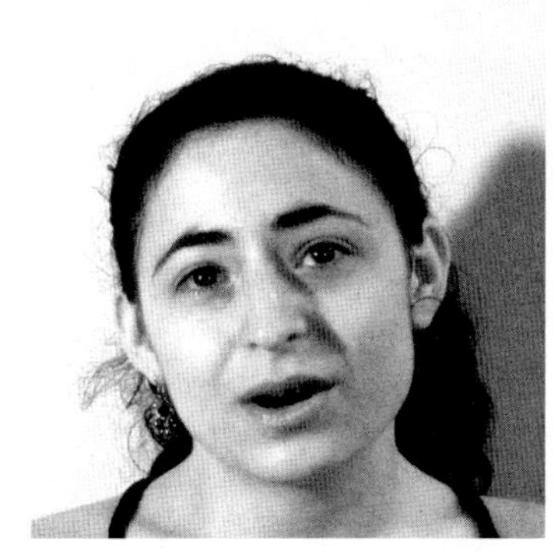
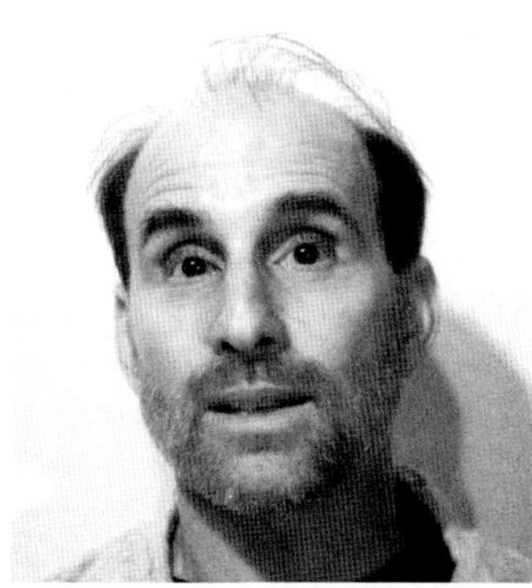
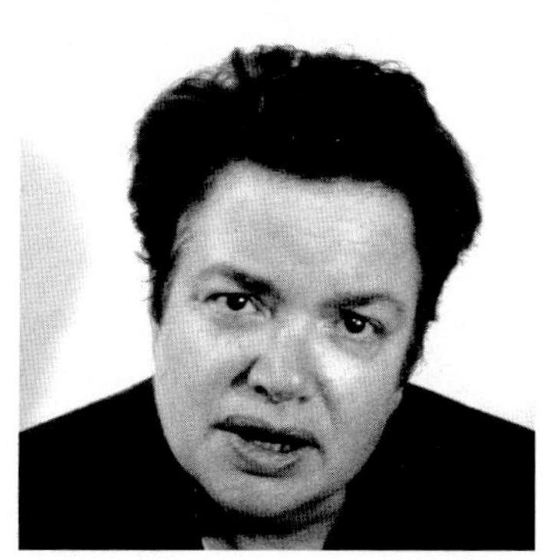

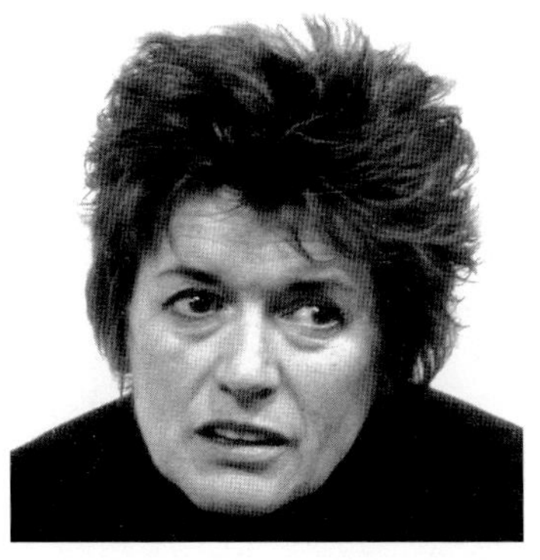
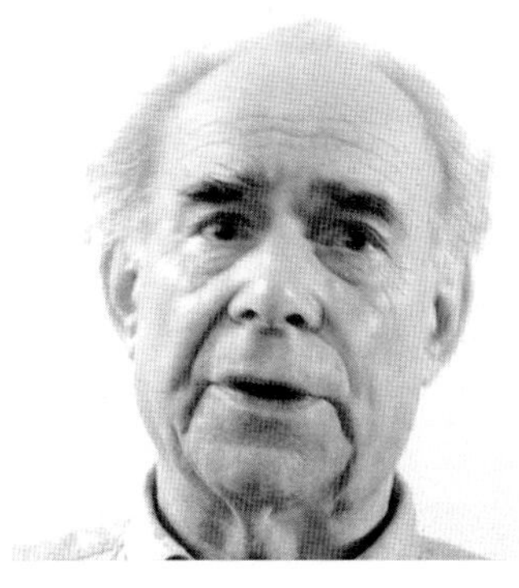
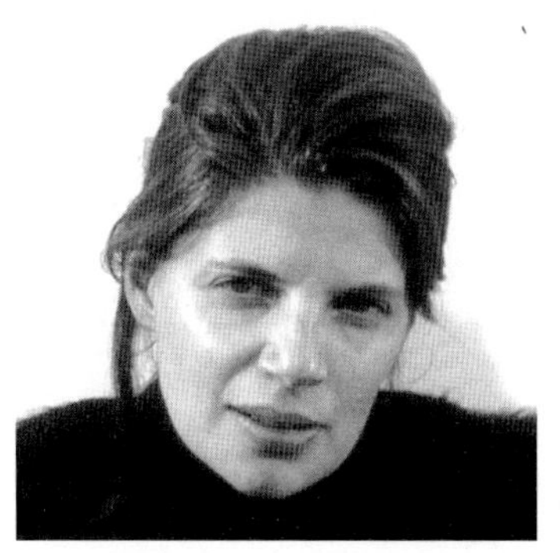
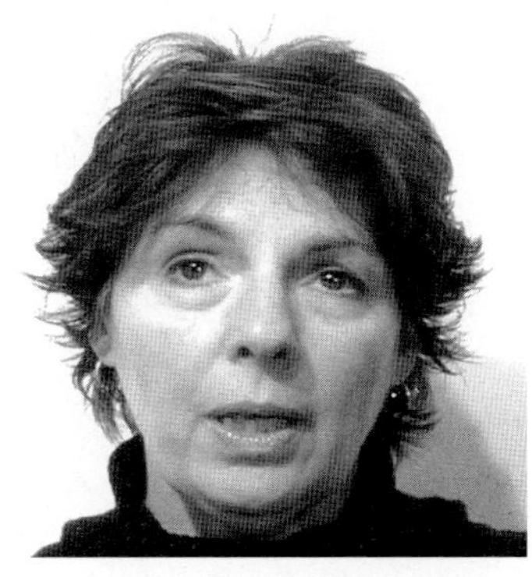
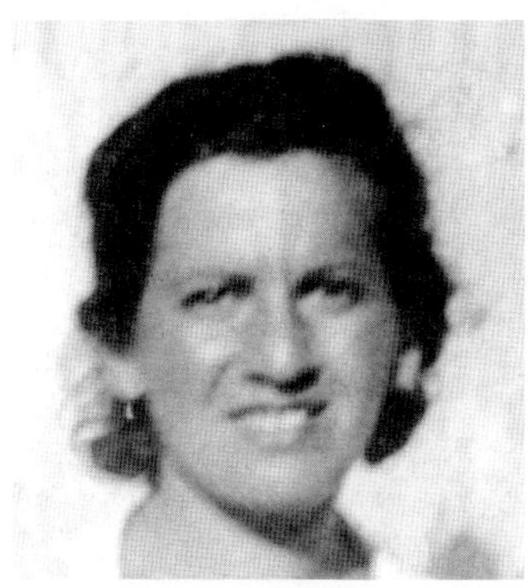
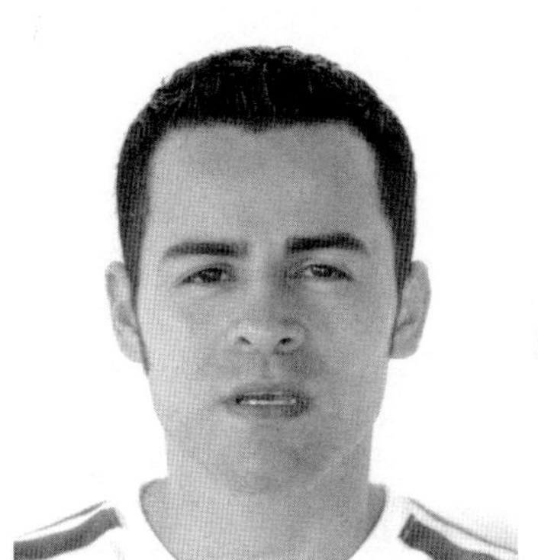

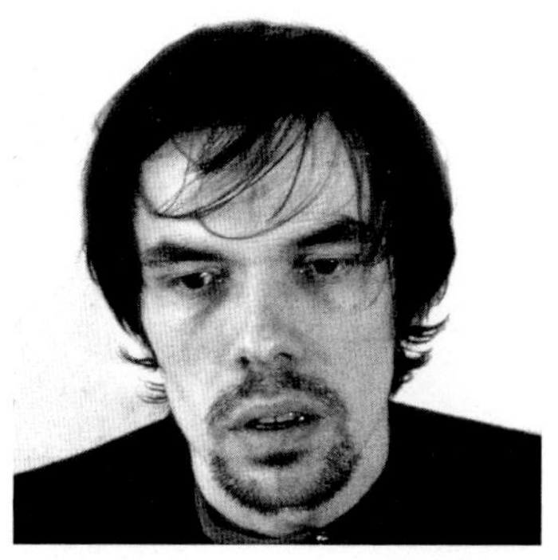
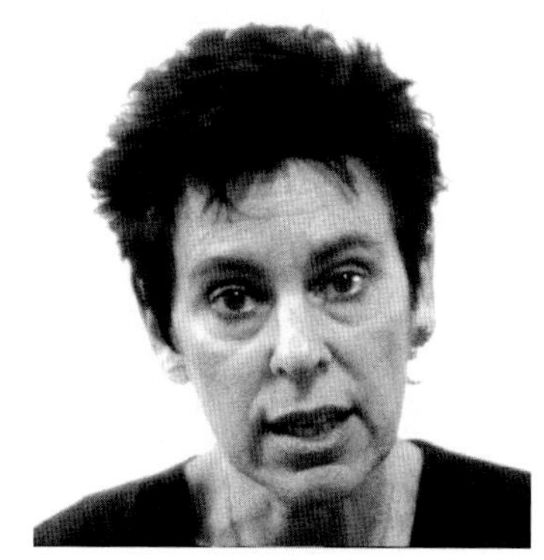
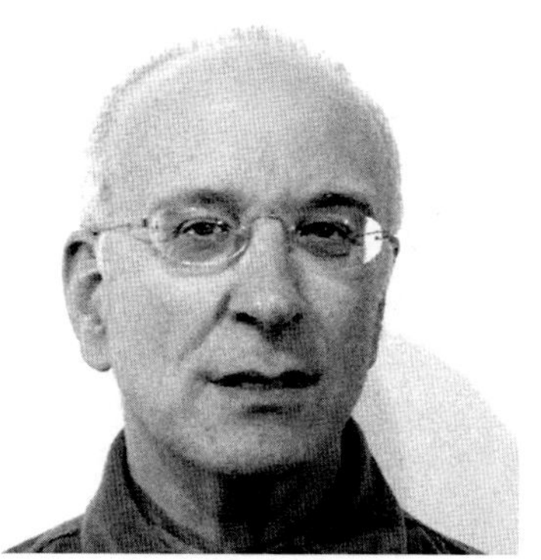
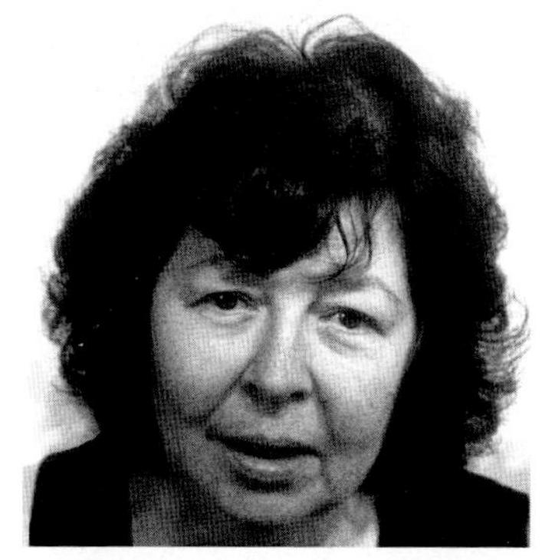
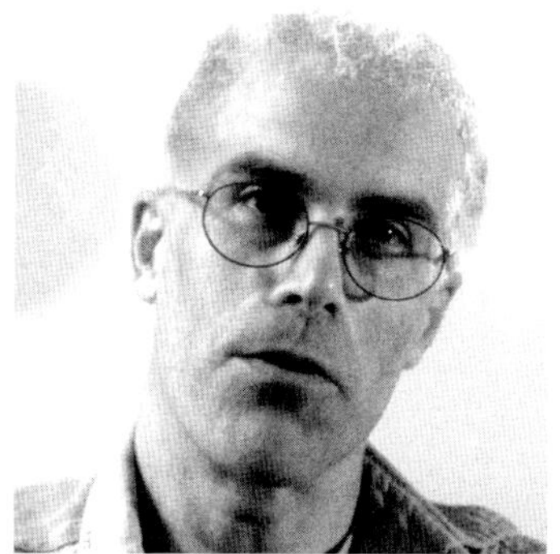
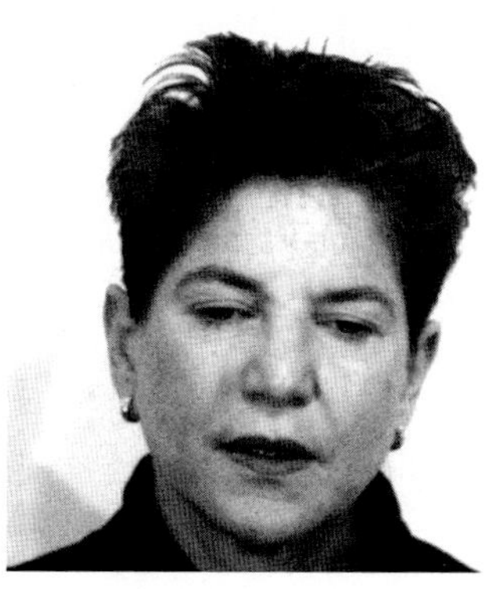

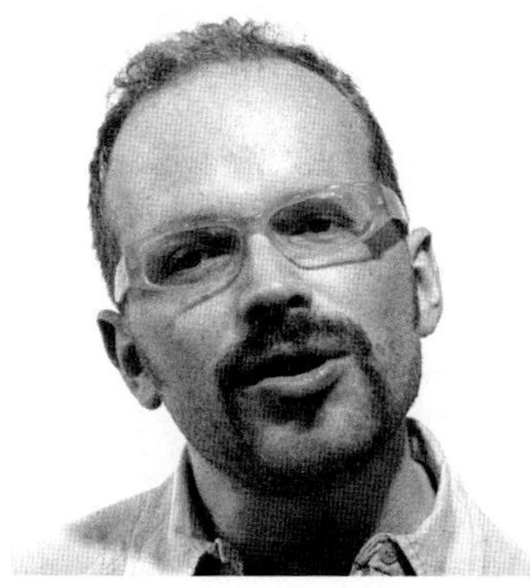
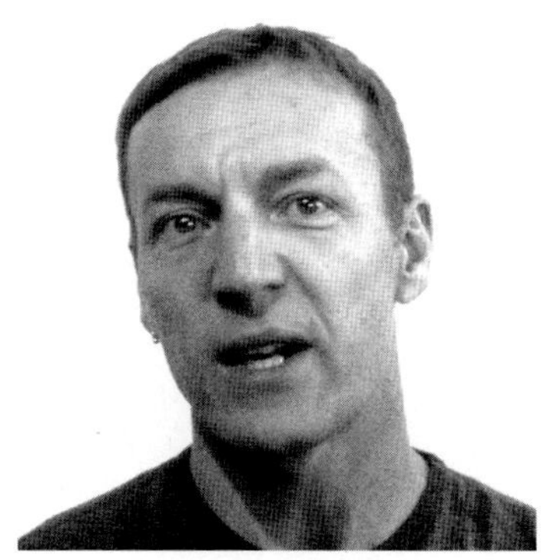
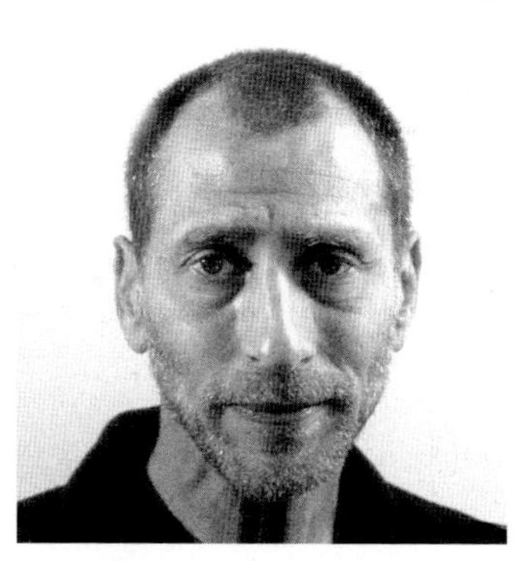
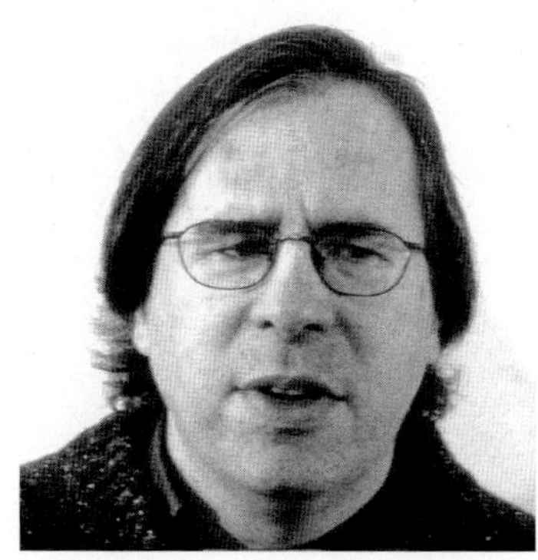
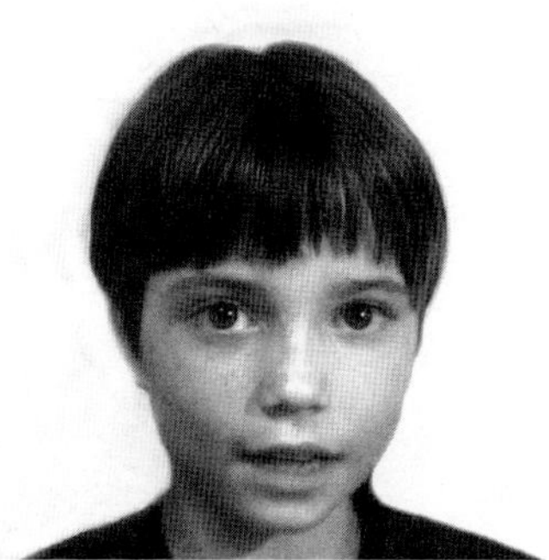
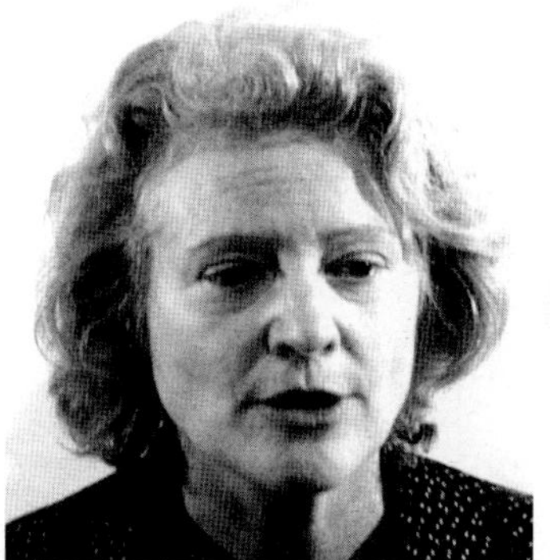

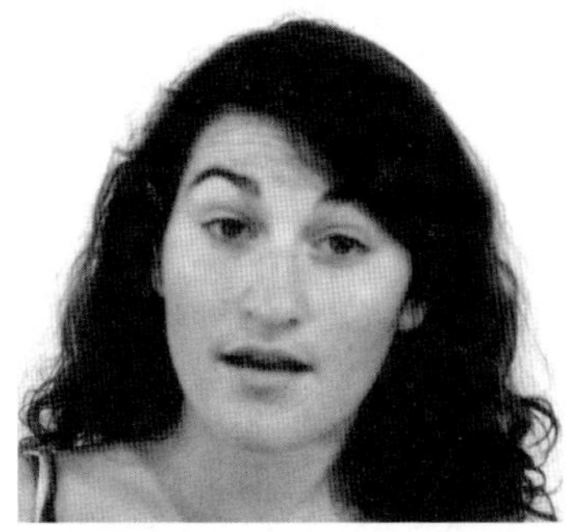
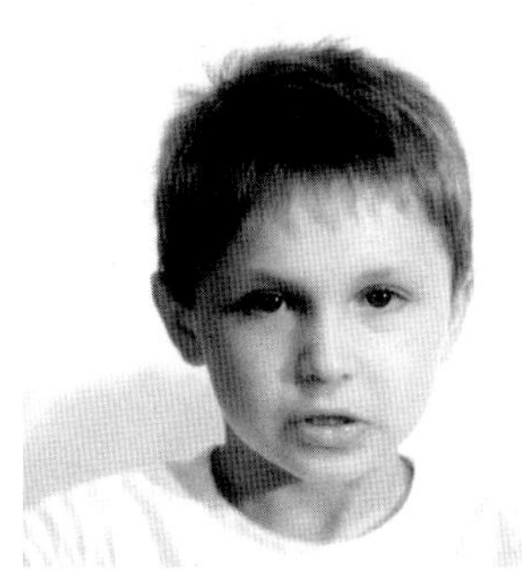
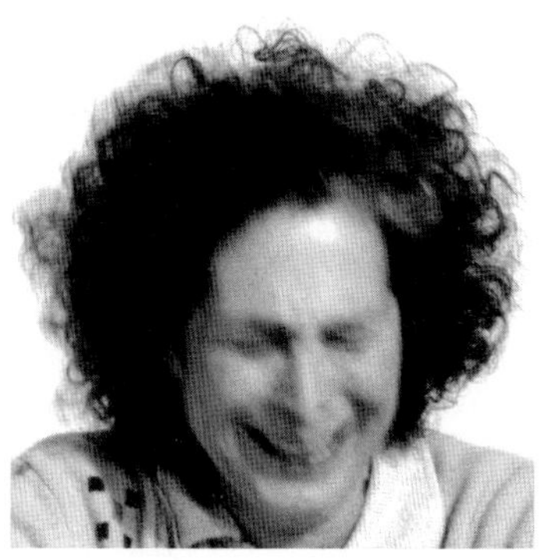
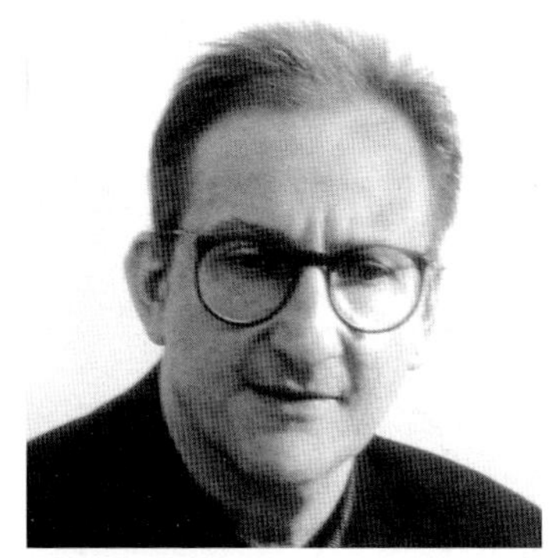
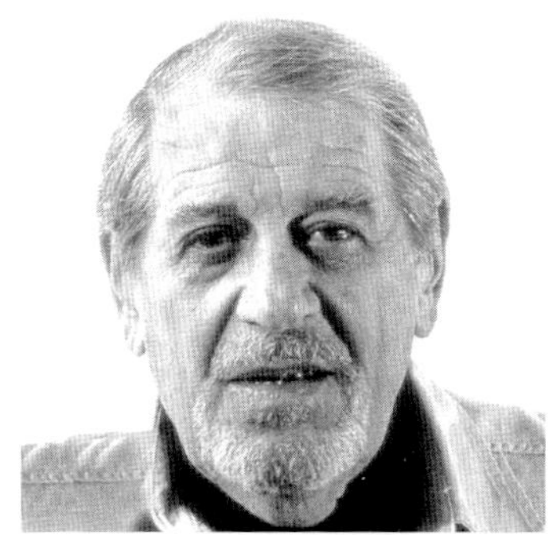
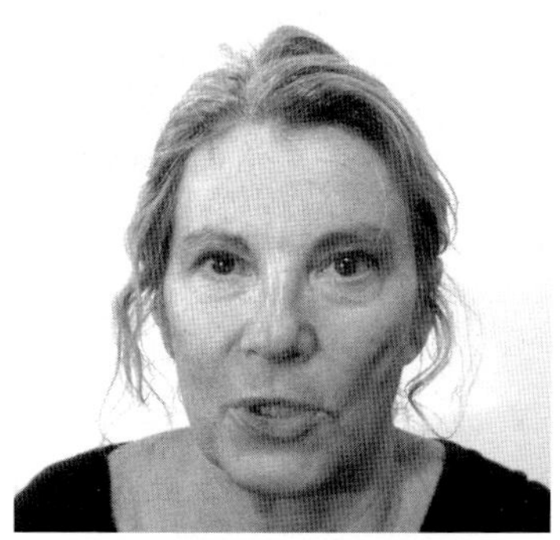

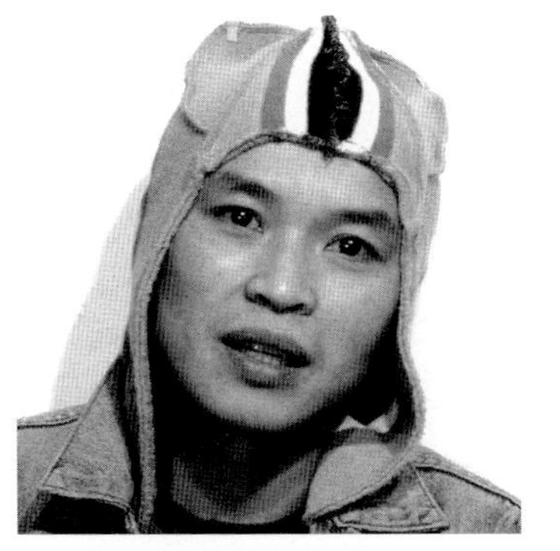
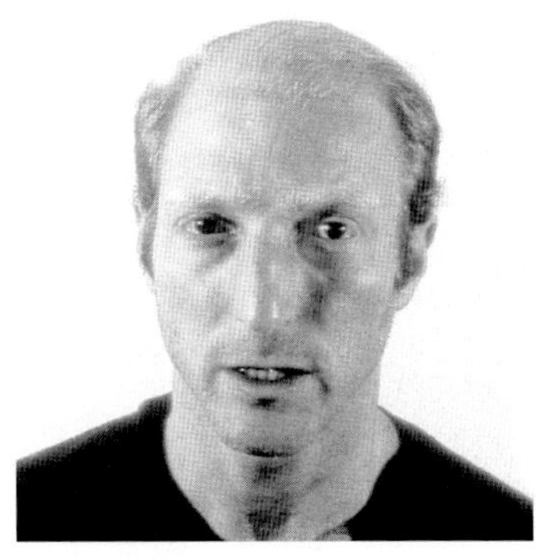
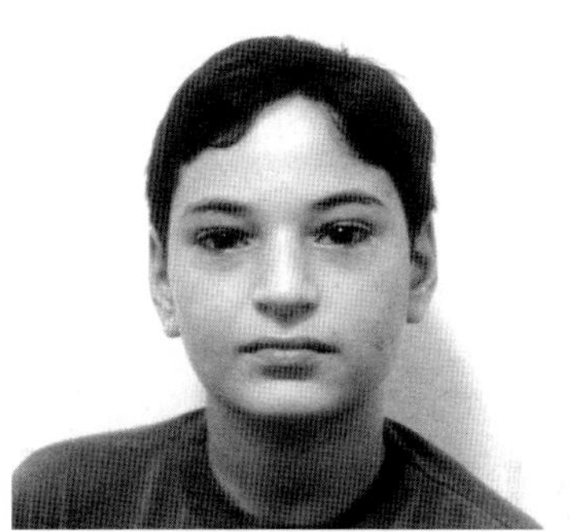
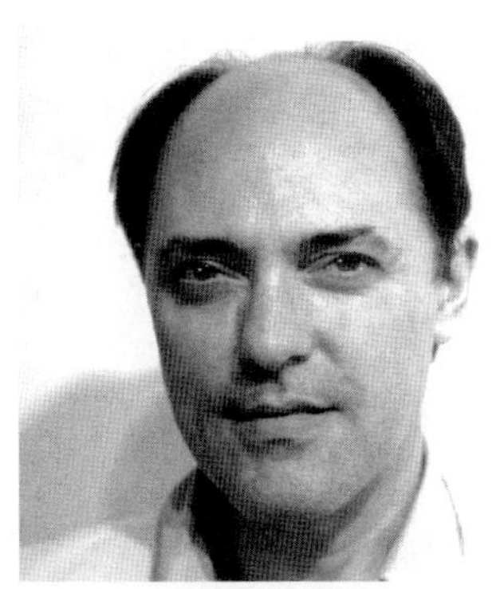
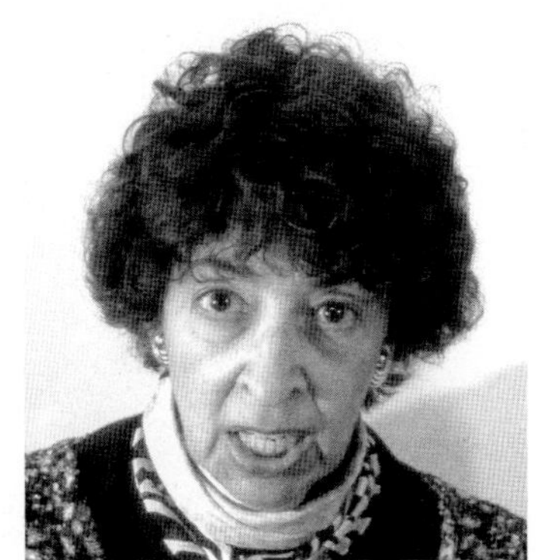
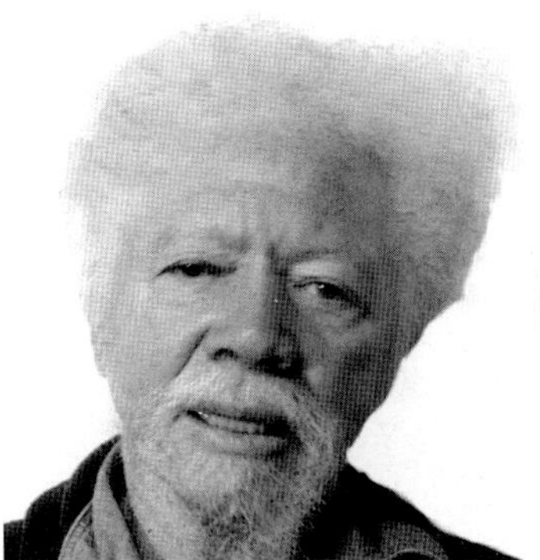

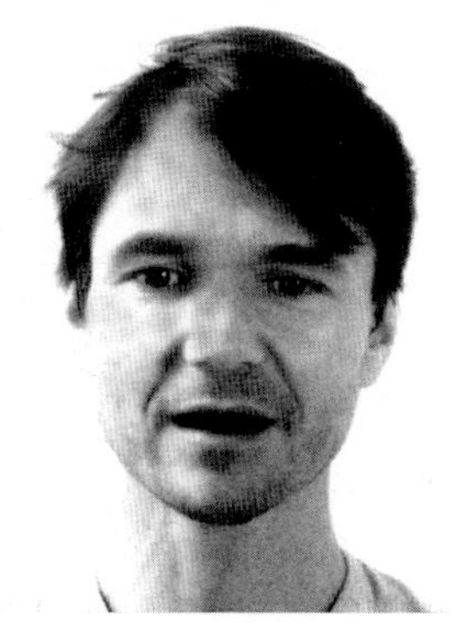
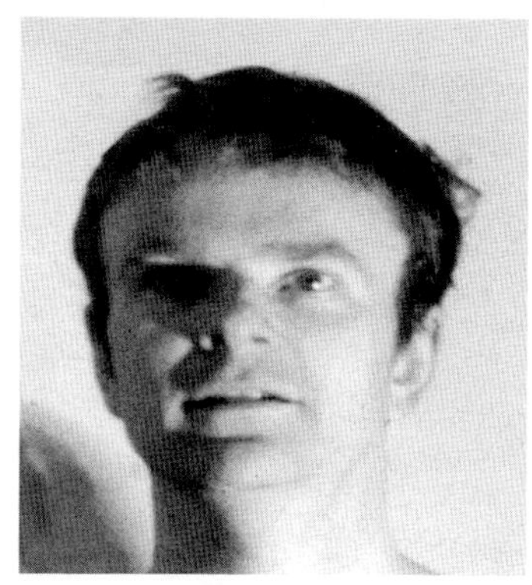
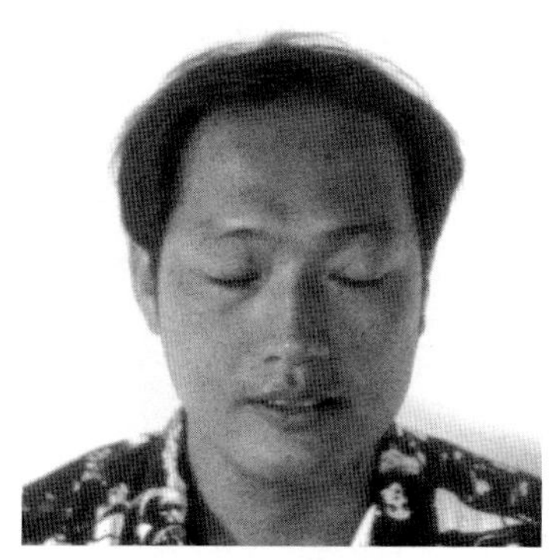
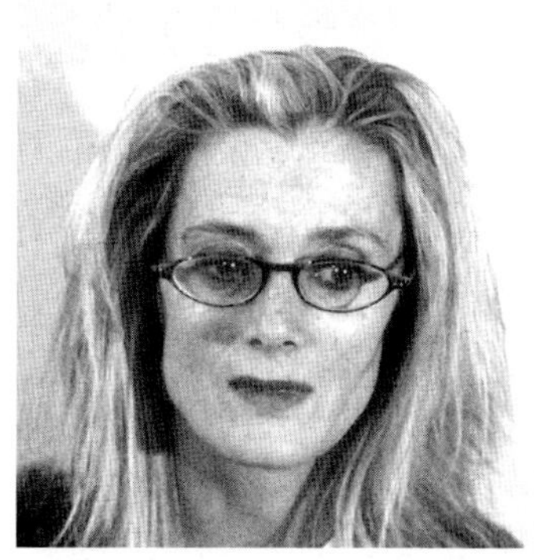
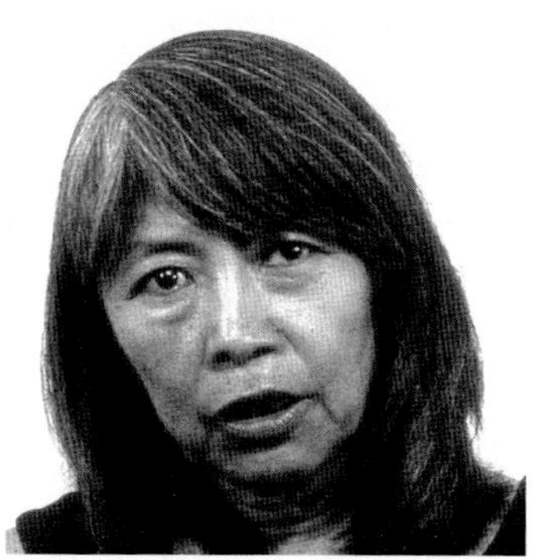
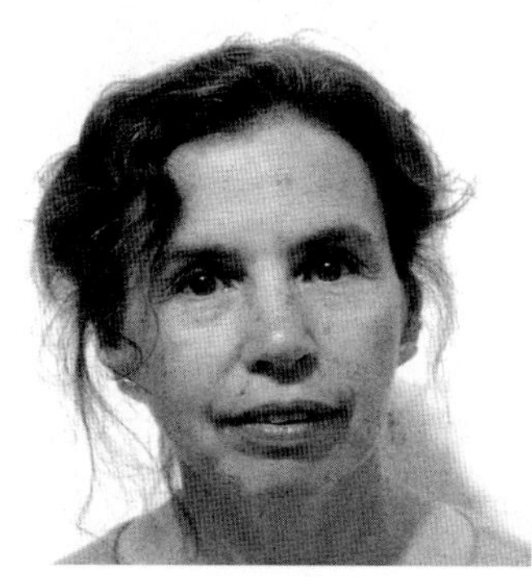

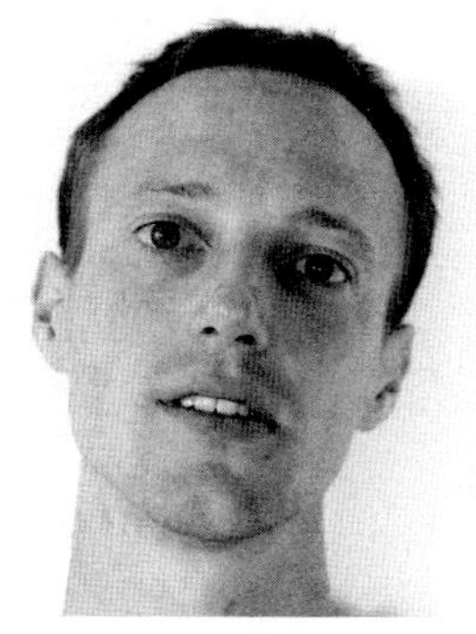
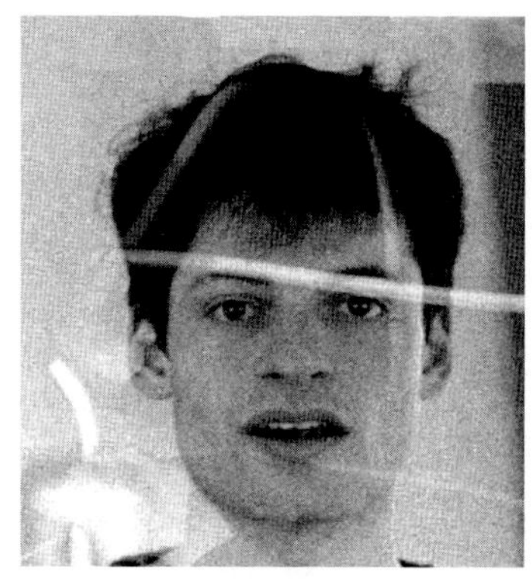
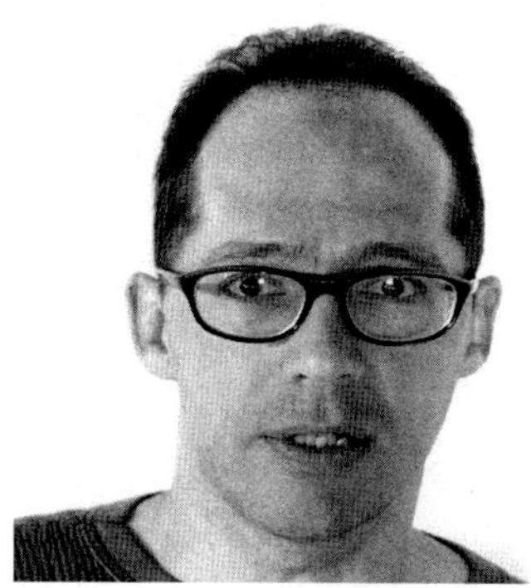
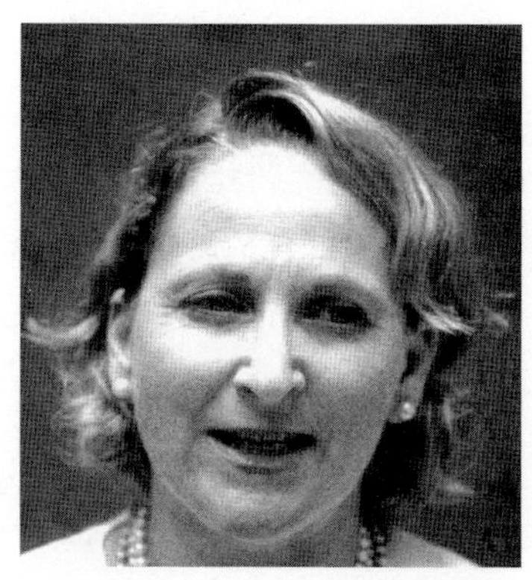
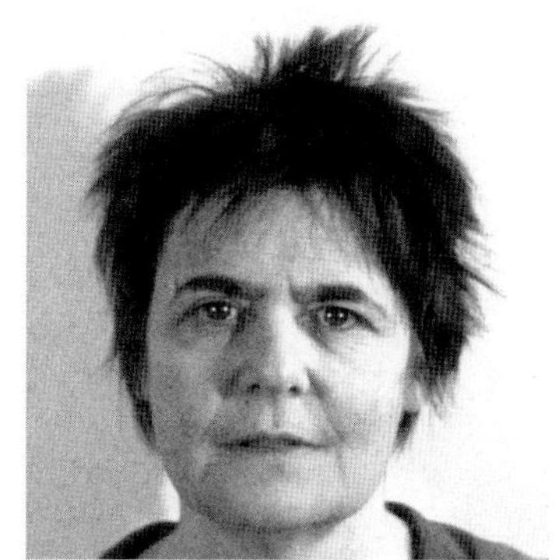
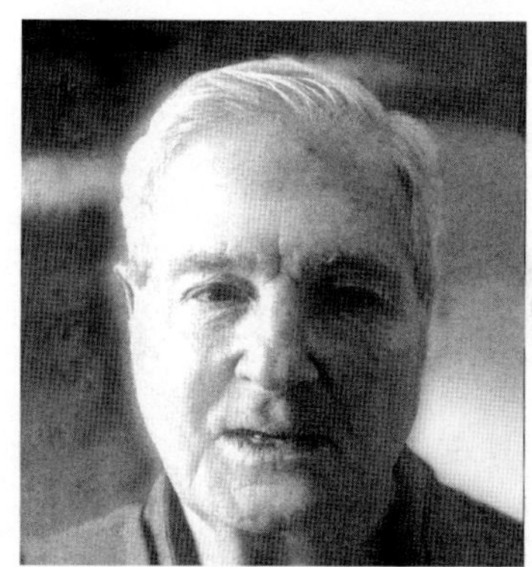

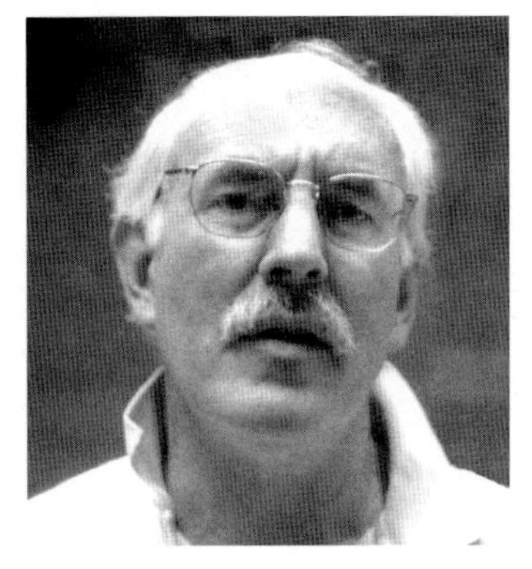
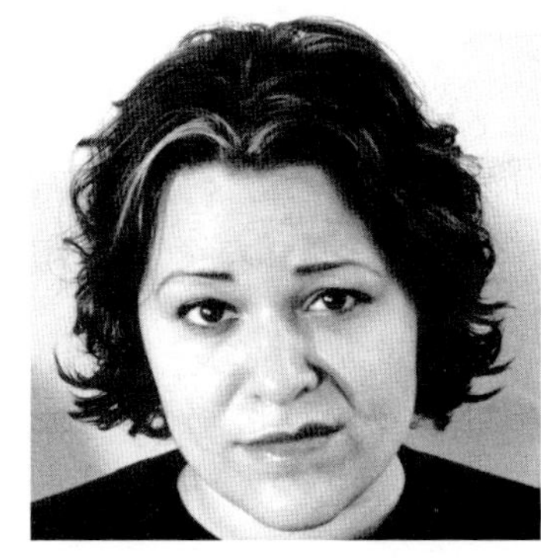
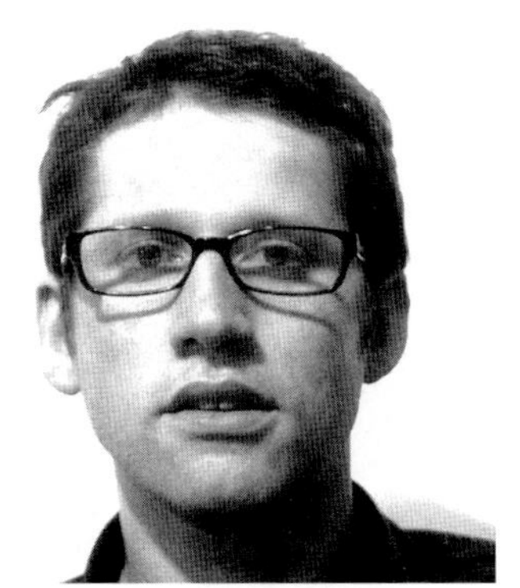
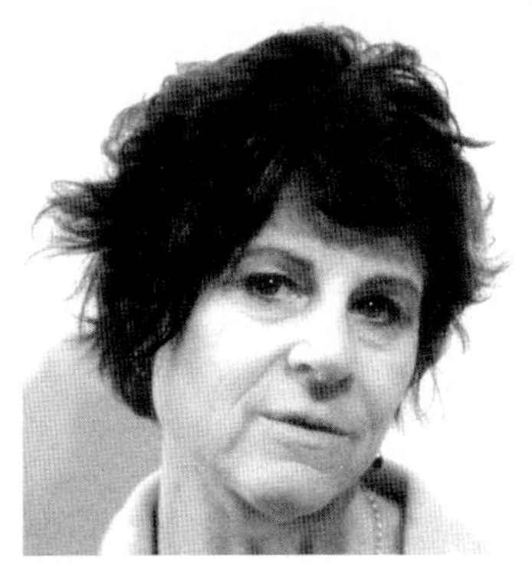
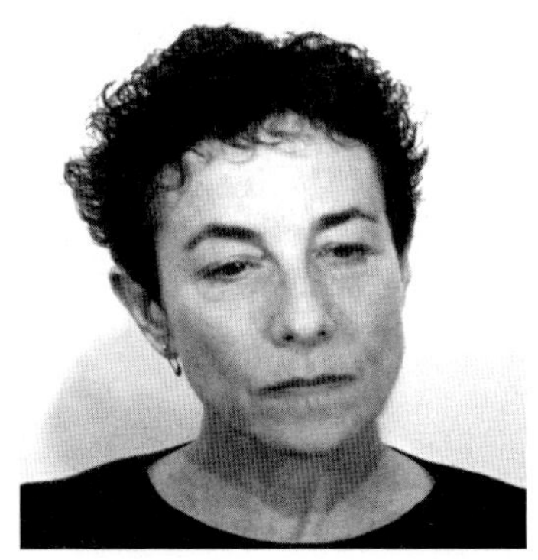
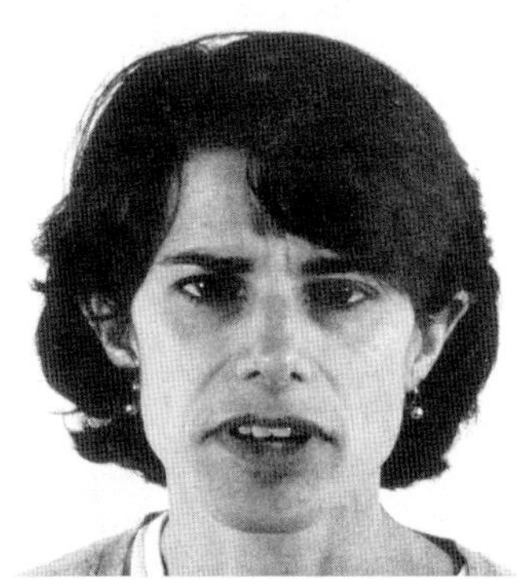

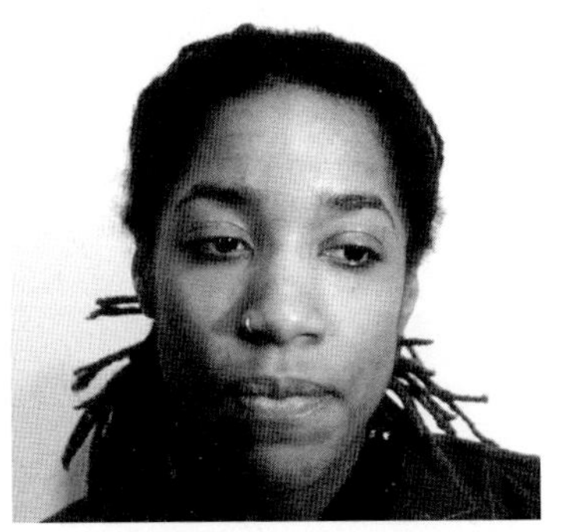
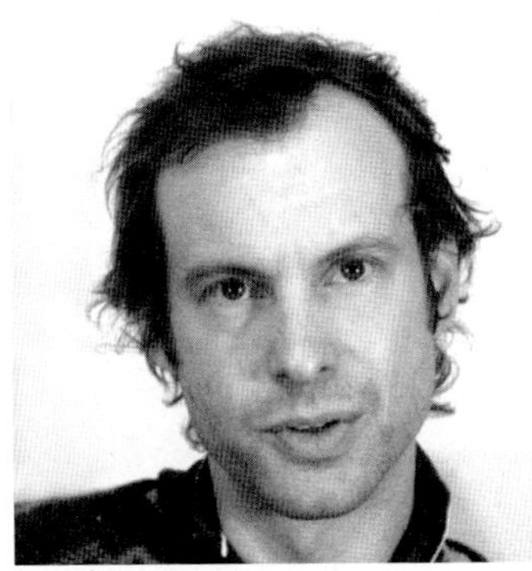
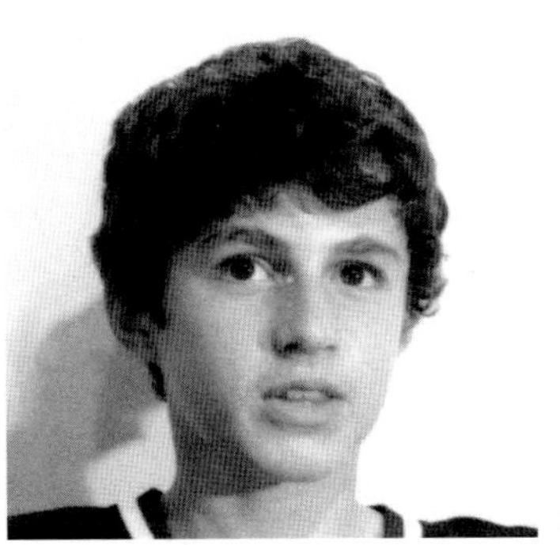
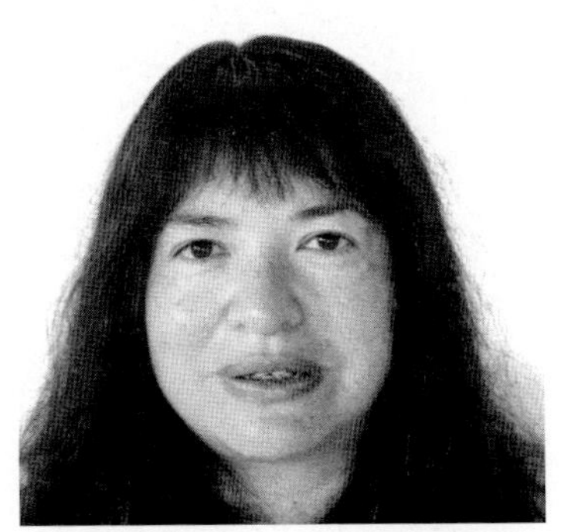
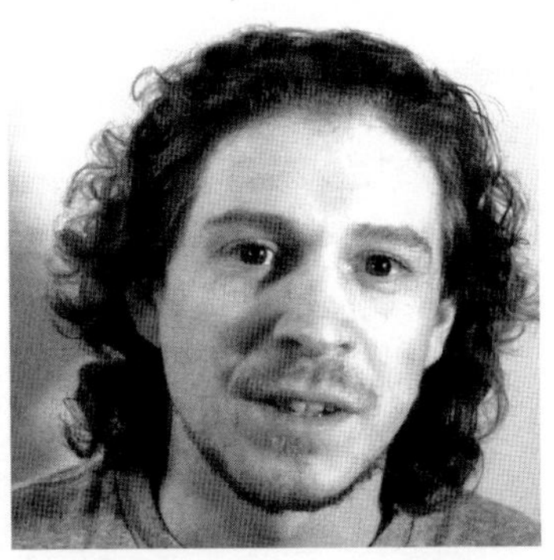
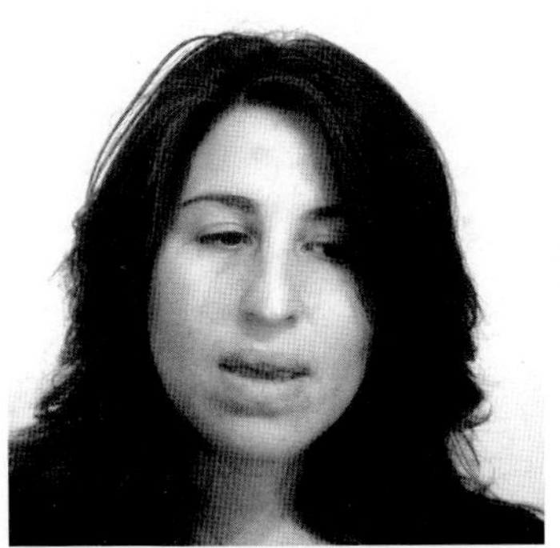

NOTES

HOW I LEARNED ABOUT THE NEW SOCIETY

1 In the *Journal of Theological Studies* (vol. 17, 1916), James Moffatt notes the parallel here between Tertullian's assertion and Aristotle's in *Rhetoric* 2.23.22, where Aristotle makes the point that an argument can be drawn from sheer improbability: Some stories are so improbable that it is reasonable to believe them.

2 "There is almost no change which happens in the heavenly bodies without its influencing the fluids and solids of our earth in agreement. Then, who would deny that the animal machine would, in these circumstances, be agitated to a certain degree by the same causes? The animal is part of the earth and is composed of fluids and solids, and when the proportion and the equilibrium of these fluids and solids are modified to a certain degree, very perceptible effects will occur from this." From "*Dissertatio physico-medica de planetarum influxu*" (*Physical-Medical Treatise on the Influence of the Planets*), Vindobonae, Vienna, Ghelen, 1766, in *Mesmerism: A Translation of the Original Scientific and Medical Writings of F.A. Mesmer, M.D.* George Bloch, Ph.D., translator and compiler. Los Altos, California: William Kaufmann, Inc., 1980, p. 13.

3 "Early Martian Magnetism Tape-Recorded in Rock," in *Astronomy Magazine*, August, 1999.

4 "I showed that the sun and the moon — as a result of their positions and distances relative to each other as well as to the earth — produce an effect on the human body which is analogous to the way in which they affect the tides, the different seas, and the entire atmosphere. I added that the attractive forces of these spheres penetrate deeply into all of our constitutive parts, solid and liquid, and act immediately on the nerves in a way so as to excite a real magnetism in our bodies. I call this property of the animal body which makes it sensitive to universal gravitation 'gravity' *(gravitatem)* or 'animal magnetism' *(magnetismum animalem)*." "*Lettre sur la cure magnétique à un médicin résident à l'étranger,*" *Nouveau Mercure savant d'Altona*, 1775. Translated by George Bloch in *Mesmerism*, 1980, p. 25.

5 In his "*Catéchisme*," Mesmer discusses the magnetization of plants:

Question: What is magnetism?

Response: It is the property which bodies have of being susceptible to the action of a universally distributed fluid, a fluid which surrounds all that exists and which serves to maintain the equilibrium of all the vital functions.

Question: Does this fluid only exist in animals, and are they the only individuals in nature which experience the effects of it?

Response: The principle is of equal necessity to vegetation. It is because of this principle that the sappy juice is able to circulate, and thereby contribute to the plant's development.

Question: How can the effects of this animal fluid be demonstrated?

Response: When a very healthy subject is in immediate contact with a sick subject, or merely with one who is defective in one of his natural functions, it means to evoke more or less sharp sensations in the sick part, like cold, heat, and sometimes even pain.

Question: Is it possible to increase the force or quantity of magnetic fluid in people?

Response: The power of magnetism is augmented by establishing a direct interconnection among several people.

Question: Are there then any other procedures which need to be followed in order to establish an interconnection among several people?

Response: It is also necessary that they be attached in the middle of the body with hemp rope having the thickness of a finger.

Question: How does one demonstrate that magnetism has an effect on plants?

Response: By establishing an interconnection among several plants or trees.

Question: How is this interconnection established?

Response: It is first necessary to bend some branches from several trees and attach them to each other . . . if the finger is then brought to a young growth [shoot or sprout] of one of these trees, all the young leaves will flutter in a more or less perceptible manner.

"Catéchisme du magnétisme animal," in *L'Antimagnétisme, ou origine, progrès, décadence, renouvellement et réfutation du magnétisme animal,* Jean-Jacques Paulet, London, 1784, pp. 113–120. Translated by George Bloch in *Mesmerism*, 1980, pp. 81–84.

6 Armand Marie Jacques de Chastenet, Marquis de Puységur, *Mémoires pour servir à l'histoire et à l'éstablissement du magnétisme animal*. Paris: Dentu, 1784.

7 Bergasse also said: "The word 'society' must not be taken to mean society as it exists now . . . but the society that ought to exist, natural society, the one that results from the relations that our own natures, when well ordered, must produce . . . The guiding rule of society is harmony." In Robert Darton, *Mesmerism and the End of the Enlightenment in France*. New York: Shocken Books, 1968, p. 118.

8 "Utopia and Revolutions," Lyman Tower Sargent and Roland Schaer, in *Utopia*, edited by Roland Schaer, Gregory Claeys, and Lyman Tower Sargent, The New York Public Library and Oxford University Press, 2000, p. 194.

9 I later wondered whether F.A. Mesmer might be the new female messiah. Ramona's rapturous declaration reminded me of the utopian ideas of French nobleman Comte de Saint-Simon (1760–1825) and his followers, who, in the 1840s and 1850s, sought a female messiah.

THE ARCHIVES ROOM

1 James Braid. *Neurypnology or, the Rationale of Nervous Sleep Considered in Relation with Animal Magnetism. Illustrated by Numerous Cases of Its Successful Application in the Relief and Cure of Disease.* London, John Churchill, 1843.

2 Ann Harrington. "Metals and Magnets in Medicine: Hysteria, hypnosis and medical culture in fin-de-siècle Paris." *Psychological Medicine* 18, 1988, pp. 21–38.

3 Peter Gay. *Freud: A Life for Our Time.* W.W. Norton & Company, New York and London, 1988, p. 49.

4 Mark Solms. (1989) "A Previously-Untranslated Review by Freud of a Monograph on Hypnotism," *International Journal of Psycho-Analysis*, 1989, 70:401–403. The review also contains an interesting reference to magnetism.

Freud wrote: "It seems to this rev[iewer] that O[bersteiner] makes an inappropriate comment on the famous experiment of Babinski with Charcot, where a suggestion was transferred from one hypnotized person to another by means of a magnet. Should one have to assume that the magnet can possibly have an effect upon a person, then it would not appear strange if this person in turn influences a second; just as a magnetized piece of soft iron acquires the property of attracting a second. To be sure, this analogy does not diminish the miraculousness of the fact that one nervous system can influence another nervous system by other means than the sensory perceptions known to us. One must rather concede that a confirmation of these experiments would add something new, hitherto unrecognized, to our Weltanschauung, and expand the borders of the personality as it were." Sigmund Freud, "Hypnotism, with special consideration of its clinical and forensic significance," *Klinische Zeit- und Streitfragen,* Vienna, 1887. Following are excerpts from correspondence between Stefan Zweig and Freud:

Kapuzinerberg 5, Salzbourg, le 6. XII. 1929
Monsieur le Professeur, . . . pour moi, Mesmer est Colomb, l'explorateur de la méthode thérapeutique psychique, mais il est aussi Colomb en ce sens que, jusqu'à la fin de sa vie, il a cru avoir trouvé la route maritime vers l'Inde, alors qu'en réalité il avait découvert l'Amerique. Avec ma sincère admiration votre toujours dévoué. — Stefan Zweig

7.XII.1929, Bergasse 19, Vienne IXe
Cher Monsieur, Ne craignez pas que j'essaie d'influencer votre prise de position. Je voudrais juste dire un seul mot en faveur des milieux officiels viennois, qui va à l'encontre de l'analogie avec Mesmer. On ne s'est tout simplement pas occupé de moi et c'était bien ainsi. Qu'aurais-je fait d'une chaire de psychiatrie ou même de psychanalyse? Elle n'aurait été que gênante ou inutile. Ceux qui se sont mal conduits, ce sont en fait mes soi-disant élèves renégats comme Jung, Adler et Stekel. "Humainement vulgaires," comme dit Heine. Cordialement Freud

MY INTERVIEWS WITH F.A. MESMER

1 MHD refers to magnetohydrodynamics, which concerns the examination of electrically conducting fluids and their interactions within magnetic fields.

2 "There are people who will frown upon me and from whom I will incur reproach when they read the title of this small thesis. They will see that a man like myself, though without importance, is undertaking, after so many efforts of the distinguished Mead, to insist on the influence of the stars, a doctrine rejected a long time ago by the action of the scientific leaders of the medical profession. Moreover, I am soliciting doctors anew in order that they study this doctrine and give it their support. I emphasize that it was during this last year that I found the time to make discoveries, which confirm my theory. In order to minimize at the outset the opposition arising in the minds of such scientists, I emphasize that I do not wish to defend the theory regarding the influence of the stars, which was formerly defended by the astrologers, who boast powers to predict events to come. . . . My purpose is solely to demonstrate that the celestial bodies act on our earth. Furthermore, that all things which are here act upon these celestial bodies in turn; that these move, act and that all parts are changing, and that our human bodies are equally submitted to the same dynamic action." From *"Dissertatio physico-medica de planetarum influxu"* in *Mesmerism: A Translation of the Original Scientific and Medical Writings of F.A. Mesmer, M.D.* George Bloch, Ph.D., translator and compiler. Los Altos, California: William Kaufmann, Inc., 1980, p. 3.

Referring to the *Dissertatio*, Mesmer wrote, "My object then was only to arouse the interest of physicians, but, far from succeeding, I soon became aware that I was being accused of eccentricity, that I was being treated like a dogmatic *'homme á systéme'* and that my tendency to quit the normal path of medicine was being construed as a crime." *Mesmerism,* 1980, p. 46.

3 *Aristotle on Sleep and Dreams*. Edited by David Gallop. Broadview Press, Peterborough, Ont., 1990.

4 The great Scottish theorist James Clerk Maxwell had an immense influence on 20th-century physics. Maxwell showed theoretically that time varying electric fields will also induce magnetic fields and that the two could be unified. Maxwell's four sets of equations describe the behavior of both fields and provide the basis for the unification of the electric field and magnetic fields, the electromagnetic description of light, and ultimately Einstein's theory of relativity. Einstein's basic contribution was to understand that Maxwell's equations required the special theory of relativity.

5 Mesmer's theories were correct except for one thing. Since he died in 1815 he never knew the real connection between magnetism and electricity. That work was accomplished in the 19th century by the English physicist and chemist Michael Faraday, who demonstrated that when a field around an electromagnet was changed, that is, either increased or decreased, an electric current could be detected. This is electromagnetic induction.

6 "The natural and perfect sleep of a man is the state where the functions of the senses are suspended; that is, where the continuity which the 'common sensorium' has with the external senses is interrupted."
Franz Anton Mesmer, *"Mémoire de F.A. Mesmer, docteur en médecin sur ses découvertes"* (1779). *Le magnetisme animal.* Paris: Robert Amadou, Payot Press, 1971.

7 "Other treatments include provoking a crisis in the form of convulsions or inducing magnetic sleep. There is also bioresonance: Imagine that you are holding a vibrating tuning fork in one hand and in the other you are holding another tuning fork, which isn't vibrating. What do you think will happen? Well, the other tuning fork also starts vibrating. It soon vibrates at exactly the same speed and frequency as the first. All body organs have their own frequency spectra. If you become weak or sick your cell frequencies change and begin to vibrate incorrectly. We can stimulate your cells to return to their correct frequency. Our treatment provides the body with the correct frequencies just as the tuning fork does.

"One of our machines is equipped with coils of a titanium molybdenum mercury nickel alloy that can set up sympathetic currents in the subjects' body for the purpose of re-orientation according to a single polarity. In other words, in combination with the right food and proper thought electromagnetic energy can flow in a direction determined by the subject's life force and will, which will be one and the same."

8 "Love is not only objectively but also subjectively the criterion of being, the criterion of truth and reality. Where there is no love there is also no truth. And only he who loves something is also something — to be nothing and to love nothing is one and the same thing. The more one is, the more one loves, and vice versa." — Principle 35. Ludwig Feuerbach, *Principles of the Philosophy of the Future.* Zawar Hanfi, translator. Indianapolis: Hackett Pub. Co., 1986.

9 F.A. Mesmer also follows the precepts of the French 19th-century utopian Charles Fourier, who believed that sensual enjoyment is essential for a life of harmony. He said, "Perfect harmony lays in complete gratification." Like Fourier, Mesmer wishes to create a society founded not on work, but on social exchange, passions, and cultural "complementaries." Tasks therefore are organized according to the principle of attraction, making them as free and interesting as possible. Borrowing from Fourier, F.A. Mesmer uses the terms "celadony" and "lubricity" to refer to platonic and sensual love.

POSTSCRIPT: THE UPRISINGS

1 Amir Aczel, *Probability 1: Why There Must Be Intelligent Life in the Universe*. London: Abacus, 1998.

2 Giuseppe Cocconi and Philip Morrison, "Searching for Interstellar Communications." *Nature*, Vol. 184, Sept. 19, 1959.

TEA WITH MME. B.

1 John Gheeraert. *De Geheime Wereld van James Ensor*, Antwerp: Houtekiet, 2001, 93.

2 See for example, Pique, "A Visit to Madame Blavatsky," *The Commercial Gazette* (Cincinnati, Ohio) October 13, 1889, 3.

3 These essays can be found on line at several websites dedicated to Mme. Blavatsky's writings. See http: //www.blavatsky.org and http://www.theosociety.org.

4 The most notable of these short stories are "The Facts in the Case of M. M. Valdemar," "A Tale of the Ragged Mountain," and "Some Words with a Mummy."

5 Ensor read Poe's 1847 collection *Extraordinary Stories*. His Poe-inspired works include *King Pest* (1886–1888); *The Black Cat* (1886–1888, Kahrlsruhe, Staatliche Kunsthalle); *The Devil in the Belfry* (1886–1888), which shows a tall man dressed all in black that looks somewhat like the artist; *The Domain of Arnheim* (1890); and *The Revenge of the Hop Frog* (1885, Brussels, Royal Library, Print Cabinet).

6 Gheeraert, 74–85;93–97.

7 Sébastian Clebois, "In Search of the "Forme-Pensée: The Influence of Theosophy on Belgian Artists Between Symbolism and the Avant-Garde (1890–1910)," in *Nineteenth Century Art Worldwide*, Autumn, 2002, 1–19 (http://www.19thc-artworldwide.org). Clerbois points out that there were theosophical societies in Belgium before the turn of the century, including branches in Charleroi in 1894 and in Antwerp, Liege, and Brussels in 1897 and 1898. The first Belgian theosophical circle might have been established in 1890 around the writer Ray Nyst and included Jean Delville, Fernand Khnopff, Émile Fabry, and Albert Clamberlani.

TWENTY-FIRST-CENTURY DEVELOPMENTS IN SPIRIT PHOTOGRAPHY AND ANIMAL MAGNETISM: A BRIEF UPDATE

1 The Fall 2003 issue of *Art Journal*, a publication of the professional organization for art historians and artists, focuses entirely on this topic. The periodical's editor, Patricia C. Phillips, lauds the "searching, open-minded speculation" of the essays contained therein, which she says invite us "to critically examine our own fear of and fascination with the mysterious and irresolute." Patricia C. Phillips, "In This Issue: Close Encounters," *Art Journal*, Fall 2003, p. 3.

2 Because these images contain privileged medical information, they cannot be reproduced without the patients' permission. Given the unsettling nature of the images and the unfortunate coincidence of timing with the new medical privacy practices law, only one of the survivors or heirs was willing to give that permission.

ACKNOWLEDGMENTS

THE NEW SOCIETY FOR UNIVERSAL HARMONY was originally conceived in February 2000 as a commission to create an institution in a new city, *une ville neuf,* for the journal *9/9 revue d'art pratique,* Paris. My thanks to the editor of *9/9,* Stéphane Argillet, for setting the stage for the project. Residencies at Yaddo in the summer of 2001 and at Blue Mountain Center in the summer of 2003 allowed me to develop it further.

Grateful acknowledgments to Ruppert Bohle for his generosity in teaching me all manner of new media. I benefited immensely from discussions with Stephen Brewer and Craig Colligan, who read the manuscript and clarified much. Many thanks to Mary Beth Brewer for her wit and patience and for demanding perfection in layout and text as she shepherded the book to completion. My thanks to Aaron Levy and the Slought Foundation and Richard Shaw at the BBC for their support.

Thanks to Kathryn Alexander, Benny Andrews, Diane Burko, Stephanie Butts, Lital Cohen, Romey Cornfield, Jeff Feld, Fredericka Foster, Elizabeth Harris, Susan Ito, Sherry Katz-Bearnot, Michael Kirk, Ellen K. Levy, Jim Lyle, Steven Margolis, David Miller, Mark Nelkin, Anne O'Connor, Marisa Ravelli Přihodvá, Rick Renner, Renée Rockoff, Karen Shaw, Maiko Shimizu, Joel Simpson, Michael Slipp, Elke Solomon, David Sonnenblick, Courtney Ulrich, Clay Ward, Annabel Wong, and so many others for their help. Grateful acknowledgments to Todd Erickson, the Vektor-Mesonen resident engineer at Athol Springs, and Ann McCoy, *l'embroiderer.*

Much gratitude goes to Julie Harrison and Russell Hassell for their marvelous design. I thank Steve Clay for believing in the project from the very start.

Romain Deplas's spirit lives in every page of the book.

My greatest debt is to the Harmonites, whom I photographed and audiotaped on so many occasions. They made all of this possible.